Evolution
of World Enterprises

Evolution of World Enterprises

Arvind V. Phatak

An AMA Research Book

American Management Association, Inc.

International standard book number: 0-8144-5267-1
Library of Congress catalog card number: 72-155827

First printing

About This Book

THIS book is based on a first-hand study of European and American companies that have substantial operations abroad. The focus is on the trials and tribulations of a multinational company as it evolves into a world enterprise or world company. The terms "enterprise" and "company" are used interchangeably. The forces that help or hinder this evolutionary process are discussed, and a comparative analysis of the managerial strategies of multinational companies with the probable managerial strategies of a world enterprise is undertaken.

I have made a distinction between a multinational company and a world company. Both are international companies because of their vast operations abroad, but the managerial strategies and practices of a world company reflect a far more world-oriented attitude than do those of a multinational company. The conclusions regarding the differences between the two types of companies are based on my observations and analyses of several European and American international companies. The information conveyed in this study relates to multinational companies that are in various stages of development into world companies. Throughout, therefore, the term "multinational company" pertains to companies that, someday, should emerge as world enterprises.

An analysis of the direct-investment flows of several leading nations of the world indicates that the United States, the United Kingdom, Italy, West Germany, Switzerland, the Netherlands, Japan, and France will, in the foreseeable future, be sponsoring many more companies with substantial operations abroad. Direct investments abroad by the United States are substantially higher than those of any other nation and have been so in the past. The number of American-based companies evolving into world companies will, however, depend on how the overall attitudes of the top management of American companies shape up. It appears that, to date, European companies have made much greater progress toward approaching the world company model than American companies have. That is largely due to the attitude of top management, which in European companies generally is much more world-oriented than in American companies.

Geography and the size of European countries have been quite instrumental in shaping the world-oriented attitude of European company managements. Small size of the domestic market, proximity to other countries on the Continent, easy access by land to the markets of other countries, and sometimes the shortage of raw material resources at home induced many European companies to establish operations abroad very early in their lives. Some European companies covered in this study set up their first manufacturing plants abroad more than a hundred years ago. That has not been true of most American companies. A vast domestic market and an abundance of mineral wealth at home made it unnecessary for American companies to venture abroad in search of markets or raw materials. Any foreign manufacturing or sales operations were therefore generally treated as an extension of domestic operations. As a result, the managements of American companies have had a far less world-oriented attitude than their European counterparts. That, at least, has been true up to now of most American international companies. Of course, there have been exceptions in both American and European companies.

The movement toward transnational ownership and management of companies also started in Europe many years ago with Royal Dutch/Shell and Unilever as the prime examples. Recent quasimergers in Europe such as those between Agfa and Gavaert, Fokker and VFW, and Dunlop and Pirelli are setting the pace and trend for amalgamation between other companies in Europe. Conditions in Europe have been responsible for the amalgamations. To a great extent these company marriages took place because of the domineering presence of American companies in Europe. No such conditions exist in the United States, and there does not appear to be any need, at present, for transnational mergers composed of American companies and their counterparts in Central or Latin America. Nevertheless, all indications are that the European companies, for a variety of reasons, will emerge as world enterprises at a more rapid pace than the American companies will.

This study is primarily based on information obtained through personal interviews with executives in 26 European and 13 American companies having worldwide operations. The details of the companies interviewed are presented in the Appendix. Executives in Belgium, Germany, Great Britain, Italy, and Switzerland were interviewed in July and August 1969; executives in Denmark and Sweden were interviewed in December 1969 and January 1970; and American company executives were interviewed in February, March, and April 1970. A report on each company was written on the basis of the interview and published data obtained from the company and from newspapers and journals. These reports form the basis of this study, although information obtained through secondary sources is also included.

A set of twelve questions was sent to each executive well in advance of the interview. The interview was not limited to those questions alone, but included numerous other subjects. All the interviews were conducted in English. I was pleasantly surprised to find that all the European executives spoke very good English.

Only a few of the companies approached refused to participate in the study. Some who refused sent speeches by their respective presidents or company notes published in journals that partly answered some of my questions.

Almost all the interviews were with top management personnel. For example, those interviewed included two chairmen of the board, one company chairman, four presidents, one executive vice-president, two senior vice-presidents, seventeen vice-presidents, five heads of international division or company, and so on.

Apart from the educational rewards that I reaped from this study, which the American Management Association asked me to undertake, there have been many other pleasant experiences. Because of the warm welcome I received everywhere, I looked forward to each next interview, even in the freezing winter (−20° F) of Sweden and Denmark, where I lived through days in almost total darkness. That was quite an experience. I had heard a great deal about the famous Boardroom of Unilever and of the adjacent offices of the two chairmen. It was a memorable experience to interview Lord Cole, the former chairman of Unilever Ltd., and to be shown around the Boardroom by him. Several such incidents made the study extremely enjoyable despite the minor discomforts inherent in such a project.

I wish to thank all the executives for their cooperation and help. Several people helped me in getting this project started. I thank Professor Harold Koontz, Graduate School of Business Administration, University of California at Los Angeles; Peter Parker, Chairman, Bookers Engineering and Industrial Holdings Ltd., London; Dr. E. B. J. Postma, President, The Netherlands School of Business; Professor Peter Drucker, Graduate School of Business Administration, New York University, and Patrick McCabe of the U.S. Department of Commerce for their timely assistance.

I am grateful to John Bunting, President, First Pennsylvania Banking and Trust Company, for lending his support to this project. Robert P. Feeser, Senior Vice-President, John Taylor, Assistant Treasurer, and Bent S. Hoyrup, Assistant Vice-President, all of First Pennsylvania Banking and

Trust Company, were very helpful in establishing contacts with European companies. I owe my gratitude to Dean Seymour L. Wolfbein, School of Business Administration, Temple University, for his consistent support to this project. Without his sympathetic and helping hand it would have been difficult for me to obtain a study leave, which made my European interviews possible. My research assistants, Gardiner L. Cameron, Philip Romano, and Jeffrey Kaneff, must be given credit for doing a great deal of the detail work. Mrs. Kathy Byrd, the management department secretary, was very helpful in putting a lot of odds and ends together. I want to thank my wife, Rhoda, not only for putting up with my idiosyncrasies during the past two years, but especially for typing up all my letters and interviews, transcribing several hours of taped interviews, and typing the entire manuscript. Had it not been for her prompt help in typing, this book would have taken a lot longer to finish. Last, but not least, I owe my gratitude to Margaret V. Higginson, formerly of the American Management Association, for her patience and ever-helping hand.

Contents

ix

The World Enterprise – Its Nature and Concept

INTERNATIONAL companies with operating subsidiaries in several countries have been, during the last few years, the center of attention of politicians, businessmen, and academicians. A great number of these international companies are multinational companies. Most of them are American-based, but several are based in Europe and Japan. Many international companies are already evolving into multinational companies and are on their way toward becoming world enterprises. This book is about the companies that are becoming world enterprises. Throughout this book they will be called multinational companies, although not all fit into the definition of a multinational company as yet.

Characteristics of a Multinational Company

The literature in the field of international business includes several definitions of a multinational company:

> A multinational corporation owns and manages businesses in two or more countries. It is an agency of direct, as opposed to portfolio, investment in foreign countries, holding and managing the underlying physical assets rather than securities based upon these assets.[1]

A multinational company's management sees its enterprise as a global entity. It sees its foreign and domestic interests interwoven into a web of carefully integrated parts. It allocates its capital, manpower, and other resources on a global basis. For such a corporation, the United States is but one of many markets, one of many sites for production or research.[2]

A nonfinancial enterprise with a base of operations in one country and more or less integrated producing-servicing subsidiaries located in a number of foreign nations . . . a corporate group or family whose members are located in different countries in order to achieve a common corporate purpose.[3]

These are only a few of the many definitions of a multinational company. Viewed together, they define a multinational company as one that has a parent company based in one country and several integrated production and sales subsidiaries in a number of other countries. The parent company manages all its operations on a global basis without making any distinction between its foreign and domestic operations. Although they are referred to as multinational companies, only some of the companies studied could strictly be so characterized.

Characteristics of a World Enterprise

What is the difference between a multinational company and a world enterprise or world company? Unlike the multinational company, which is predominantly owned and managed by the nationals of the country in which it is legally based, the world enterprise typically has the following characteristics:

1. The parent company is owned by nationals of several countries.
2. The board of directors of the parent company is manned by nationals of several countries.
3. Management at both parent company and subsidiary level has a global outlook and attitude.
4. Top management personnel in the parent company and in the various subsidiaries are selected on the basis of ability to do the job well, and not on the basis of nationality.
5. Integrated plans for the entire enterprise are formulated on a global basis by using the systems approach. The plans provide for the worldwide deployment of financial, material, and human resources in a manner that produces a synergistic effect that is beneficial to the enterprise as a unit even though one of its parts, such as a subsidiary, may suffer in the process.

6. Subsidiaries involved in manufacturing and sales are located in a number of different countries.
7. A substantial portion of its total sales volume and earnings derives directly or indirectly from operations abroad.
8. Top management at the parent company level is concerned with formulating strategic plans and policies for the entire enterprise and for coordinating and controlling global operations. Operating authority is delegated to lower levels.
9. The organization structure provides top management with globally organized functional, product, and geographic inputs and makes no distinction between operations at home and abroad.

No one organization pattern is typical of a world enterprise. An organization structure that a company adopts is a function of several factors such as size, type of industry, product mix, number and geographic spread of operating units, complexity of technology, and, most importantly, the philosophy and attitudes of top management, especially the chief executive. Top management must have a world-oriented attitude if a world enterprise is to emerge. The organization structure adopted by a world enterprise must reflect that attitude. Hence, any structure that emerges should reflect top management philosophy of giving equal importance to all operating subsidiaries, regardless of their location.

Institutional Predecessors of the World Enterprise

The Intercity Global Trade System

The ancestry of the world enterprise can be traced to the Mesopotamian, Greek, and Phoenician merchants who dealt in wool, spices, leather, jewelry, coral, pearls, and slaves nearly 6,000 years ago. Great trading colonies such as Carthage, Corinth, Miletus, Rhodes, Syracuse, Tyre, and Sidon developed as overcrowding in the earlier cities forced people to move into less inhabited lands at home or abroad. The trading towns reached their peak around the sixth century B.C., and the intercity system of "global" trade continued for the next 300 years. Its decline began with the rise of first the Greek and later the Roman empires.

The Roman Republic and then Empire dominated the world scene from 146 B.C. until about A.D. 500, when it vanished in the West and was succeeded by barbarian kingdoms. Although the Romans, like the Greeks, held business and businessmen in contempt, they did value the role of the businessman in financing military expeditions and selling off the loot obtained in war. They therefore made the sea routes safe from the threat of pirates and built fine roads that enabled trade to flourish as it never had before. With the demise of the Roman Empire, Europe declined into feudalism, which was little better than anarchy. "World" trade was almost impossible, and each feudal unit was forced to be independent and self-reliant. The church became the most influential political and social institution in Europe in the Middle Ages. At one time it controlled over one-third of the land in Europe. Constant warfare between the feudal units plus the restriction placed by the church upon trade with the Moslems were impediments to world trade.

The Crusades, beginning in 1095, brought the Europeans in contact with the civilization, culture, and wealth of the East. City-states of Genoa, Venice, Florence, and Pisa served as staging areas and supply depots for the Crusades. The barter economy was replaced by the money economy. This period also marked the development of banks and financial institutions that charged interest on loaned money, although that was contrary to church doctrine.

The Commenda

Until the sixteenth century, foreign trade was characterized by independent merchants transporting and exchanging goods across national boundaries. Commercial enterprises consisting of formal associations of individual financiers, traders, and merchants were nonexistent. However, by the end of the Middle Ages (around 1450) some temporary commercial organizations known as commenda began to grow. The commenda consisted of temporary contractual agreements between the financier—who supplied the funds and stayed at home—and the merchant-adventurer, who ventured abroad and actually performed the trade. The contractual agreement was task-oriented and hence was dissolved once the expedition was successfully terminated. The commenda were the embryo of the more complex commercial enterprises of later years.

The development of ocean-going ships and the magnetic compass made navigation much safer and more reliable. Feats such as the discovery of America in 1492, the voyage of Vasco da Gama to India by sailing around the Cape of Good Hope in 1498, and the 3-year voyage of Magellan beginning in 1519 led to the growth of powerful nation-states based on commercial rather than military exploitation. The Italian city-states slowly faded away in importance in world trade.

The Colonial Enterprise

The European national powers began to take considerable interest in the wealth of the new world as well as the old. The doctrine of mercantilism, which was based upon the thesis that the wealth of the world was limited and therefore the only way for a nation to get rich and prosper was to accumulate wealth by exploiting other countries, lead to the growth of colonialism. England, France, Spain, Belgium, Portugal, and the Netherlands emerged as the dominant colonial powers. The government's authority in all foreign development matters was unwillingly accepted and it was then granted to one or more individuals, who thereby gained the exclusive right to exploit, trade with, and govern a certain colony. In accordance with their mercantilist philosophy, the colonial powers forbade their colonies to trade with other nations.

The huge amount of capital required to exploit, govern, and trade with a colony led to the chartering of the British East India Company, the Hudson Bay Company, the Levant Company, and the Dutch East India Company. The monopolistic colonial enterprises, although primarily concerned with trade and raw materials exploitation in the colonies, also got involved, albeit in a small way, in the manufacture of finished goods required for consumption in the home country or re-export from the home country. But the home countries did not allow the colonial monopolies to manufacture goods that were already being manufactured in the home country and hence to compete with home-country products.

This period marked the emergence of export-import houses, commercial agencies, and financial institutions to serve the growing needs of world trading institutions. The colonial monopolies dominated the world trade scene until the late eighteenth century.

The mercantilist doctrine gave birth to the modern-day type of trade barriers, subsidies, production quotas, and price regulation, all of which, as today, were meant to support domestic industry and protect it from foreign competition. The Industrial Revolution marked the demise of mercantilism and the beginning of the free-trade era.

By the nineteenth century, new technology had come to England and to all Europe: the invention of the spinning jenny, the development of steam power, and breakthroughs in the art and science of steelmaking. The factory system replaced cottage industry throughout Europe, and the Industrial Revolution was underway. The factory system encouraged specialization and concentration of production, and that forced the nations and governments to change their attitude from protectionism and self-sufficiency to free trade between nations. The movement toward *laissez faire* was supported by philosophers such as John Locke and by classical economists, of whom the most prominent was Adam Smith.

World trade tripled during the late nineteenth and early twentieth century. The pattern of world trade also shifted significantly during that period, which saw the beginning of direct investments of a more permanent nature by the industrialized nations in their colonies in Asia, Africa, and Latin America. Less emphasis was placed on the exchange of goods between countries. The factories of Europe required raw materials, and therefore greater emphasis was placed by them on exploiting colonial raw materials sources through permanent capital investments in operating subsidiaries, particularly in the mining industry. Perhaps it can be said that these colonial parent-subsidiary company relationships marked the beginning of the present-day multinational company.

But there are great differences between the colonial company of the past and the present-day multinational company. For instance, the colonial companies operated mainly within the colonial territories or spheres of influence of their own nations, rather than under the jurisdiction of foreign sovereign states. Also, the colonial company's primary interest was in the extractive field, whereas we see today's multinational companies operating in varied fields, expecially in manufacturing. The colonial company's interest in the economic development of the colonized region was minimal. That does not happen to be the philosophy of the modern multinational company, which is generally oriented toward the betterment of the region in which its operations abroad are located.

A major difference between the colonial company of yesterday and today's multinational company is that the colonial company was production-oriented and the output of its subsidiaries in the colony or colonies was for its own use or for further processing or resale. The prime objective of the subsidiary was to exploit the local region to serve the interests of the parent company. In contrast, the modern multinational company's main emphasis at the outset is on marketing the parent company's products in the local region. The subsidiary abroad is therefore first used as a marketing arm of the parent; production abroad follows once the market for the product is developed. And, unlike the colonial company, the multinational company of today produces abroad primarily for consumption in the local market. Whereas the colonial company exported goods produced by its subsidiaries abroad to the company's traditional markets, today's multinational company attempts to export products made by its subsidiaries to the host country's traditional markets and thus it serves the economic interests of the host country as well.

With the crumpling of the colonial empires during the late nineteenth and the mid-twentieth century came the decline of the colonial companies. The rise of nationalism, the two world wars, the Great Depression, the emergence of the Communist bloc of nations, and the growth of voluntary associations after World War II such as the International Bank of Reconstruction, the International Monetary Fund, and the GATT agreement of 1947 have changed the traditional patterns of trade among nations.

These developments have contributed substantially, if not totally, to the enormous growth of direct investments abroad by the United States and most nations of Western Europe since World War II and to the subsequent growth and development of the present-day multinational companies. We shall, therefore, examine the recent trends in international business and direct investments abroad by a select group of industrialized countries of Europe, Japan, and the United States.

The Pattern of Direct Investments Abroad

The multinational company is one of the most important vehicles of direct investments abroad. By identifying the countries from which the direct investments originate, we could make generalizations as to which countries are most likely to be the bases of future multinational companies. By pinpointing the countries where the direct investments are made, we could generalize as to the countries in which the subsidiaries of multinational companies are most likely to be located. Also, by locating the industries in which the direct investments abroad are made by the country making the biggest such investments, we could estimate which industries are most likely to give birth to future multinational companies.

Data presented in the various tables were collected from various sources. It is very easy to get statistics on U.S. direct investments abroad by country and industry from the U.S. Department of Commerce. Similarly, the Department of Commerce has rather complete statistics on foreign direct investments in the United States by country and industry. But comparable statistics on the direct investments abroad by the leading industrial nations of the world, particularly the European nations and Japan, are difficult to get. Those countries do not compile such statistics. Often when a country does report the amounts of its capital exports to another country, those amounts and the recipient country's estimates of its capital imports from the exporting country do not match. In many cases there is no uniformity in the methodology used to classify the statistics.

Neither the European Economic Community (EEC) nor the Organization for Economic Co-operation and Development has as yet attempted to compile comparable statistics on direct investments abroad and foreign investment inflows of member countries. The only source of comparable statistics, and the one used in this study, is the International Monetary Fund's *Balance of Payments Yearbook*, which reports inflows and outflows of direct investments on a country basis. But even that source does not contain complete and comparable statistics for all countries. For example, statistics on direct investment outflows and inflows for Switzerland are

Table 1. Direct investment flows of selected countries from 1964 to 1968 (millions of dollars)*

Year		Japan[1]	West Germany[2]	Belgium and Luxemburg[3]	France[4]	Norway[5]	Sweden[6]	Denmark[7]	Netherlands[8]	Italy	Spain	United Kingdom[9]	United States
1964	Inflow	109	531	242	232	15	39	82	164	536	79	454	322
	Outflow	57	231	108	132	2	93	8	116	136	1	737	3759
1965	Inflow	45	823	142	237	23	87	90	153	286	123	551	415
	Outflow	77	263	40	189	2	102	16	148	178	7	862	5010
1966	Inflow	30	860	140	293	28	139	43	158	384	134	546	425
	Outflow	305	306	8	170	7	118	6	256	130	6	773	5378
1967	Inflow	45	699	230	338	70	101	110	241	434	86	461	698
	Outflow	122	247	52	228	N.A.	110	N.A.	298	407	6	770	4752
1968	Inflow	76	401	250	196	28	104	N.A.	308	529	152	588	807
	Outflow	220	396	72	343	7	45	N.A.	346	424	9	1029	5167

SOURCES:

International Monetary Fund. *Balance of Payments Yearbook*, Vol. 21.

EEC Commission, *The Development of a European Capital Market*, Brussels, November 1966, Table 14, for 1964 and 1965 data for France and Italy.

Statistics for Italy for years 1966 to 1968 from Bank of Italy reported in OECD *Economic Survey on Italy*, Table H, August 1969.

1966 and 1967 data for France obtained from International Monetary Fund *Balance of Payments Yearbook*, Vol. 20.

Data for Japan, Sweden, United Kingdom, and United States including undistributed earnings. Estimates of undistributed earnings for all countries except United Kingdom and United States are not available.

*See definitions on facing page.

unavailable and those for France are incomplete. Often there is a discrepancy between the International Monetary Fund's statistics and those reported by the U.S. Department of Commerce.

In spite of these difficulties, an attempt has been made to answer the questions raised earlier in this section.

Direct Investment Outflows

There is certainly an upward trend in the direct investments abroad not only by the United States but by almost all the leading industrial nations of the world. Table 1 presents direct investment outflows and inflows for selected leading industrial nations from 1964 to 1968. The United States had by far the largest direct investments abroad, which stood at about $5.2 billion in 1968. The United Kingdom had the second largest direct investments abroad in 1968, which then amounted to $1 billion. Following those two nations were Italy at $424 million, Germany at $396 million, the Netherlands at $346 million, France at $343 million, and Japan at $220 million. Those seven countries were thus the leaders in direct investments abroad in 1968. Also, back in 1964 the United States was the leader in direct investments abroad, which amounted to $3.7 billion, followed by the

---

Definitions of Direct Investment
1. Inflow entries cover total foreign investment in direct-investment enterprises, that is, investment both by controlling and by minority interests.
2. The separation of direct investment from other private long-term capital is incomplete. Some loans to direct-investment companies appropriate here are classified under other private long-term capital.
3. Entries cover long-term investment. Short-term transactions and reinvested earnings are not included.
4. For years 1964 and 1965 direct investment is undefined in *The Development of a European Capital Market*. For 1966 direct investment as defined in *Balance of Payments Yearbook*, Vol. 20, excludes intercompany loans and includes all investment in real estate.
5. Inflow entries for 1965 to 1968 include loans extended by foreign parent companies to their subsidiaries in Norway. Separate data for these loans in 1964 are unavailable. The inflow entry for 1967 includes the direct investment caused by the purchase by a Canadian company of Norwegian government-held shares in two Norwegian companies. The proceeds were used by the government to purchase shares in the Canadian company.
6. Reinvested undistributed earnings are included, but the undistributed earnings figures are incomplete.
7. Not defined.
8. Net of liquidations and repayments.
9. Investment in United Kingdom excludes oil and insurance companies. Investment abroad excludes oil companies. Subsidiaries include associated companies. Investment is net of disinvestment. Investment by United Kingdom insurance companies in their overseas branches and subsidiaries is included.

United Kingdom, West Germany, Italy, France, the Netherlands, and the Belgium and Luxemburg Economic Union. Japanese direct investments abroad were relatively small in 1964 at $57 million; in that year they were less than those of Sweden, at $93 million.

Japanese direct investments abroad have been on the rise since 1964. The increase has amounted to 286 percent from 1964 to 1968, an average increase of 72 percent per year. Japan in 1964 ranked eighth in direct investments abroad; now it ranks sixth.

Italy and the Netherlands also have shown a substantial increase in direct investments abroad, with an increase of over 200 percent from 1964 to 1968 for the former and 198 percent for the latter, an average growth per year of 53 and 49.5 percent respectively.

France comes next in growth rate of direct investments abroad; it amounted to 160 percent from 1964 to 1968, an average growth rate of 40 percent per year. West Germany was next with a growth of 71.5 percent for the period, an average growth rate of 18 percent per year, and was fol-lowed by the United Kingdom with a growth rate of 40 percent, an aver-age of 10 percent per year, and the United States with 37 percent growth rate and an average of 9 percent per year.

Countries that have shown not growth but an actual decline in their direct investments abroad from 1964 to 1968 are the Belgium and Luxem-burg Economic Union and Sweden, both of which were among the leaders and ahead of Japan and almost equal to the Netherlands in 1964. Direct investments abroad by the Belgium and Luxemburg Economic Union fell 93 percent from 1964 to 1966, but they rose again 800 percent from 1966 to 1968 and 38 percent from 1967 to 1968. Yet on the whole, the Belgium and Luxemburg Economic Union has shown a drop of 33.3 percent in its direct investments abroad from 1964 to 1968. Swedish net direct invest-ments abroad grew at the average rate of 9 percent per year from 1964 to 1967, but dropped 59 percent from 1967 to 1968. This has accounted for an overall drop of 52 percent from 1964 to 1968 and an average drop of 13 percent per year since 1964. Sweden's investment abroad in 1968 amounted to $45 million.

The pattern of direct investments abroad by the leading industrial nations indicates that although the total United States direct investments abroad are the largest and have been so for quite a few years, they have not been growing as rapidly as those of some industrialized countries. United States direct investments abroad in 1968 showed an increase of 9 percent over the 1967 figure, whereas in comparison Japan registered a jump of 80 percent, West Germany a jump of 60 percent, and the United Kingdom an increase of 34 percent. For Italy and the Netherlands the increase for the period amounted to 4 and 16 percent, respectively. All indications are that, although the United States in the future will be a dominating force abroad because of its huge base of direct investments overseas, countries such as Japan, the Netherlands, Germany, Italy, France, and the United Kingdom will also have their presence felt in the international direct investments scene. Not to be forgotten is Switzerland, whose statistics on direct investments are not presented because of their nonavailability but whose aggregate foreign investment as a percent of GNP is believed to be larger than that of any other country.

Direct Investment Inflows

As far as inflows of direct investments are concerned, the biggest recipient in 1964 was Italy, followed closely by West Germany. The United Kingdom was the next biggest recipient of such investments followed by the United States. Direct-investment inflows into West Germany were largest until 1966, at which time they stood at $860 million. They dropped by 19 percent in 1967 to $699 million. Direct-investment inflows into the United States were $425 million in 1966, but they jumped by 64 percent in 1967 to $698 million. Thus West Germany and the United States had almost identical amounts of direct-investment inflows in 1967. German direct investment inflows fell again by 43 percent to $401 million in 1968, but during the same period inflows into the United States grew by 16 percent to $807 million in 1968. Thus the United States became the biggest recipient of direct-investment inflows among the leading industrial nations of the world. Similarly, the United Kingdom, which lagged behind Germany in its inflows of direct investments, moved ahead in 1968 with a jump of 27.5 percent to a total of $588 million.

The leading recipients of direct foreign investments in 1968 in their order of importance were the United States, the United Kingdom, Italy, West Germany, the Netherlands, Belgium and Luxemburg Economic Union, and France. It should be noted that the average inflows from 1964 to 1968 for Germany and France have been declining at the rate of 6 and 4 percent respectively. (Inflows into France dropped by 42 percent from 1967 to 1968.) Inflows into the Belgium and Luxemburg Economic Union for the same period have grown at an average yearly rate of about 1 percent, but they grew 79 percent from 1966 to 1968. During the 1964 to 1968 period, average inflows into the United States and the Netherlands have grown at the rate of 38 and 22 percent, respectively.

Also significant, although not in terms of absolute dollar amounts, has been the growth of direct investments into Sweden, which grew from a low of $39 million in 1964 to $104 million in 1968, an average yearly growth rate of 42 percent. Inflows into Japan have been historically low, mainly because of restrictions by the Japanese government. But with the recent relaxation of the restrictions on foreign investments in Japan, inflows increased from $45 million in 1967 to $76 million in 1968, a growth of 69 percent.

Table 2 shows the direct-investment inflows and outflows of the different countries as a percent of respective gross national products for 1968. The figures throw further light upon how deeply involved a country is in the direct-investment field.

Table 2. Direct investment flows of selected countries as a percent of GNP (1968).

	Japan	West Germany	Belgium and Luxemburg	France	Norway	Sweden
GNP (In billions)	$141.92	$132.20	$20.28	$126.28	$9.01	$25.54
Inflow, %	0.05	0.30	1.20	0.15	0.31	0.41
Outflow, %	0.16	0.30	0.34	0.27	0.08	0.18

	Denmark	Netherlands	Italy	Spain	United Kingdom	United States
GNP (In billions)	$12.41	$25.30	$74.96	$25.26	$101.86	$865.70
Inflow, %	N.A.	1.22	0.70	0.60	0.58	0.09
Outflow, %	N.A.	1.37	0.56	0.04	1.01	0.60

Countries Likely to Generate Multinational Companies

From the analysis of outflows and inflows of direct investments by a select group of industrial nations, certain generalizations can be made. One note of caution should be injected at this point. It is not at all clear how much of these inflows and outflows is contributed by the foreign subsidiaries of multinational companies. For example, how much of the direct-investment inflows into the Netherlands is contributed by a Swiss subsidiary of a U.S. company? And how much of the direct investments flowing out of Italy should be attributed to a U.S. company's subsidiary located in Italy?

Taking those limitations into consideration, it seems that, provided the current growth trends in direct-investment outflows continue, the countries that should provide the most fertile ground for the birth, growth, and development of multinational and world companies in the foreseeable future are the United States, the United Kingdom, Italy, West Germany,

Switzerland, the Netherlands, Japan, and France, more or less in that order.

If the United Kingdom can enter the EEC, solve its economic problems, and show an improvement in its balance of payments, then a subsequent relaxation of its curbs on British business investments abroad could make the United Kingdom a very solid base for the growth of multinational companies.

Tight labor market conditions at home are forcing West German industry to move its production facilities abroad. Besides, West Germany now has ample foreign exchange reserves and balance-of-payments surpluses. Direct investments abroad by West German firms are bound to rise by orders of magnitude in the next decade. The revaluation of the West German mark in 1969 has made it cheaper for West Germans to build plants abroad or to buy into foreign countries. This is yet another factor that could stimulate the growth of multinational companies based in West Germany.

Switzerland, like West Germany, is also faced with an extremely tight labor market both for skilled and unskilled labor. Whereas in West Germany there are no restrictions on the importation of labor from neighboring countries, Swiss industry has to live with stiff governmental restrictions on such imports. The desire to preserve the Swiss identity and heritage in a country with a population of about 6 million people is the motivation behind the tight curbs imposed by the Swiss government on the importation of foreign workers. Economically, like West Germany, Switzerland is very healthy. For these and other reasons that will be discussed in later chapters, Swiss industry, like West German industry, is bound to establish a great number of its new production facilities abroad. Thus, in the foreseeable future, Switzerland should generate a great number of new multinational companies.

Countries that should be favorites for the location of foreign subsidiaries—wholly or partly owned—are the United States, the Netherlands, Italy, the United Kingdom, Belgium and Luxemburg, and West Germany, approximately in that order. Although growth rates of investment inflows into Japan have been high during the past few years, the Japanese government, despite its moderate change in attitude recently, has definitely been inhospitable to foreign private investment and ownership. Clamor against such restrictive policies of the Japanese government by the Japanese business community as well as the international business community, particularly in the United States, may force a further relaxation of the capital import restrictions.

Thus far, Japanese companies have been able to grow to a great extent by purchasing technology abroad and adapting it to various uses and environments. But if that method of acquiring new technology proves to be inadequate in the future—and indications are that the Japanese companies have already reached that stage and are making their predicament known to the government—then Japan may have to open its doors to foreign private investments as a means of obtaining the required technology.

Industries Likely to Generate Multinational Companies

Which industries are most likely to support the growth of multinational companies? Statistics for capital-exporting countries, other than the United States, pertaining to the inflows and outflows of direct investments classified on the basis of industry are almost nonexistent or obscure. The paucity of such data for other countries should not deter us from making certain broad generalizations based upon the figures we have available for the United States. Although the United States has no monopoly on international investment—the ready availability of U.S. statistics in the absence of similar statistics from other countries has tended to give the contrary impression—it is still true that U.S. investments abroad are quite significant and larger than those of any other country.

It has been estimated that the ratio of the book value of U.S. direct investments abroad to the value of the output of such investments abroad is 2 to 1. For 1968 the book value of U.S. direct investments abroad was close to $65 billion (Table 3). It follows that the output of all foreign affiliates of United States companies abroad was a monumental $130 billion during 1968.[1]

At the end of 1968 the book value of direct investments abroad was $64.7 billion, more than twice the amount at the beginning of the decade and about 44 percent of all U.S. investments abroad during 1968. About 41 percent of the total was in manufacturing affiliates, 29 percent in petroleum, 8 percent in mining, and 22 percent in all other industries. At the end of 1960, petroleum and manufacturing affiliates each had 34 percent of the total book value of investments for that year. But from 1960 to 1968 manufacturing has been the fastest-growing category with a growth of 131 percent for the period and an average yearly growth rate of 16 percent.

Latin America and Canada were the most favored areas of investment at the end of 1960; they accounted for approximately 25 and 34 percent of the total book value of direct investments, respectively, and Europe got about 21 percent. By the end of 1968 the book value of direct investments in Europe had risen to 29 percent of the total book value of direct investments. The direct investments in Latin America and Canada had dropped to 20 and 30 percent, respectively. Thus in 1968 close to 60 percent of the

Table 3. Book value of United States direct investments abroad from 1960 to 1968 by area and industry (millions of dollars).

		Book Value at Year's End			
	Total	Mining and smelting	Petroleum	Manu-facturing	Other
All areas, total:					
1960	31,865	2,997	10,810	11,051	7,007
1961	34,717	3,094	12,190	11,997	7,436
1962	37,276	3,244	12,725	13,250	8,057
1963	40,736	3,419	13,652	14,937	8,728
1964	44,480	3,665	14,328	16,935	9,552
1965	49,474	3,931	15,298	19,339	10,906
1966	54,777	4,365	16,200	22,078	12,134
1967	59,486	4,876	17,404	24,167	13,039
1968	64,756	5,370	18,835	26,354	14,196
Canada:					
1960	11,179	1,325	2,664	4,827	2,363
1961	11,602	1,367	2,828	5,076	2,331
1962	12,133	1,489	2,875	5,312	2,457
1963	13,044	1,549	3,134	5,761	2,600
1964	13,855	1,713	3,196	6,198	2,748
1965	15,318	1,851	3,356	6,872	3,239
1966	17,017	2,089	3,608	7,692	3,628
1967	18,097	2,342	3,819	8,095	3,842
1968	19,488	2,636	4,088	8,546	4,219
Latin America:*					
1960	8,365	1,319	3,122	1,521	2,403
1961	9,239	1,332	3,674	1,707	2,526
1962	9,524	1,321	3,642	1,944	2,617
1963	9,941	1,353	3,636	2,213	2,739
1964	10,254	1,404	3,589	2,507	2,754
1965	10,886	1,474	3,546	2,945	2,921
1966	11,498	1,565	3,475	3,318	3,141
1967	12,044	1,708	3,472	3,581	3,283
1968	12,989	1,875	3,643	3,990	3,480
Europe:					
1960	6,691	49	1,763	3,804	1,075
1961	7,742	48	2,152	4,255	1,287
1962	8,930	50	2,385	4,883	1,612
1963	10,340	55	2,776	5,634	1,875
1964	12,129	56	3,122	6,587	2,364
1965	13,985	54	3,427	7,606	2,898
1966	16,212	54	3,981	8,879	3,297
1967	17,926	61	4,423	9,798	3,645
1968	19,386	61	4,640	10,778	3,908
Other areas:					
1960	5,630	304	3,261	899	1,166
1961	6,134	347	3,536	959	1,292
1962	6,689	384	3,823	1,111	1,371
1963	7,411	462	4,106	1,329	1,514
1964	8,242	492	4,421	1,643	1,686
1965	9,285	552	4,969	1,916	1,848

*Includes "Other Western Hemisphere."
SOURCE: U.S. Department of Commerce, *Survey of Current Business,* October 1969, Table 8, p. 30.

total book value of foreign investments was concentrated in Europe and Canada. Other areas of the world accounted for 20 percent of the total.

Around 17 percent of the total book value of direct investments in 1968 was concentrated in Europe in the manufacturing sector. That amounted to 58 percent, or more than half of the $19.3 billion total book value of direct investments in Europe at the end of the year.

Other areas of the world besides Canada, Latin America, and Europe received in 1968 about 10 percent of the $12.8 billion total book value of foreign investments. Of that amount almost 50 percent represented investments in the petroleum sector. They included petroleum investments in Libya, the Middle East, and the West African countries.

The above analyses show that a large amount of direct investments abroad by the United States has been made in the manufacturing and petroleum sector. If the behavioral patterns in world business of the industrialized nations during the last two decades are taken as reliable indicators of the current and future patterns, then we could make a general prediction that they will react positively to face the American challenge head-on. That would involve their entering the United States market as well as third-country markets in fields in which American industry is concentrating. Hence, in all probability, the manufacturing and petroleum industries will be the two biggest fields in which we shall see the birth and growth of new and existing multinational companies.

REFERENCES

1. Neil H. Jacoby, "The Multinational Corporation," *The Center Magazine*, Vol. 3, No. 3 (May 1970), p. 38.

2. "Multinational Companies," *Business Week*, April 20, 1963, pp. 63, 64.

3. Virgil Salera, *Multinational Business* (Boston: Houghton Mifflin Company, 1969), p. 9.

4. Judd Polk, *U.S. Exports and U.S. Production Abroad* (New York: U.S. Council of the International Chamber of Commerce, Inc., 1967), p. 5.

2

The Impact of Multinational
Market Organizations

THE growth of regional economic blocs was pointed out by American and European companies interviewed as one of the biggest stimulants to the growth and development of multinational companies. In this chapter we shall take a look at the phenomenon.

Since the end of World War II, we have witnessed efforts on the part of nations in different regions of the world, particularly those in Europe and Latin America, to integrate their economies. The European Economic Community (EEC), the Latin American Free Trade Association (LAFTA), the European Free Trade Association (EFTA), and the Central American Common Market (CACM) are results of such efforts. The trend toward integration of economies of countries is likely to increase and spread to countries of Asia and Africa. There are presently thirty countries that are members of one or another of the four leading multinational market organizations just mentioned. The trade patterns of the world have been substantially altered because of the global rush toward economic integration.

The principal objective of economic integration is the widening of markets and the increase in size of the economy or the business system of the group of countries as a whole in order to permit member countries to take advantage of economies of scale. Large markets permit greater efficiency in production and larger investments and provide investments in new fields. The assumption is that the productive efficiency of the integrated business system will rise to a higher level than the respective levels of productive efficiencies of the member countries as autonomous economic entities. It can very well be argued that the growth of giant American companies is the result of there being a large United States market free from interstate trade restrictions.

A logical consequence of the widening of the market is the rise of multinational companies in the multinational market organizations that take advantage of the opportunities created by the linking of previously disconnected economies. In this chapter we shall first discuss the four leading multinational market organizations (EEC, EFTA, LAFTA, and CACM), their objectives, and the extent to which those objectives have been achieved to date. Next we shall focus on the EEC, which is the most advanced regional economic bloc of all, and see how American companies in Europe have stimulated the birth and growth of European giants.

The European Economic Community

The formation of the European Economic Community, generally referred to as the European Common Market, was the culmination of several earlier efforts by European nations to form regional economic groupings of one kind or another.

Historical Antecedents

Until World War II, the main objective of European countries was to be as self-sufficient as possible and thereby minimize interdependence among nations. To achieve that objective, each country adopted policies aimed at promoting its own self-interest and independence at the expense of the interests and independence of other countries. The rise of nationalism during the interwar period saw nations formulating their economic policies on a basis not of economic considerations, but of political ones. That led to various forms of trade and currency restrictions, bilateral trade treaties, and other types of discrimination in the trade relations among nations. The economic warfare among European nations ultimately resulted in armed warfare in 1939.

The European participants in World War II suffered great losses of life and property. What the economists refer to as social capital—roads, bridges, public utilities, and transportation facilities—was terribly depleted. Factories, mills, and other production facilities that survived enemy action were run down, outmoded, and inefficient because of nonreplacement and overuse during the war. Agriculture also was in disarray because lack of fertilizer and overexploitation had made the land infertile. Trade was brought to a standstill and required normalization. The European countries were on the verge of total disaster and ripe for Communist subversion and takeover. The Soviet Union had already taken over Eastern Europe, and it was decidedly unfriendly to American efforts to negotiate the restoration of freely elected governments in the countries there. On the contrary, the Soviet Union had designs to take advantage of the weak economic conditions and convert the Western European countries to its political ideology.

The only way to save Western Europe from total collapse was through a massive foreign aid program to rebuild the devastated countries. That idea was the basis of the European Recovery Program, commonly known as the Marshall Plan. There was a general concern in the United States that the funds allotted by it to be used for the rebuilding and effective integration of the European economies might be used not for those purposes, but instead for paramilitary or nationalistic ones. The Marshall Plan was offered under the condition that the recipient countries make concrete organizational arrangements that would dispel U.S. fears.

The U.S. demands were met when in Paris, in April 1948, Austria, Belgium, Denmark, France, Greece, Ireland, Iceland, Italy, Luxemburg, the Netherlands, Norway, Portugal, Sweden, Switzerland, Turkey, the United Kingdom, and Western Occupied Germany signed the convention creating the Organization for European Economic Cooperation (OEEC).

The main purpose of the OEEC was to administer the Marshall Plan from 1948 to 1952 and that main purpose was achieved admirably. But in addition, OEEC served as the main vehicle that set in motion the wheels of European economic integration by embarking upon three additional programs. It created a subsidiary organization, the European Payments Union (EPU), that served as an international clearinghouse and helped in the settling of currency claims among member nations on a collective or multilateral basis. The EPU helped to restore regional convertibility and monetary stability of currencies in Europe, which enabled businessmen to use resources with maximum efficiency and best results. As might be expected, trade, investments, and production in Europe registered a marked increase.

The OEEC was also interested in trade liberalization. Although member nations agreed with the general principle of trade liberalization, conflicts arose over the means to be used in realizing the objective. One group, led by Britain, advocated global free trade as an objective to be pursued. The other group, led by France, advocated free trade among member nations and argued that any global free-trade scheme within the framework of the OEEC was unrealistic. Since the two factions could not be reconciled within the framework of the OEEC, the French-led group went ahead and signed at Paris, in April 1951, the Treaty Establishing the Coal and Steel Community (ECSC). The countries that signed the treaty included France, Belgium, West Germany, Italy, Luxemburg, and the Netherlands. The objective of the ECSC was to integrate the coal and steel production of member countries by creating a kind of customs union for those two products. A common intertariff against nonmembers was imposed, and internal tariffs on the two products were eliminated. A supranational high authority was created to govern the pooled industries.

Greatly encouraged by the success of the ECSC, the six member countries began active planning for an enlargement of the basic idea behind the ECSC to include many more products than just coal and steel. Their efforts culminated in the signing of the Treaty of Rome in 1958, establishing the European Economic Community (EEC). All other European countries were invited to join the EEC, but none did. Hence the EEC was left with the same membership as the ECSC.

EEC Goals and Achievements

The EEC member nations have agreed that the goals of the EEC should be implemented within 12 to 15 years. Since the treaty was signed in 1958, the goals should all be achieved and an integrated European community completed by 1973. We shall see now what goals were stipulated in 1958 and to what extent they have been achieved to date. The treaty called for a common market and unification of certain national economies. The goals discussed in the following paragraphs were to be achieved in order to accomplish this overall goal.

The common-market goals. The treaty called for the abolition of internal custom duties and the creation of a common external tariff applicable to imports from nonmember countries. All customs duties on trade in industrial goods within the community were eliminated on July 1, 1968. On the same date, the tariffs on goods imported from nonmember countries were fully harmonized.

The treaty's second important feature provided for the elimination of all quotas and other nontariff barriers to internal trade within the community. Although all quotas on trade in industrial goods among member nations have been removed as of July 1, 1968, other nontariff barriers remain. Plans are to remove them by the end of 1972. Thus although the tariff barriers have been eliminated, the goal of free and unimpeded movement of industrial goods among the member countries has yet to be fully realized. The import quotas on certain goods manufactured in other EEC countries imposed by France in 1968—at a time when France was in serious economic crisis—have set an unhealthy precedent for other EEC members to follow. The nontariff barriers have been the most difficult to abolish, and it remains to be seen when the goal of abolishing them will be achieved.

Another major goal is to create a common agricultural policy that provides for free trade within the community and unified marketing and pricing for farm goods both within the community and in trade with nonmember countries. Common policies have been established for most products, but there is not yet agreement on final agricultural financing arrangements. The devaluation of the French currency and upward revaluation of the West German currency have created temporary problems for the pricing of farm goods.

Little progress has been made on the goal of a common commercial policy involving harmonizing of national export assistance programs and establishing common trade agreements with nonmember countries. The goal of harmonization of indirect taxation to eliminate export subsidies and border taxes on imports has been partially achieved. All members, except Italy and Belgium, have adopted the value-added tax system; unification of rates is yet to be achieved. The three Benelux countries—Belgium, Luxemburg, and the Netherlands—have abolished all border taxes on imports from each other.

The unified-economy goal. The treaty called for the abolition of restrictions on movement of workers and capital and on the right to establish business anywhere in the community. Now there is almost unrestricted movement of workers and considerable freedom for direct investment among the member countries, although other types of capital movement are still controlled. Labor mobility is promoted by social legislation among the member countries that has been so well coordinated that workers can now move freely and continue to build social security rights by making contributions wherever they are employed within the community. EEC nationals can establish businesses in many sectors without legal constraints, but some national health and safety regulations still discriminate against foreign companies.

The EEC treaty provides for the establishment of antimonopoly measures and common rules against practices that distort or restrain competition by either private or public sectors of member countries. The community has clarified what constitutes an unfair business practice in a body of case law, but work remains to be done to eliminate discrimination due to national public procurement policies and national aid programs. An important goal of the treaty is to have each member nation formulate its own monetary and fiscal policies in coordination with the others in the community. Not much progress has been made in that area; national monetary and fiscal policies of each member nation are still set independently and with consideration of domestic needs only.

An important move was recently made by the finance ministers of the EEC toward the monetary integration they foresee by 1980. The finance ministers have decided that under no condition will they widen the margins of fluctuation between their currencies. Ever since the EEC was formed, the members have maintained a margin of no more than 0.75 percent on either side of parity. The ministers have agreed to progressively narrow the margins, but they have postponed a decision on just when the process should begin. If the EEC can fulfill its aspirations, the six currencies may eventually fluctuate as one in the foreign exchange markets. In the more distant future, it could even lead to the creation of a single monetary unit for all of the EEC that would replace national currencies.

Another prominent goal of the community is to create a common industrial policy that would eliminate the current obstacles to transnational mergers. The objective is that the common policy would include the adoption by member nations of a uniform company law. Little progress has been made in this area as well, primarily because of opposition to the creation of one EEC company law.

Thus EEC has made progress in some areas and has a long way to go in others. It has succeeded in creating a viable customs union. Members have abolished all tariffs on industrial goods for intracommunity trade. They have common tariffs on goods imported from non-EEC members. Quotas on industrial goods manufactured within EEC have been almost eliminated for intra-EEC trade. There is almost complete free movement of workers from one member country to another. Yet EEC members have not succeeded in sufficiently integrating the economies of the six member countries into one unit that in any way resembles the United States unit in either size or degree of integration. EEC members are, in effect, hoping to create total unification of their countries short of political unification. And there are many who hope that political unification will follow economic unification. The problem that EEC members are facing is that of surrendering national sovereignty and control on issues such as price levels, employment levels, transportation policies, and even currency values. But the overall impression that I received after talking with several European top management executives is that they all expect that EEC will succeed in further integration of the economies of its members and that more countries will join. They also assume that EFTA, which includes England, Norway, Sweden, Denmark, Austria, Portugal, and Switzerland, and EEC will merge in a few more years and that more countries will gain associate membership of the EEC. Therefore, companies in EEC as well as in EFTA are making their strategic decisions in areas such as plant location, R&D facilities location, and marketing on that fundamental assumption.

In sum, we can say that EEC has been more successful than not in achieving its overall mission, and all indications are that the progress made to date should proceed in the years ahead.

European Free Trade Association

EFTA was set up at the instigation of Britain at a time when Britain wanted to stay out of the EEC. It was created when Britain found that, contrary to her and many other countries' expectations, the EEC members' economies began to flourish. A club to rival the EEC therefore had to be formed. After a series of conferences, an international convention establishing the European Free Trade Association was signed at Stockholm in January 1960 by countries that were not willing or able to be associated with EEC, namely, Britain, Austria, Denmark, Portugal, Norway, Sweden, and Switzerland. The group has been dubbed the outer seven and is regarded as a defensive arrangement against the so-called inner six of the EEC.

The chief goal of EFTA was to liberalize trade in manufactured goods among the seven member countries. The goal has been achieved, since almost all industrial tariffs among the EFTA countries have been eliminated. Unlike the EEC, which is a customs union, EFTA is a free-trade area since the group does not seek to establish a common outer tariff against nonmembers. Importers could take advantage of the absence of internal tariffs by importing their products into the member country that had the lowest tariff on the particular product and then redistributing it to other EFTA countries duty-free. To prevent such practices, the Stockholm Convention required that every shipment moving from one EFTA country to another have a certificate of origin. Thus if a particular product was not produced in an EFTA country, the certificate of origin would identify the country of manufacture and the appropriate customs duty, if necessary, would be imposed. There is also a provision that products that are made with ingredients imported from nonmember countries in combination with domestic ingredients are to move free of customs duties if more than 50 percent of their value is created internally; if not, full customs duty is charged.

Unlike EEC, EFTA has not attempted to minimize constraints on the free flow of workers and capital among its members. Like EEC, it has been trying to reduce trade barriers on agricultural products, though it is not making as concerted an effort in that area as EEC is.

By and large, EFTA is a more loosely integrated union of member nations than EEC and makes much fewer demands on its members than EEC makes. Is EFTA a defensive success against EEC, and has it demonstrated its ability to negotiate and bargain with EEC on an equal footing? The answer is clearly no. Perhaps the best measure of the relative success of EFTA versus EEC is available from the persistent efforts made by Britain to enter EEC, the very group that Britain refused to join earlier. And if Britain succeeds in getting membership in the exclusive club of the inner six, then in all probability the other EFTA members will gain admission also as full members or associate members. Entry of EFTA members into EEC would be beneficial to Europe because most EFTA members are very actively promoting the economic unification of all of Europe.

Regardless of the form that it might ultimately take, the unification of EFTA and EEC is bound to happen. The movement toward increasing trade liberalization should push the two major economic blocs to an ultimate merger in the near future, and consequently we would see a huge market emerging in Europe, almost as large as in the United States.

Latin American Free Trade Association

Both the Latin American Free Trade Association, and the Central American Program of Economic Integration, commonly known as the Central American Common Market, took their initial conceptual and organizational ideas from EEC. We shall be considering the Central American Common Market later in this chapter and therefore the following discussion will be limited to the Latin American Free Trade Association.

LAFTA was created with the signing of the Treaty of Montevideo, Uruguay, in February 1960 by Argentina, Brazil, Chile, Mexico, Paraguay, Peru, and Uruguay. Bolivia, Colombia, Ecuador, and Venezuela joined the union later.

The long-term objective of LAFTA is to create a South American common market on the model developed by EEC. But in the meantime, LAFTA members hope to integrate their economies and expand the market area to enable them to pool their scarce resources to finance fundamental developments such as power and agricultural projects, transportation networks, and roads on a cooperative basis. The objective of LAFTA is much more than the mere expansion of trade among member nations; it includes economic growth of the LAFTA region as the prime goal.

The provisions of the treaty are to be implemented gradually over the

12-year period starting in June 1961. The treaty calls for the creation of a free-trade area during that period. There is no requirement to establish a common external tariff against nonmember countries. The treaty virtually excludes agricultural products except those that member countries voluntarily choose to include in a common schedule of items of intra-area trade that are to be free of customs duties by the time the 12-year period is over. The treaty calls for annual cuts of at least 8 percent of the average of duties applicable to imports from non-LAFTA countries. LAFTA members are free to determine the products on which they want to make reductions; thus the logical move for each country is to reduce tariffs only on the products that do not compete with domestic industry during the earlier years of the 12-year period.

Another objective of LAFTA is to promote Latin American economic development on the principles of "reciprocity" and "complementarity." Under the principle of reciprocity, members of the LAFTA group will negotiate reductions in tariff and nontariff barriers with each other by using the overall guideline that any concessions made would not harm the balance-of-payments and industrialization programs of the country making the concessions. The principle of complementarity urges the member countries to cooperate with industry and establish regionally integrated complementary industries located in different countries. The principle urges balanced economic growth for the entire region. The emphasis is upon planning and negotiation, rather than the market forces, to bring about the required specialization and complementarity with respect to various industries within Latin America. It recognizes that many countries cannot widen their industrial base within the confines of national markets. There is a hope that the various LAFTA countries will specialize and concentrate on the production of various products and intermediate goods to be sold in the entire LAFTA region.

Under a special provision of the treaty, less-developed countries are given special consideration in their reduction of tariffs and other restrictions on imports from other LAFTA countries. Such countries are also permitted to adopt special measures such as import quotas for the protection of their domestic industries, for balance-of-payments reasons, or for the sake of economic development.

Thus we can say that the LAFTA countries are trying to create, over a 12-year period, a free-trade zone that would permit goods to flow freely from one member country into another and that would allow each country to impose an independent tariff structure on goods it imports from third countries.

What has been the performance of LAFTA to date? Progress has been slow in promoting free trade among member nations because of the great amount of influence exerted by businessmen upon government leaders. As a result, the latter find it very difficult to override specific vested interests in favor of long-range LAFTA goals. There is also great dissimilarity in the economic development levels of different countries. As a result capital, management, and technology have tended to gravitate to the richer countries such as Argentina, Mexico, and Brazil. Inflation and currency instability in the region have created balance-of-payments problems in certain countries and forced them to resort to tariff restrictions. If the trend continues because of the disparities in the economic health of the member countries, it will be difficult for LAFTA to achieve its overall objectives.

The Central American Common Market

The Central American Common Market (CACM) came into being with the signing of the General Treaty on Central American Economic Integration in December 1960 at Managua, Nicaragua, by Costa Rica, El Salvador, Guatemala, Honduras, and Nicaragua. The treaty calls for the elimination of all tariffs and free intra-area trade for goods originating in the CACM countries. The treaty also provides for a common external tariff to be achieved in 10 years. Under the treaty, members are forbidden to grant tariff relief to goods produced outside the CACM if they are also produced within the CACM. Direct and indirect subsidies on exports by member countries are forbidden, as is discriminatory treatment of capital investments made by nationals of any country within the CACM. The member countries also hope to be able to effectuate the industrial integration of their economies. The CACM is thus aimed at creating something that is more than a customs union yet is not quite a common market.

As far as the progress made by CACM is concerned, the goal of a free-trade area has been achieved and common external tariffs have been agreed upon for approximately 85 percent of the total CACM imports from the rest of the world. The member nations have a market clearinghouse and monetary council through which monetary cooperation is achieved. There are also plans to establish a common currency. The similarities of the CACM countries certainly helped the countries in their integration efforts; a comparable similarity is not true of LAFTA members. All five countries are at an early stage of industrialization, and all five have enjoyed fairly stable currencies.

It can be said that on the whole the CACM has been much more successful than LAFTA. The CACM makes much greater demands on its members that LAFTA makes, but that is understandable, given the similar levels of economic development of the CACM members.

There are now plans for the merger of CACM with LAFTA into an all-inclusive Latin American common market, which would be open to other Latin American countries by 1985. The agreement was reached by the presidents of the Americas in a conference at Punta del Este, Uruguay, in the spring of 1967. The conference obtained a pledge from the United States for foreign aid to help finance the project. The plan could bring together into a single market countries that currently have a rapidly expanding population in excess of 250 million and a combined GNP that exceeds $100 billion. If successful, it could bring to Latin America economic and social progress of a magnitude never imagined in the past.

Toward a Global Business System

In spite of the problems encountered by the countries of Europe and the Americas in integrating their economies, the message that clearly comes through is that more and more countries of the world are realizing that in the long run, protectionism does not pay. There is emerging an understanding, an acceptance, of the basic premises on which capitalism is based: (1) that the marketplace is the best mechanism for the allocation of resources of production such as labor, capital, and management, (2) that the marketplace should decide what to produce, where to produce it, and in what quantitites, (3) that the marketplace should set the price on the products to be sold, and (4) that profit is the best measure of efficiency and business performance. There is also a greater acceptance that, again in the long run, it is more advantageous and in the national interest to search for new markets instead of closing doors and thereby protecting old markets from competition.

There is still a great amount of suspicion of and apprehension about foreign investments on the part of the developing nations, and that is especially true of direct foreign investments. But we are witnessing efforts by the countries of Asia, such as Indonesia, the Philippines, Thailand, Malaysia, and Singapore, to link their countries economically. Japan is also showing interest in some sort of a Far Eastern common market. Eighteen former African colonies of some of the EEC members, as well as Greece and Turkey, have associate membership with the EEC. Countries of East Africa have made attempts in the past to form and are still interested in forming some kind of customs union or free-trade area of their own. As the nations of the world progress economically, they will be much more receptive to foreign investments. And as they band together into regional economic units, their receptivity should increase. Thus, there is undoubtedly a worldwide trend toward economic integration.

Although formal trade blocs are the most evident signs of the trend toward economic integration of different national economies, other forces are helping the process. Many private and government-owned agencies designed specifically to assist and stimulate direct international investment make direct loans and finance projects. For example, Adela Investment Co. S.A. is a private international finance corporation based in Luxemburg that is oriented exclusively to the financing of private sector projects in Latin America. Other agencies that aid international direct investment are the International Bank for Reconstruction and Development (IBRD), popularly known as the World Bank, International Finance Corporation (IFC), Agency for International Development (AID), Inter-American Development Bank (IADB), and Institute for Latin American Integration (INTAL). Dozens of international organizations, including the Organization for Economic Cooperation (OECD) and the UN's regional economic commissions, are actively engaged in economic integration. All these agencies are laying the groundwork for balanced economic development on a regional basis in various parts of the world that would serve the purposes of increased trade and regional economic integration.

We are now witnessing efforts to merge the two major trading blocs in Europe, the EEC and the EFTA. At the Punta del Este conference, the presidents of the Americas pledged to merge LAFTA with CACM. Jamaica and the Dominican Republic have shown an interest in joining CACM. The former British colonies in the Caribbean (with the exception of British Honduras and the Bahamas), namely, Jamaica, Trinidad-Tobago, Barbados, and Guiana, have most recently formed a free trade zone called Caribbean Free Trade Association (CARIFTA). Independently of the new CARIFTA arrangement, negotiations are proceeding on the establishment of a Caribbean Development Bank, with financial backing from the United States, Canada, and the United Kingdom. The Caribbean economic integration scheme may, at a later date, serve as a bridge to some kind of cooperation with the CACM and eventually with the Latin American Common Market. Thus, the effort on the part of small groups of nations toward group protectionism and away from free trade might, in the long run, lead to greater free trade among an increasing number of countries. That could happen as more and more countries in similar stages of economic development form small regional economic groupings. And if the merger of the EEC with EFTA is consummated and is successful, that could very well serve as a driving force for the various regional economic groupings, at similar levels of sophistication, to merge to form larger market areas. And what could be more favorable to the development of multinational companies, which thrive upon the opening of national markets and the formation of large economic areas?

EEC Influence on Multinational Company Growth

The establishment of the EEC gave rise to a large increase in the multinational action of American companies within the Common Market region. Why were American companies much more effective in taking advantage of the community than were the European companies themselves? In spite of the great success of the Common Market, the industrial power gap between the United States and Europe, in terms of relative corporate strength, has not been significantly reduced.[1] I asked several top management executives in European companies for the reasons why American companies were so much more successful than European companies in creating large European operations. Almost all credited the superiority of American company research, finance, and management as the crucial factor.

What has been the European response to the American onslaught? A great number of European executives are realizing that the mere opening of national markets in the Common Market will not automatically bring about an organic growth of companies, and therefore a regrouping or merger of firms is a must to attain the managerial, technological, and financial capability in basic economic sectors necessary to compete successfully with the American giants. That conviction is manifested by the growth of mergers and cooperative deals now taking place within and between countries. The merger trend is most evident in the chemical, textile, automobile, computer, aircraft, and electrical industries.

Initially most mergers were confined within national frontiers, but now we see mergers across national frontiers. Many of those mergers were consummated with encouragement of the national governments, who were wary that key industries might succumb to American competition because of their small size. We shall now take a look at mergers within national boundaries.

England. (1) A giant computer group, International Computers (Holdings) Ltd., was formed after a series of mergers involving nine British-owned companies or divisions of companies. Sales in 1969 totaled more than $276 million. ICL is the only British maker of commercial and scientific computers. (2) British Leyland Motor Corporation was formed after a merger of eleven automobile manufacturers. Sales in 1969 were $2.3 billion, which makes the company the second largest European manufacturer of cars and trucks. (3) One large company in the field of electrical equipment and telecommunications, called General Electric and English Electric, was formed after a series of mergers that combined four large companies. Sales of the company in 1968 totaled more than $2 billion, which makes the company the second largest in the industry in Europe. (4) Rio

Tinto-Zinc Corp. Ltd. merged with Borax to form one large company with sales in excess of $697 million in 1968.

France. (1) Two giant electrical equipment manufacturers—Cie Générale d'Électricité and Thomson-Brandt, whose sales in 1968 were in excess of $900 million each—seem to be on the verge of merger. (2) A series of mergers have led to the formation of Rhône-Poulenc S.A. Sales in 1969 were estimated to be $2.1 billion, which makes the company one of the giants in the European chemical industry.

The Netherlands. The merger of Algemeine Kunstzijoe Unie (AKU) and Koninklijke Zout-Organon (KZO) will form a giant company in the chemical and textile industry with sales of over $1 billion.

West Germany. With the Bonn government actively supporting concentration of industries, we have seen the shipbuilding industry already concentrated. The aircraft industry has seen the merger of Messerschmidt and Boelkors. *Business Week* reports[2] that:

> The three all-German-owned companies—Volkswagen, Daimler-Benz, and BMW—can probably hold out separately for awhile. But VW officials expect that in five to ten years the industry will be narrowed down to one big company centered around VW and Daimler-Benz. BMW, small but profitable, has already made known that it is interested in talking to would-be partners.

Three of the largest chemical companies in Europe are located in Germany—Farbwerke Hoechst (sales in 1968 in excess of $1.9 billion), Farbenfabriken Bayer (sales in 1968 in excess of $1.7 billion), and BASF (sales in 1968 of more than $1.3 billion). All three have been engaged in taking over small companies for quite some time. BASF has taken over Wintershall AG, which is engaged in oil refining and chemicals and has sales of over $300 million. BASF has also acquired Nordmark, a drug manufacturing company.

Fortune reports that during 1969 there were 46 sizable mergers.[3] They include the pooling of the conventional and nuclear power plant businesses of Siemens and AEG Telefunken—the country's number-one and number-two electrical companies. That could lead to merger of the two companies. Similarly, Mannesmann AG and the Thyssen Group have created a jointly owned subsidiary that will produce about two-thirds of the national production of steel tubes.[4]

Italy. There were 176 major mergers in Italy from 1961 to 1967, reports *Business Week*.[5] Montecatini and Edison merged to form Montecatini Edison S.p.A., Italy's largest industrial company with sales of over $2.3 billion. Italy's two state-owned companies—ENI and IRI—then acquired almost complete control of Montecatini Edison. Two big petrochemicals makers of Italy—Società Italiana Resine and Rumianca S.p.A.—probably will merge.[6] Fiat has taken over Ferrari, a car maker whose specialty was in racing car manufacture.

Sweden. The United States is beginning to challenge Swedish markets in Europe in the pulp and paper industry, in which there is a great deal of activity to promote mergers of small, marginal companies.[7] The government is also creating conglomerates of nationalized companies.[8] Two large steel makers—Grangesberg Co. and Stora Kopparbergs Berlags AB—have coordinated their production facilities and formed a joint export company.

Belgium. The two largest steel companies in Belgium, Cockerill-Oug-rée-Providence and Longdoz S.A., have decided to merge.

Switzerland. Brown Boveri and Sulzer Brothers, both makers of turbines, have combined their turbocompressor and gas turbine businesses and formed a joint subsidiary. Brown Boveri said that the agreement represented "another important step towards combatting steadily rising costs, the fierce competition with much larger firms abroad, and the evermore acute lack of staff in Switzerland."[9] Brown Boveri also acquired the Oerlikon Engineering Company "with the intention of uniting its staff and production facilities with those of Brown Boveri and so eliminating duplication of effort in their respective activities."[10] The Swiss chemical and pharmaceutical giants, CIBA and Geigy, have now also merged.[11] Sales of each in 1968 were over $600 million. The merger had not been accomplished until now, mainly because of the uncertainty over how the U.S. Justice Department would view it. Both companies have sizable interests in the United States.

Transnational Mergers

Competition from U.S. companies has set off a wave of national mergers in Europe, but now there are signs that U.S. competition is also igniting transnational mergers and cooperative arrangements that fall short of merger. To date there have been only two transnational mergers since World War II. The first came about five years ago when Agfa, a German subsidiary of the German company Bayer, and Belgium's Gevaert Photo-Producten merged. The two separate photographic companies were facing fierce competition from Eastman Kodak. Agfa had a good name in the amateur market, and Gevaert was well known in the industrial and technical market.

The other transnational merger took place more recently between Fokker, a small aircraft company partly owned by the Fokker family, the Dutch government, and the American Northrop, and Germany's VFW, a privately owned aircraft firm in which the American United Aircraft has minority interest. The two companies had previously done a considerable amount of joint project work. The arrangement may lead to a multinationally owned European aircraft company. But what is significant is that these two transnational mergers took place in industries that are dominated greatly by American companies and in which independent existence and growth were most doubtful. The American companies had overwhelming research superiority in both cases. In fact, it was the need to pool their research capabilities together that accounted for the Agfa-Gevaert and Fokker-VFW mergers.[12]

A most recent transnational venture was announced in March 1970 when Dunlop, an English company, and Pirelli, an Italian company, formed an alliance of unusual significance, one that may set the example for other European companies to follow. Under the agreement, each agreed to take a 49 and 40 percent interest in the other's domestic and overseas facilities, respectively. The combined gross sales of the two companies will total more than $2 billion, which will make the combine the third largest rubber-processing venture in the world behind Goodyear and Firestone. To circumvent legal complications, the two companies will remain independent but will operate as holding companies.

There have been many transnational arrangements that fall short of merger. Nestlé and Unilever have combined their frozen food and ice cream subsidiaries in Austria, Germany, and Italy. Hoechst, the German chemical concern, has bought a minority interest in Roussel Uclaf, a French chemical and drug maker, and the two companies have agreed to cooperate worldwide in production, research, and marketing. Roussel Uclaf has its own arrangement with Boehringer Mannheim, a large German pharmaceuticals firm, to cooperate in sales and production. AKU, prior to its merger with KZO (referred to earlier in this chapter) bought Fabelta, a Belgian company, in order to solidify its position in the synthetic fiber industry. Demag AG, a large German machinery producer, and Richier, International Export, a large French construction company, have agreed to cooperate in R&D marketing, joint planning, and exchange of know-how. Fiat, the Italian car maker, has a 15 percent interest in France's Citroen, and the two have formed a joint company to cooperate in certain technical and commercial areas.

Many European executives when I interviewed believe that there are still many barriers to full-scale mergers across national boundaries, but that there are ways of getting around them. Nationalism seems to be the big barrier, especially if a transnational merger involves a firm that is a country's largest or the only firm in the particular industry. If that were not so, transnational mergers would be consummated rather easily, and often with the help of the national governments concerned. Many executives referred to the numerous transnational cooperative arrangements between companies in R&D, production, marketing, and exchange of know-how as the kind of arrangements that will grow in the future and lay the foundation for transnational mergers and integration of industry in Europe.

REFERENCES

1. Doina Thomas, "Europe Calls for Combines," in Etienne Cracco, ed., *International Business—1970: A Selection of Current Readings* (East Lansing, Mich.: Division of Research, Graduate School of Business Administration, Michigan State University, 1970), p. 82.

2. "Europe's Merger Boom Thunders a Lot Louder," *Business Week*, November 23, 1968, p. 56.

3. Philip Siekman, "Europe's Love Affair with Bigness," *Fortune*, March 1970, p. 98.

4. Ibid.

5. *Business Week*, op. cit., p. 55.

6. Ibid., p. 53.

7. Ibid., p. 56.

8. *Fortune*, op. cit., p. 98.

9. Brown Boveri, annual report, 1967–68, p. 7.

10. Ibid., p. 27.

11. Letter from CIBA regarding CIBA-Geigy Merger.

12. Doina Thomas, op. cit., p. 84.

3

Forces Favoring the Development of World Enterprises

THERE are several forces other than those discussed in the preceding chapter that not only aid in the growth and development of new multinational companies but also serve as catalysts in the evolution of multinational companies into world enterprises. Some of them can be considered as being internal to the company in the sense that they could be altered or modified by the company's owners, board of directors, or top management. Others are not directly controllable by the company, although company actions could have an indirect influence upon them. They could be considered as external to the company. In this chapter five internal and six external forces specified by companies interviewed will be discussed.

Forces Internal to the Company

Quality and Attitude of Management

Executives in fourteen companies interviewed referred to the importance of skilled management, top management support, and proper attitude toward international operations at the top management level to a company that aspires to become globally oriented in its operations. The executives spoke about the importance of good management not only in the parent company but in the subsidiaries abroad as well. Here are a few examples of the importance of good management to the company cited by the top management personnel of some multinational companies interviewed:

> Excellent management at the "nerve center" in Vevey and the will of the people who run the company to grow big and multinational. The excellent "comaraderie" between the different foreign nations at the head office. The head office is like a miniature United Nations—34 percent of a total staff of 1,500 persons at the headquarters are foreigners. More than 50 percent of Nestlé upper management are foreigners. *Pierre Liotard-Vogt, managing director, Nestlé Alimentana S.A., Vevey, Switzerland.*

> The top management of Dunlop realizes that decisions taken by them will have an effect 10 to 15 years from now. Dunlop's top management have the professional pride and motivation that they do not want, when they retire, to leave behind a weakness that will be discovered later. *Sir Reay Geddes, chairman, The Dunlop Company Ltd., London.*

> Good people in any enterprise today is the key to success. It is not your products. It is not your technology. It is your people. If you have attracted good people, there will be a great deal of self-generated drive which is partly ambition provided it is reasonably healthy and controlled. These people want to go places. They will see to it that there will be enough new opportunities being brought to the attention of the corporation, being investigated, being pursued, and being fought for. I think the biggest internal force is a good, dynamic, management team. *W. E. Lehmann, vice-president and director for Europe, Africa, and Middle East, Johns-Manville Corporation, New York.*

The importance of an international attitude on the part of management also was stressed by executives interviewed. For example

> The company had to go abroad for rubber, its main raw material, well before the turn of the century. Thus, from the very beginning, the Dunlop organization has been international-minded. This attitude proved to be a stimulating factor in the company's expansion overseas. *Sir Reay Geddes, chairman, the Dunlop Company, Ltd., London.*

> Here throughout the Scott operation, there is a very sympathetic understanding of the international market, a very strong feeling that we should be in international business in a major way. Therefore, we have very powerful support of recommendations from our international division at the top level of business. *James D. Stocker, Jr., division vice-president, international services, Scott Paper Company, Philadelphia, Pennsylvania.*

The crucial role played by the top management and especially by the chief executive was stressed by many executives. An executive of a major American company expressed it as follows:

> I am going to give you a controversial but honest answer. There has
> been very little stimulation on the part of corporate management until
> the present chief executive took over. He has been the first president
> of the company who took more than a casual interest in the interna-
> tional operations. He has encouraged us to grow. . . . It was a hard fight
> [before] to get even a hearing and hard to get meaningful support in terms
> of people, money, and facilities to make a start. Once we got going and
> standing on our feet, with the new chief executive who has been with us
> now for about ten years, the thing has radically changed. Today, interna-
> tional [Division] is one of the not only accepted but important parts of the
> corporate image and purpose.

A company can grow abroad rapidly if it has top management support and good management at the corporate level. But an important role is also played by the management of the subsidiaries or affiliates abroad, who often come up with new ideas and recommendations. That was mentioned by numerous executives interviewed and was stressed by executives in companies such as Imperial Chemical Industries Ltd., Unilever, Royal Dutch/Shell, Brown, Boveri and Company, Ltd., and The East Asiatic Company Ltd. The executives gave many examples of how new manufacturing and production subsidiaries were established abroad based upon recommendations made by managers of foreign subsidiaries. The East Asiatic Company, of Copenhagen, has had several manufacturing facilities abroad set up on the recommendations made by its trading branches abroad.

Nature and Type of Products Produced

The products that a company produces have an effect on the extent of its international operations. For example, Alfa-Laval AB, of Sweden, mentioned that certain products that the company makes, such as tanks, steel sheet work, piping, and fittings, cannot take costs of exportation and therefore have to be manufactured abroad where the local market exists.

There are companies who make products whose demand is positively correlated with the standard of living of the world and that can be consumed by almost everybody. Consequently, if the standard of living goes up, then the demand for the products also goes up. An example is that of

Scott Paper Company, whose products—paper towels, facial tissues, and so on—help the pursuit of cleanliness and hygiene. The desire on the part of people to be clean and hygienic is bound to go up as their living standards rise, and as a result the demand for paper towels and tissues is also likely to rise. Scott Paper has a good reputation worldwide, and that has accounted for private industrialists abroad approaching Scott with proposals to go into business in collaboration with them.

Nestlé Alimentana S.A. and Unilever are also producers of products. such as condensed milk, margarine, butter, and chocolate, that are connected with the standard of living of people. The increased standard of living of people all over the world should help Nestlé and Unilever, because both produce inexpensive, subsistence foods as well as prepared foods that are a little more expensive. Referring to Nestlé's products, Pierre Liotard-Vogt, managing director of Nestlé, says "Nestlé products help fight famine as well as furnish feasts." The same is true of Unilever.

The Metal Box Company Limited is yet another firm whose product sales are based upon derived demand. The company makes containers of all sizes to perserve food. K. D. Brough, the managing director of the company, is of the opinion that the need for preserving food is going to increase, since food may have to be grown and preserved in areas that do not necessarily need the food. And although the can is not the only way to preserve food, it is widely used for the purpose. For example, Hawaii is becoming such a favorite and popular holiday resort that land prices there are skyrocketing. As a result of the escalation of land prices, leases on the pineapple lands are falling through. That means that before very long there will be no Hawaiian pineapples left. The American pineapple growers are now looking for other areas suitable for growing pineapples. The east and west coasts of Africa, Kenya, Formosa, Malaysia, and the Philippines are possible areas.

The need to preserve the food grown in distant lands for use somewhere else will put demand on cans. That is where The Metal Box Company comes into the picture. Metal Box will go abroad wherever the packagers will go, provided, of course, that there is a packager abroad who will buy cans in sufficient quantity to enable Metal Box to build a plant that is economically feasible.

The big force that will promote the growth and development of Metal Box as a multinational company is the increasing demand for containers of all sizes to preserve food. The more multinational that this demand for containers becomes, the more multinational will the company become.

The bread-and-butter product of Landis and Gyr AG, of Switzerland, is meters. The meters are bought by public utility companies, and every country's public utilities have their own specifications. Also, each country, for nationalistic and precautionary reasons, prefers to buy locally made meters. The company therefore began to produce meters abroad in wholly owned subsidiaries, which became the nucleus for further expansion abroad into other product lines formerly marketed in Switzerland alone. Besides, meters are also used in private homes for heating and cooling—known as the comfort market. The increase in per capita income and the associated growth of consumer buying power all over Europe and elsewhere will rapidly expand the market for capital and consumer goods in the comfort market and consequently for meters as well.

There are certain products that have to be produced near the source of supply of raw materials. For example, Nestlé Alimentana S.A. is engaged in making milk products, among other things. Milk spoils if it is transported over long distances. Hence, the production and distribution units of milk products have to be built near the source of supply of milk. Nestlé has management, production, and distribution facilities in almost every country. Thus it found itself ideally placed when it decided to diversify its product line. The mechanics of making and distributing milk products provided Nestlé with a ready-made base for expansion abroad.

All companies that make soups, such as Campbell Soup, Nestlé, Unilever, and General Foods, have to locate their production and distribution units near the source of raw materials and water. Tomatoes cannot travel across oceans without spoiling and have to be used soon after they are picked. The same limitation is true of other kinds of vegetables that are used in making soups. Duty and freight considerations prohibit shipping cans of soup over long distances and across national boundaries. Because of all those considerations, plants have to be located in strategically selected sites all over the world where markets exist. Many of the products made by these companies, such as ice cream, chocolates, and pies, have a short shelf life, which means that they must be produced close to the ultimate customer. And customers of companies such as Unilever, Nestlé, and General Foods are spread throughout the world, which accounts for the numerous multinational operations of the companies.

Absence of a domestic market for diesel engines for ships is responsible for the international licensing operations in that field of Sulzer Brothers, of Switzerland. Sulzer developed the first diesel engine but found that there was no Swiss market for it because the engine was used in ships and Switzerland, being a landlocked country, does not build any ships. Also, the diesel engines were far too big and would have been quite far away from the shipbuilders had they been manufactured in Switzerland. Besides, the costs of transporting them would have added substantially to the cost of the engine. For example, transportation of a diesel engine from Switzerland to Japan would have added 15 percent of the cost of the engine to the final price.

Sulzer found that big shipbuilders do not like to buy their engines, but instead prefer to make their own engines and thereby produce the entire ship in their shipyards. So for those reasons Sulzer had to license the manufacture of diesel engines abroad. Presently, Sulzer has 33 percent of the world market for diesel engines with its licensees. A similar situation exists for large industrial utility and boiler plants. Switzerland uses only hydroelectric plants for the generation of electricity, and so Sulzer had to start a wide licensing policy in various countries. For this, the foreign manufacturers pay Sulzer royalties.

Economies of scale force Sulzer to manufacture all textile machines in Switzerland. The machines are not so large, and so the transportation costs are not high. The product is made in series and has to be made in one place to permit the building of large plants for its manufacture to facilitate economies of scale. Sulzer does not intend to license the manufacture of textile machines abroad; it does not have to.

Research and Development Capability

A great number of company executives said that one of the most important forces that stimulated the expansion of their operations abroad was the necessity to raise revenues to cover the huge expenditures in research and development. For example, Pirelli, the Italian cable and tire manufacturer, is one of the largest producers of cables in the world. That position has been possible because of Pirelli's independent advanced technology in its field. Developing such a technology requires huge expenditures in R&D. The company is forced to go abroad wherever there are markets that would help pay for the R&D efforts. Pirelli also had to expand abroad to defray the R&D costs of tire technology, and so did Dunlop, the tire manufacturer based in the United Kingdom.

For a Swiss chemical company, successful diversification of research opened the way for new contacts in new countries with new markets. The huge costs of R&D in the chemical industry means that new specialty products must be marketed on an international scale. That requires building more factories abroad and strengthening the international sales organization. Similar reasons for expansion abroad were given by Unilever, Bayer, American Cyanamid, and others.

Ownership of a unique technique was mentioned by Brown, Boveri and Company, of Switzerland, as an important catalyst in its growth and development as a multinational company:

The company wants to be known as a multinational company. It has had considerable success in becoming a multinational company because it has developed its own technique. It does not have to obtain a license for manufacturing turbines and generators, for example. Competitors have obtained licenses from U.S. firms; Brown Boveri does not own any licenses from outsiders except for one or two small items.

European companies mentioned yet another research-related reason for expansion abroad. Some executives referred to the growing trend toward joint ventures in the United States between European and American companies. A major factor responsible for such joint ventures was said to be the desire of European companies to gain easy access to American technology. Many European companies are now involved in acquiring small and medium-sized research-based American companies for that reason.

Quite a few European chemicals and pharmaceuticals companies interviewed said that they were establishing research laboratories in several technologically advanced countries such as the United States, Canada, the United Kingdom, Japan, and Germany, in order to tap the local educational and scientific talents. European companies realize that one of the major factors responsible for the American invasion of European industry is the superiority of American technology. The talent that gave the technological superiority to American companies is what the European companies are after when they locate their research laboratories in the United States. Research laboratories often precede, follow, or come along with the setting up of production facilities in the United States and in the other technologically advanced countries.

The Desire to Grow ·

A senior vice-president of a large American pharmaceuticals company that does not wish to reveal its identity said, "The desire of this company is to be a growth company. The responsibility of this management is to make the company grow both here and abroad, to be a growth company. Otherwise, we are not doing our job."

Most companies interviewed emphasized that merely "being a profitable company" is not good enough in today's world of international business. A small but profitable company cannot possibly face up to the competition offered by giant multinational companies. The desire to survive is what motivates the small companies to grow. Profit is important to these companies, but to insure a continuous flow of reasonable profits over the long run, they must grow. And if they are to grow, expansion of manufacturing and sales abroad is a must, because either the home market is not big enough or the domestic economy is not growing fast enough to sustain the company's desired growth. Here are some quotes from my interviews:

> In order to make a profit in a manufacturing company, you obviously first must sell something and sell it to someone who wants it. In general, I feel the market for most, if not all, of what we make is larger abroad than what it is here. If you want to be larger and make more profit, which has as a precondition that you sell more, you have to sell it to the people who want it, and they are not here. They are abroad. Therefore we have to go abroad to find them. Certainly this is a point that we just take for granted, and maybe we always have. But, as I see it, this is the basis for it [the company's expansion abroad]. There are, of course, some very big advantages in being bigger than in being smaller, and this relates . . . to . . . foreign competitors. To the extent that we would try, if we wish to do so, to restrict ourselves to a purely domestic operation, we may then find that we are by that policy made smaller, that we are less able to develop new machines, less able to be efficient in manufacturing, and an easier prey for this [foreign] competition. *D. C. Garfield, executive vice-president, Ingersoll-Rand Company, New York.*

> It is one of Dunlop's objectives to double net after-tax profits during the next ten years and to increase its average rate of return on net funds employed to a minimum of 17.5 percent per annum before interest and taxation. The U.K. market—from which some 40 percent of the company's earnings arise—is not growing fast enough to achieve the desired level of growth. The company has to get less dependent on the U.K. economy, and so it is seeking greater tire market share together with investment opportunities in faster-growth areas overseas. Dunlop is making forecasts of areas that have a better than average growth potential over the next decade, and from this will evolve a geographic pattern of development consistent with an acceptable level of political and economic risk. *Sir Reay Geddes, Chairman, The Dunlop Company Ltd., London.*

Similar opinions were expressed by a senior executive of one of the world's largest chemical companies:

> The growth rate of the U.K. has not been as high as some other industrialized nations. ICI cannot limit its growth rate to the growth of the British economy. If it does, it would be consigning itself to a diminishing place in the world markets. The Japanese, German, and American companies have been prospering and growing partly because the economies of their countries have been growing rapidly. ICI has to go abroad and locate itself in these and similar other growing economies. *Sir Cyril Pitts, general manager, overseas, Imperial Chemical Industries, Ltd., London.*

Faster-growing markets overseas was the reason given for expanding abroad by John R. Torrens, Norman Nichols, and Robert A. Lasley, senior executives of General Foods Corporation:

> The opportunities for growth in the businesses that we know something about had ceilings on them here in the U.S. There were great opportunities in the rest of the world. The urge to expand is just that, a force encouraging us to grow everywhere, be it the U.S. or overseas. . . . Another way of saying this is that we turned outside the U.S. because there were potentially faster-growing markets.

Similar viewpoints were expressed by many executives interviewed in both United States and European companies. In sum, the executives interviewed were emphasizing that a company must look for growing markets abroad if the domestic market is not large enough or is not growing fast enough to support the company's growth objectives.

Financial Strength

It was indeed a surprise to note that only one executive interviewed mentioned financial strength as one of the factors responsible for his company's growth and development as a multinational company. It is possible that financial strength was taken for granted by the others. I made it a point to ask each executive toward the end of the interview what role financial strength played in the growth of the company. A large number of executives said that the factor was important, but an equally large number of executives said something to the effect that if a company has sound management, and a desire to grow, then it can consider half the battle won, because management, if it takes the trouble, will find the way to raise the capital to support research and to implement its growth strategies.

We should consider those opinions in their proper perspective. The executives interviewed belonged not to small or medium-size companies, but rather to fairly large or giant companies that have already reached a point of financial self-sufficiency for normal growth. It is not very difficult for such companies to raise capital in the capital markets of the world provided they have sound projects based upon realistic plans. And that is where the managerial and technological capability of the company becomes very important. If management can plan for the proper growth strategies, taking into account the company's critical strengths and weaknesses, then the results should show up on the company's financial statements, which investors, whether private or institutional, would not fail to recognize!

Forces External to the Company

Competition

Competition from local or other foreign companies was often cited as a major force stimulating the expansion abroad of companies interviewed. The manner in which competitors launched their attack varied considerably. But the response of the defending company resulted in its setting up manufacturing or production facilities in the market attacked by the competitor. Here are a few examples:

A major chemical company in Switzerland was forced to manufacture abroad in quite a few cases because patent laws in certain countries require a company to exercise patent on a product within a prescribed period. If the company holding the patent does not comply, then a competitor may claim a compulsory license from a local court and start producing the product. In return, the producer has to pay the company that once held the patent royalties for using its patent.

The desire to be in a market before the competition was one of the reasons given by Pirelli, of Italy, for its growth abroad. "Pirelli was the first in tires to go to Greece and Turkey. Now there are three companies making tires in Turkey and Goodyear has joined Pirelli in Greece." Pirelli also entered the German and French markets to attack the competitor on his home ground. Pirelli entered the German market when Continental Tire Company from Germany entered the Italian market. When Michelin entered Italy from France, Pirelli invaded France. Volvo, the Swedish car manufacturer, decided to enter the United States, French, and German markets to fight competitors from those countries who were fast penetrating the Swedish car market. D. C. Garfield, executive vice-president of Ingersoll-Rand Company, had these comments when asked what were the major forces that stimulated his company's overseas expansion:

> One has certainly been competition, existing and potential, from foreign manufacturers. A realization on our part that we might better compete forcefully with those fellows abroad than to try to defend ourselves here. Of course, we are doing both at the same time; they are trying to sell here, we are trying to sell there. So this is like the typical adage that a good defense is a strong offense. That motivates us very much. There are some good foreign companies in our general line of business and we are trying to compete with them by carrying this fight over there.

The "need to have centers of production, especially in the fibers business, in various parts of the world if you are going to hold your own in the international fibers field" was cited by Sir Cyril Pitts, general manager, overseas, Imperial Chemical Industries, as one of the key driving forces that stimulated the company's expansion abroad in the past and will in the future. Competition in the fibers field is very tough, especially from American giants such as Du Pont, Monsanto, and Celanese. ICI has to compete with those giants at home and abroad often by setting up plants abroad if the capability of production is there.

The need to become as large as the competitor and to enjoy economies of scale, coupled with the fact that the home market could not by itself support large-scale production, is one of the reasons that Dunlop gave for setting up production facilities abroad in a number of countries. Sir Reay Geddes, chairman, The Dunlop Company Ltd., London, put the problem this way:

> The tire is a component for the car; where the car goes, there must be replacement tires. Having been producers of tires in countries which design and produce motorcars and trucks, Dunlop has had to provide a service in *their* export markets. Dunlop has to provide this service against competition from American, European, and now Japanese tire companies which have a much larger home market than Dunlop's. Therefore, Dunlop can only hope to get economies of scale by a geographical spread, and even then it cannot grow as big as the American companies have grown. So the company has this particular competitive reason and the particular reason of service that the component manufacturer must give to his main product acting as stimulants for its overseas expansion.

A large Swiss chemical company found itself pushed into expanding its markets abroad because competitors were diversifying into its product lines. The company has relatively high-priced and profitable products. A strategic decision was made not to diversify into the competitors' product lines, which would have meant a diluting of its own profits, but to expand abroad and find new markets for current profitable products.

A classical reason for massive world expansion was given by H. J. Taufen, general manager, international department, of Hercules Inc., when he said that:

> I do not think any company can let its competitor have a world position and it be content with a national position. It is a kind of a threat to survival. This is a driving force that makes companies, if they think about it, think globally.

Expansion abroad as a defensive measure was mentioned by Alfa-Laval, of Sweden, and Bayer, of Germany. Alfa-Laval went to Denmark and bought the Titan Company because Bendix and Westinghouse were interested in it too. In the case of Bayer, the company came to know that some United States firms were planning to set up isocyanate plants in France. Bayer also had the need for expanding its isocyanate production. The company therefore came to an agreement with two French companies and established a firm for the manufacture of isocyanates.

Constraints by Foreign Governments

Various kinds of governmental tariff and nontariff constraints are used by foreign governments with the objectives of (1) providing local manufacturers with a large enough market to permit use of economies of scale, (2) conserving scarce foreign exchange, (3) protecting infant domestic industry from the competition of a more mature foreign industry, and (4) encouraging local manufacture of a product or group of products to minimize or eliminate imports of the product or products. These constraints serve as incentives to direct investments abroad by multinational companies, as we shall see in the following examples.

The necessity to jump over the tariff barriers was given as the main reason for setting up manufacturing facilities abroad by a number of executives interviewed. The alternative was to lose the market, because of the high costs of importation due to the high tariffs, either to a local producer or to a competitor who can manage to set up local manufacturing facilities in order to avoid the tariff costs.

For example, Alfa-Laval, of Sweden, a maker of milk-processing plants among other things, was induced to establish plants in Argentina because of the 100 percent duty on imports of milk-processing plants. Volvo of Sweden was forced to set up a plant in Belgium because of high tariffs on car imports in that country. Sweden is in the EFTA, whereas Belgium is in the EEC, and that accounted for the tariff imposed by Belgium on imports from Sweden.

Many companies located in the EFTA countries cited their non-EEC status as one of the main reasons for setting up plants in one or more of the EEC countries. That was the reason mentioned, for example, by Landis and Gyr, of Switzerland; ICI, the giant chemical manufacturer of England; and Atlas Copco, of Sweden. Both Brown Boveri and Sandoz, of Switzerland, and Ingersoll-Rand, of the United States, referred to the tariff barriers raised by foreign governments as inducements to their expansion of production facilities abroad. In the case of Brown Boveri, newly imposed custom barriers is what forced it to set up production plants abroad, especially in South America. Similarly, high tariffs by countries in which Pirelli, of Italy, already had a big export market for its product are what forced the company to erect manufacturing subsidiaries in those countries.

Nontariff barriers, such as import restrictions on products to support their local production or to conserve foreign exchange, and foreign exchange controls were cited as strong incentives for production in the country or countries raising such barriers. According to a senior executive of a large American chemicals company:

> The availability of foreign exchange, or import restrictions, is a fairly powerful incentive to produce there (abroad) if you are going to stay in business. The simple requirement that you must produce locally, or not import, implies on the other hand that the country is willing to protect the market from other influences that would make it possible to do business in that particular country. So, you develop into a protective market.

A problem arises if the market is not large enough to justify the investment. One way to meet that problem was given by executives of a major Swiss chemicals and pharmaceuticals company. Their approach is to join hands with another foreign firm or firms active in the country concerned, and to undertake investment projects with allied firms rather than alone. For example, two European chemicals and pharmaceuticals companies are engaged in pharmaceuticals in Venezuela, and in Brazil three European companies jointly operate a dyes and pharmaceuticals factory. Pakistan has a well-developed textile industry, and the government wanted the country to be more independent of dyestuff imports. So two German companies, Bayer and Hoechst, participated jointly to 30 percent in a project of the National Pakistan Industrial Development Corporation for the erection of a dyestuffs factory. High tariff barriers and foreign exchange controls forced Bayer to set up dyestuffs plants in Brazil, Argentina, and India. Nestlé, of Switzerland, has manufacturing plants in several countries because, an executive explained, "agricultural products are among the most protected products in every country and thus Nestlé was forced to produce within the country where markets existed."

Inducements by Foreign Governments

Many developing countries as well as countries making an effort to develop depressed areas are now using a great number of methods to encourage foreign and domestic companies to set up new factories to assist them in their developmental efforts. The host countries offer incentives such as exemption from taxation for a cerfain number of years, loans at low interest rates, donation of huge tracts of land to build the factory, assistance in the recruiting of labor, and protection from imports. Landis and Gyr, of Switzerland, erected a production plant in Italy because of the financial incentives offered by the Italian government. There the company began the manufacture of thermostats for all of Europe by combining its technology with ample availability of labor in Italy. A Swiss chemical company that wishes to remain unidentified said that it went into production in Scotland and Nicaragua because of the financial incentives offered by those countries. Invitations from foreign governments to companies to set up plants in their countries have induced many companies to set up factories abroad. For example, a Swiss chemical company has been invited by many countries where its products are popular to come and establish production facilities, and the company has responded positively in certain cases. Also, 70 years ago Brown, Boveri and Company, of Switzerland, was asked by Germany to set up a small power plant, which it did. Now the power plant has grown to be one of the biggest investments abroad of Brown Boveri. Tires are high on the list of priorities of any developing country, and therefore Dunlop, of England, has been approached at times by foreign governments with a proposal for Dunlop to manufacture tires in their respective countries. In a few cases Dunlop has responded positively.

A good example of how a government can use tax incentives to attract foreign investment is that of Brazil. The government desires to develop northeast Brazil, which was found to be "among the unlikeliest spots for industrial development."[1] Under the fiscal incentives offered by the government,

> Companies operating in Brazil can elect to invest in the Northeast the equivalent of half their tax instead of paying it to the treasury. The money is deposited in blocked accounts of the development bank for the region, and companies have three years [recently reduced to one year] to start a project or select others to invest in.[2]

The incentives have worked, and foreign investors have flocked into the region. Some big United States companies include Dow Chemical International, Union Carbide Intl. Co., Ford Motor Company, Mohawk Rubber Co., and Lone Star Cement Corporation.[3] Similar schemes to attract foreign investments have been utilized by both developing and developed countries.

Availability and Cost of Labor

Labor shortages at home plus the availability of ample and sometimes cheap labor abroad are forcing many companies to expand their production operations abroad. The problem of labor shortage is extremely acute in Switzerland because the Swiss government has put severe restrictions on the importation of skilled and unskilled labor from abroad. Executives in all Swiss companies interviewed mentioned the problems facing them because of labor shortages. They talked about the difficulty of finding qualified people both in management and the R&D field, which is forcing them to transfer not only more production but also research to countries where qualified personnel are available.

West Germany is also facing the problem of labor shortages; but unlike the Swiss government, the German government has not placed any restrictions on the inflow of foreign labor. Still, there are presently on an average more jobs available than there are people available to fill them. That is a major reason why more and more German companies are beginning to move their production abroad.

An increasing number of American and European companies are now moving their production into countries such as Taiwan, Mexico, Hong Kong, and South Korea. Companies domiciled in the developed countries, where labor is expensive, scarce, or both, are now aware of the profitable use that can be made of the low-cost labor that is available in the developing countries, to produce goods for export markets. The developing countries are welcoming the foreign companies with open arms because exports by the subsidiaries of the foreign companies help in alleviating their own balance-of-payments problems. The productivity of labor in the developing countries is lower than that of labor in the advanced countries, assuming that mechanization and economies of scale are the same, but the wages in most developing countries are significantly lower than in the advanced countries. Hence, distinct advantages would accrue to a company that, in developing countries, produces products by labor-intensive methods with labor as a substantial part of the total production costs. Textiles, sewing machines, small motors, electrical parts and assemblies, lathes, small machine tools, and canned or frozen fruits and vegetables meet those criteria. That is why Philco-Taiwan Corporation, a subsidiary of Ford Motor Company, began to manufacture television sets, radios, and other electronic products in Taiwan for export to the United States.[4] Even the Japanese have turned to the low-priced labor in Taiwan. There are more than 250 Japanese companies in Taiwan and they use the country as a base from which to invade the world markets.[5] The average wage in Taiwan is only 80 cents to $1 a day, which is substantially lower than in Japan. The government of Taiwan is inviting new companies that require huge amounts of skilled labor to produce goods not to serve the Taiwan market—the government would prefer to let local industrialists do that—but for export.

And nowhere has that campaign been more successful than at the export-processing zone at Kaohsiung harbor. There, on a 170-acre spit of land reclaimed from the sea, 82 plants employ 19,000 workers to make $60 million of products for sale outside Taiwan. Within the duty-free zone are American concerns making video tape recorder heads and computer memory cores, Japanese companies turning out portable radios, and local Chinese companies making wigs, textiles, and hundreds of other products. One company produces helmets and army uniforms for Arab and African countries.[6]

Examples of companies migrating to developing countries to utilize the cheap labor available are many. American food-processing companies have operations close to the food crops, particularly vegetables and fruits, in Mexico, the Philippines, Kenya, Greece, Portugal, and Morocco. The output of such plants is mainly exported.

Section 807 of the U.S. Tariff Code has spurred American companies to set up assembly or processing plants abroad. Under its provisions, tariff is levied only on the value added by foreign labor and upon non-U.S.-made parts and materials. *Business Week* reports[7] that:

> In the next five years, Fairchild Hiller Corporation plans to sell about 24 Dutch-built, short-haul, jet passenger planes to American customers. The 65-seat F-28s cost $2.65 million apiece, but Fairchild will pay U.S. tariffs on only 80 percent of their value. The reason is that each Fokker jet contains $465,000 worth of U.S.-made parts that were exported to the Netherlands for inclusion in the F-28. As domestic products under Section 807 of the U.S. Tariff Code, these parts are not subject to duty.

Thus, an American company could produce these parts that are capital-intensive at home, ship them to be assembled abroad, produce the labor-intensive parts in countries where labor is cheap, assemble the whole product abroad, and ship it back to the American market at favorable tariff rates. Section 807 of the U.S. Tariff Code is to a large extent responsible for the numerous assembly and processing plants set up by American companies throughout the world where labor is cheap and economies of transportation permit. But the biggest such activity has been in nearby Mexico.

> [Last year] some $145 million worth of imports containing U.S.-made parts came from Mexico; three years ago, the figure was practically zero. These products use lots of semiskilled hand labor—clothing, toys, television sets—and the proportion of U.S.-made parts was much higher in them than in other goods assembled abroad.

Size of the Home Market

Companies interviewed in Sweden, Switzerland, and England talked about their small domestic markets as being one of the dominant forces that stimulated their expansion abroad. Sweden has a population of 7.8 million people, Switzerland has 6 million, and England has 55 million. All three countries are in EFTA region. I asked one executive in a Swedish company why his company could not consider the entire EFTA region as one big market as the companies in the EEC countries do. His answer was that the EFTA countries, in spite of the abolition of tariffs on goods originating in the region, have not been able to integrate their economies because of economic nationalism. England, for example, would not buy Swedish goods even though at times they were cheaper and better.

The balance-of-payments problems of England also hurt the integration efforts of EFTA nations. In his opinion, England posed the same type of problems for EFTA that France did for the EEC. But the fever for economic and eventual political unity of Europe is much greater among the EEC nations than it is in the EFTA group. The geographical separation of the EFTA nations has also hurt their integration efforts. Trade between the EFTA nations has not grown as fast as between the EEC nations. Besides, the competition from foreign companies has been growing consistently. Therefore, for all practical purposes, the effective market for companies in the EFTA region is small.

Companies in England, Sweden, and Switzerland said that there was no room for growth for them in the domestic market alone and therefore the only way to survive in the highly competitive environment was to grow abroad. For example, Sir Cyril Pitts of Imperial Chemical Industries said that the company had to grow abroad because of "the realization that ICI could not keep its place in the world chemical league if it confined itself to a country with 55 million people. ICI had to treat the world as its potential market."

Other Reasons for Expansion Abroad

The growth of the regional economic blocs in Europe and Latin America was mentioned by several companies to be a driving force in their growth as world companies. Economic unification is permitting Nestlé "to serve larger markets and to manage its vast confederation of food factories more rationally." The national tradition of traveling abroad was mentioned by The East Asiatic Company, of Denmark, and by some Swiss companies as a driving force for their expansion abroad. Pierre Liotard-Vogt, managing director of Nestlé, put it as follows:

The Swiss people, because they live in a small country that has poor soil with no minerals, are inclined to travel abroad and find what cannot be found at home. The Swiss are quite adaptable to most foreign countries. These factors account for the growth abroad of Nestlé and other Swiss companies.

That may be applicable to companies in countries, such as England and Sweden, with similar traditions.

REFERENCES

1. "Industry Tries to Stir a Brazilian Backwater," *Business Week*, March 29, 1969, p. 147.

2. Ibid., p. 148.

3. Ibid., p. 147.

4. *Wall Street Journal*, Thursday, March 27, 1969, p. 36.

5. Ibid.

6. Ibid.

7. "Will the Multinationals Lose a Loophole?," *Business Week*, May 2, 1970, p. 28.

8. Ibid.

4

Forces Constraining the Development of World Enterprises

I N the preceding chapter we discussed the forces that help in the growth and development of multinational companies and world enterprises; in this chapter we shall examine some of the factors that serve as constraints. All seven of the constraints discussed are beyond direct management control. That does not imply that management can do nothing to minimize the impact of constraints on the company; it means only that each constraint owes its existence not to a company policy or program decision, but to one made by an external institution.

Restrictions on Outflow of Capital

To be able to grow and prosper, a multinational or world company should be able to transfer capital freely from one subsidiary to another. For example, it should be able to borrow capital wherever the cost of capital is low or raise capital in a country where the capital market is well developed, loan the capital thus obtained to a subsidiary in a country where either the cost of capital is high or the capital market is not developed, retransfer the profits of the borrowing subsidiary either to repay the borrowed capital or pay dividends or interest charges to the investors, and so on. The objective of all such transactions is to make the most efficient use of the financial resources of the whole company. Host nations that do not permit the parent company to transfer loaned capital, dividends, or royalties from the subsidiary abroad when such actions are in the interests of the entire company were mentioned by executives of more than a dozen companies as obstacles to multinational actions.

The balance-of-payments problem in host countries is the reason for stringent regulation of the repatriation of funds of multinational companies. Several company executives said that such regulations dampen incentive and discourage further investment when it is most needed and that they restrain managements of multinational companies from venturing even when the normal commercial risks are acceptable.

Balance-of-payments difficulties in the developed countries that have the capabilities to serve as base countries for multinational companies have led to regulation of direct investment outflows. Companies in Sweden, Italy, Belgium, and the United Kingdom claimed that such regulations confine and limit their growth abroad. It is worth noting that, of all the developed countries, only Canada, West Germany, and Switzerland are free from exchange controls. France, Italy, Austria, Belgium, Holland, and Luxemburg have certain restrictions, whereas the United Kingdom, Ireland, Japan, Spain, Australia, Norway, Sweden, and Denmark have a great number of foreign exchange controls for balance-of-payments and monetary policy reasons.

Import Tariffs and Quotas, and Host Country Market Size

In the preceding chapter it was said that tariffs and import quotas levied by nations were considered by multinational companies to be stimulants to the expansion of production facilities abroad. The stimulus was to jump over the barriers raised by the foreign countries, so it might appear to be a contradiction to say that tariffs and quotas act as constraints to the multinational activities of companies. If the domestic economy of the country that imposes tariff and nontariff barriers is "technologically optimal," for example, it can consume as well as provide outlets for the output of the most efficient plant in a certain industry, then a company might be induced to erect a plant in the country if there is not already one. But if there is a domestic producer and the country is technologically optimal for the operation of one plant only, then it is unwise for a foreign company to establish a competing plant. That is why Pirelli, of Italy, did not set up tire manufacturing operations in Mexico, where American tire companies are firmly established. Sulzer, of Switzerland, also said that sometimes markets are too small in some countries to justify local manufacture of some of its products such as textile weaving machines.

The EEC has a common tariff against goods originating in non-EEC countries. But the EEC market is large enough and technologically optimal for the operation of several large plants in most industries. Hence, as was pointed out in an earlier chapter, the tariff and nontariff barriers erected by the EEC act as stimulants to companies in non-EEC countries to erect production facilities within the "protective" walls. But a large number of countries do not belong to the EEC and do not have large domestic markets. If those countries erect tariffs and import quotas against foreign competitors, then the measures that are meant to support and encourage domestic producers and conserve foreign exchange act as disincentives to foreign companies because of the small size of the domestic markets. More than a dozen companies interviewed referred to tariffs and import quotas plus small market size of many countries as constraints to their expansion abroad and to their own growth and development as multinational companies.

Double Taxation

Several company executives interviewed said that income taxes, which vary from one country to another, and additional taxes on net income every time money is transferred from one country to another are creating severe problems of tax discrimination against the multinational company. The double taxation question becomes quite complicated for a company that tries to find the best solution to the international tax problem, because a solution that is supposed to be optimal this year may not be so next year. Quite often a host country discriminates by levying higher taxes on the income of foreign companies than that of domestic companies.

Several countries have bilateral tax treaties to provide for reciprocal tax credit. The treaties also generally provide for either an exemption or a lower rate of withholding tax for royalties, dividends, and interest income. In addition, the newer treaties provide for an exchange of information, and they occasionally operate to avoid double taxation by providing authority for the two governments to consult. But the older treaties do nothing to prevent double taxation that results from different interpretations of "income" by different countries.

Measures to avoid double taxation have included a credit given by the multinational company's home country against its own tax for taxes on income and dividends paid by the company's subsidiary to its host country. However, the credit is usually less than expected because countries have different concepts of "income."

A senior executive of a large American chemicals company having worldwide operations had this to say:

> Another thing which can be and maybe will be an even more significant obstacle to worldwide enterprises is incompatible systems of taxation. This may result in double taxation on the same income. Let me give you an example. Europe's tax system under the EEC is becoming more and more based on turnover tax. The U.S. system is based on income tax, not turnover tax. They are basically incompatible.

Nationalization and Confiscation

Perhaps the most serious constraint on the multinational company, especially in the developing countries, is the specter of nationalization and confiscation of foreign subsidiaries by host countries. The threat of a takeover by the host country, plus local pressures and harassment, was specified by 19 companies interviewed as obstacles that restrain their multinational growth and development. Executives interviewed stated that they would have liked to expand their operations in a certain country but decided against such a move because of the host country's policy, which appeared to be drifting more and more in favor of state-owned enterprises at the expense of private enterprise. The nationalization of the banking system in India was cited by many as a deterrent to the inflow of direct foreign investments into that country. The outright confiscation of foreign concerns with or without appropriate compensation in Indonesia during the Sukarno regime was certainly a deterrent to any new inflow of direct foreign investments to that country. The uncertainty regarding the role of the private sector in the developmental plans of newly emergent nations, especially in Asia and Africa, was mentioned by some executives as a constraint to foreign investments.

From the comments made by various executives, it appears that a foreign subsidiary that uses sophisticated and complicated technology is less susceptible to a takeover by the host country than one that does not use sophisticated technology if there is a shortage or unavailability of skilled personnel to run the plant. Lord Cole, chairman of Unilever, stated that Unilever's subsidiaries are vulnerable to nationalization because, from the host country's point of view, the technology of soap or margarine manufacture appears simple enough and Unilever does not control the import of any essential raw material. Unilever subsidiaries in Algeria, Burma, and, for a while, Indonesia were nationalized.

The subsidiaries of a multinational company are very vulnerable to local pressure by the host country. For example, many of Unilever's subsidiaries abroad operate as self-contained units and they are therefore subject to local pressure and harassment. A margarine factory has to have its product on the shelf of a local store within 24 hours of manufacture; it cannot pack its bags and leave the country and supply from abroad. Consequently, the host country can, by putting pressure such as price controls and import restrictions on the vulnerable subsidiary, put pressure on the Unilever group as a whole. Another example of host country pressure is that of Union Carbide's subsidiary in India, which might be forced to go into the business of exporting frozen Indian shrimp for the United States market in response to the Indian government's demand that it bring in foreign exchange. Otherwise, Carbide might not be permitted to import essential goods for its battery production. The subsidiary was able to convince the Indian government that it could not export batteries, because they are not competitive, but could export shrimp at a profit.

Natural resource companies and utilities seem to be the favorite targets of takeovers. Recent examples of takeovers of such subsidiaries are many; two of them are the seizure by Peru in 1968 of International Petroleum Company, Ltd., a subsidiary of the Standard Oil Company of New Jersey, and the nationalization of the sugar plantations of W. R. Grace and Company during the summer of 1968. The International Telephone and Telegraph Corporation in Lima was also taken over by the Peruvian government, and during November 1969 so was a telephone company owned by L. M. Ericsson, of Sweden. A subsidiary of the Gulf Oil Corporation was expropriated in Bolivia. In the early part of this year (1971), the fate of the big mining companies in Peru and Bolivia is hanging by a hair!

The reasons for the hostility of the host countries against the multinational companies are many; some are justified and some are not. But yet another problem confronted by multinational companies in the developing countries is concerned, as one executive put it, "with domestic businessmen [who] in order to protect their own interests, create false propaganda against the multinational companies which affects the thinking of politicians." This problem does not arise to any great extent if the host country is not committed heavily to a process of rapid industrial development. If it is not, the leading local businessmen are not competing with but complementing the foreign company's activities in the country. They are engaged in producing feeder goods or services, providing transportation, running local banks, and so on. The long-term interests of the local businessman and the foreign investor in such instances are not in conflict.

But the situation changes drastically the moment the host country decides to embark on a program of rapid industrialization. Generally, a developing country formulates a plan of development for a certain number of years, usually five. At the end of the five years, a second five-year plan is usually formulated, and the process continues over a number of years. Most countries that have launched plans for economic development have come to realize that they are short of a very important resource, namely, foreign exchange reserves to pay for imports of capital goods and raw materials, so foreign exchange and import restrictions are applied to conserve foreign exchange.

At the same time, tax exemptions, special industrial credits, and various other inducements are offered to attract foreign and domestic companies that are either export-producing or import-replacing. Once the inducements and restraints are applied, new entrepreneurs generally come on the scene. Some of the newcomers are foreign, but most of them are local businessmen who are willing to stake their fortunes in a protected market. The government next applies strict licensing rules to control the establishment of new plants in an industry and the expansion of those already in operation. The purpose of such licensing controls is to protect the companies already in business and prevent overcapacity in an industry. What that amounts to is nothing less than a guaranteed near monopoly or partial oligopoly market for a handful of firms in a particular industry.

The situation changes when a foreign company, accustomed to competition as a way of life, appears on the local scene and makes life "difficult" for the local businessmen. The foreign subsidiary generally introduces new methods and processes of production and new marketing techniques, and slowly but surely it begins to erode the market share of the local businessmen. Some local businessmen fall by the wayside, and in most cases a few local and foreign companies are left in the market. The local businessmen now raise the familiar cry of "foreign imperialism and domination," and, ironically, they get the support of their arch enemies—the leftists and Communists.

A market characterized as a partial oligopoly provides a fertile ground for the use of product variation, advertising, and other forms of selling activities. Price tends to stabilize at a certain figure; and although companies are anxious to increase sales in order to lower average costs, price reduction is not the answer because other firms will do the same thing. Firms therefore resort to various forms of non-price policies and competition. The largest share of the market may go to a company that does the best job in non-price competition. The firms that fail may be those that make mistakes in their product and marketing planning. Local businessmen then charge the foreign subsidiaries with unfair competition. They claim that the foreign subsidiary has the advantage (which it often has) of a famous brand name or has easier access to international credit; whereas the local producer pays anywhere from 10 to 25 percent interest rate for short-term borrowings—a rate that is typical of countries in Asia and Latin America—the foreign parent can loan the foreign subsidiary funds that it needs at much lower interest rates.

It is no secret that big local businessmen have great influence on the local political authorities who run the government. That is true in highly industrialized countries such as the United States and is equally true in the developing countries. The local businessmen use their influence with the government to curb the activities of the foreign subsidiary. For instance, imports of an important ingredient that were previously allowed may suddenly be cut off or the foreign subsidiary may be forced to share a much greater portion of its equity with local investors. That is the trend in Mexico, Brazil, and several other developing countries.

The insistence of some host countries that not only ownership but also management of the subsidiary be turned over to locals, who are not yet ready for the responsibility, was a problem referred to by K. D. Brough, deputy chairman and managing director of The Metal Box Company Overseas Limited, London.

> Metal Box strongly insists on maintaining control of the management responsibilities even though it may not own a majority of the equity capital of the overseas subsidiary, as was the case in Tanzania where the government insisted on acquiring a 60 percent ownership of Metal Box's subsidiary there. Finally, after long negotiations it was agreed that Metal Box and the government of Tanzania would each own 50 percent of the equity capital. But Metal Box Overseas Limited still retained control through its having earned the right (through negotiations) of keeping a majority of its nominees on the board of directors of the subsidiary there.

Many executives interviewed said that the trends discussed in this chapter will continue in the next decade and might even get worse if the economic disparities between the "have" and "have-not" nations remain the same or continue to widen. One executive of a prominent Swiss company was very candid in his remarks that "because multinationality is an achievement in many ways, it creates jealousy locally and politically as well, which attempts to kill multinational companies." There is some truth in that statement.

Shortage of Globally Oriented Managerial Talent

A multinational company needs at the top management level of its subsidiaries and affiliate companies abroad managers with a global viewpoint and global experience. That is a problem for many companies interviewed. One way to provide an executive with such a viewpoint is to place him in a suitable job in the headquarters. But that is easier said than done, because the subsidiaries abroad of most companies are growing so fast that they cannot spare good men for positions at headquarters. Another problem with the executives heading up the subsidiaries abroad has to do with their loyalty. Quite often, to the dismay of the parent company, subsidiary heads have had financial interests in local competitor companies. And that has often caused conflict-of-interest problems.

There is also an issue that Sir Reay Geddes, chairman of Dunlop, mentioned in reference to the United Kingdom but is equally applicable to other countries. It has to do with "whether the educational system both in knowledge and character training is well fitted to make what used to be called adventurous entrepreneurs who liked to go out and build businesses abroad." According to Sir Reay, "the political and social pressures in Britain were much more favorable to this, but lately have not been."

Price Control Imposed by Host Governments

If a multinational company's subsidiary abroad has a substantial share of the local market for its products, then it often comes under increasing pressure from some host nations who suspect that it is misusing its dominant market position to price its products at levels that disregard the public interest. Lord Cole, chairman of Unilever Ltd., of the United Kingdom had this to say about the problem as it concerns his company:

> Unilever's pricing policy is important to host governments because they are concerned about rising living costs, and Unilever happens to be producing products which make up the market basket from which the cost-of-living index is calculated. Unilever has been subjected to various forms of price controls by host governments—ranging from voluntary price controls by Unilever in Germany to a fully fledged quota system for margarine in Holland.

Companies that are in the pharmaceuticals field are frequently subjected to price controls because of local charges of excessive profits levied against them. Several executives in European companies mentioned this as being a very severe problem, one that threatens the survival of some companies in light of the high R&D expenditures and competition from the capital-rich American companies.

Currency Instability

The devaluation of the French franc on August 10, 1969, and of the English pound on November 18, 1967, led to the same percentage devaluation of the currencies of French and English colonies. Because Denmark has close trade relations with England, the devaluation of the pound also led to the devaluation of the Danish currency three days later, on November 21, 1967. Similar currency devaluations have been taking place in many countries, especially in Asia and Latin America.

Sudden and unpredictable devaluations of currencies cause considerable harm to a multinational company. Imports into the country whose currency has been devalued become more expensive and exports become cheaper to the degree that the currency has been devalued. Thus if a subsidiary of a multinational company has been importing certain essential raw materials or components from the parent company to provide goods for local consumption only, then it is going to incur higher costs of production owing to the higher import bill. It is very difficult for a subsidiary caught in such a bind to raise the price of its product. First, if the subsidiary is the only producer of the product, then raising the price of the product is likely to cause adverse reaction from the government, the local business community, and the public. Charges of exploitation would most likely be made against it. Second, if the subsidiary is one of a few or many other firms producing the product, then raising the price of its product would only lead to a loss of sales revenues as customers shifted to products offered at a cheaper rate by competing firms. Hence, the only alternative for the subsidiary is to suffer a drop in its profits until it can find methods to cut costs elsewhere or increase its sales volume.

Another problem arises when a country devalues its currency, because more of the local currency is then required than before to buy the same number of dollars, marks, or whatever. That means the parent company and its owners get less out of the foreign subsidiary in terms of profits and dividends. Thus even though the local profits of the subsidiary may be high, the dollar or mark profits of the multinational group are reduced. More than half a dozen companies interviewed referred to unexpected currency devaluation as an obstacle that restrains their multinational financial activities. The problem becomes much more acute when a multinational company expects a country to devalue its currency but cannot move its funds out of the country because of foreign exchange restrictions on the outflow of hard currency.

5

Global Planning

A WORLD company that has some or all of its production, marketing, purchasing, finance, and R&D operations diversified worldwide must plan on a global basis. It bases its plans for the immediate and distant future on an evaluation of the threats and opportunities that it is likely to experience in the different environments in which its subsidiaries operate. In this chapter we shall discuss the concept and process of global planning. The planning strategies adopted by companies in the different functional areas will also be analyzed.

What Is Global Planning?

Global planning is the application of the principles and processes of comprehensive business planning on a global scale. It involves the determination that will regulate the acquisition, use, and disposition of the company's global resources to achieve the company mission. Global planning is concerned with the uncovering of future opportunities on a worldwide basis and the making of plans to exploit them after the company's strengths and weaknesses, and also the anticipated driving and constraining forces that may act as catalysts or roadblocks, are taken into consideration. Under global planning, current decisions in areas such as production, marketing and R&D, are made after an evaluation of their long-range implications on the objectives of the company. An attempt is made to make decisions that result in actions such that the company's entire global network of operations as a system is optimized. Global planning requires that the headquarters of a world company move its products, ideas, money, and people in such a way that synergistic benefits of global coordination become available to the total organization.

How Companies Plan Expansion of Operations Abroad

Not all companies studied had planned the expansion of their operations abroad by using the global planning approach. Some companies said that they were lucky to be successful abroad without much planning; others said that they wished that they had planned carefully. Various factors prompt a company to start operating in a foreign country. For example, a decision to commence production in Belgium may be made by the president of a company because he likes the country and its people or because he knows a prominent businessman or government official there. A company may decide to go abroad in response to an invitation by a foreign government that promises to give the company incentives such as a protected market, tax concessions, low interest loans, and help in finding local manpower. Many companies go abroad because their main competitor has done so or in response to an offer by a foreign company to form a joint venture in the domestic market of the foreign company or in a third country.

Some companies do not adopt this ad hoc approach but instead use a more systematic approach in moving abroad that falls short of what may be called the global approach. For example, if the feasibility of manufacturing in a certain country is identified, then management at the headquarters conducts a study of the market potential in the country, the investment required, and the probable financial returns. It does so on the basis of information obtained from reference materials available at headquarters plus the company's past international experience. On-the-spot investigation is made by specialists drawn from the relevant functional departments, which results in initiation, postponement, or rejection of the project. That approach is becoming quite common. It is useful, but it contains inherent dangers of becoming quite misleading. For example, a certain company decided to establish manufacturing facilities in country A because the market potential showed that it could earn a fair-size return on investment per year. But there was another country, country B, where the company could have had a 25 percent return that it had not even considered.

Yet another example was given by an executive of a company that decided to set up a plant in England to serve the market in the EFTA region and another plant in Germany to serve the EEC region. Many companies interviewed in the EFTA region are expecting that in the near future EEC and EFTA will merge to form one big market bloc. If the company that established two separate plants to serve the two regional blocs had done some planning; it might have decided to set up one large plant in a suitable location in light of the long-range merger prospects of the two blocs. Then again, it might not have, but the very exercise in global planning would have revealed opportunities and threats that lie covered under an ad hoc or country-by-country approach to planning operations abroad.

So far in this chapter we have discussed mainly the expansion abroad of companies in terms of their production facilities. The global approach to planning is not restricted to production alone but is equally applicable to making decisions such as where to set up R&D facilities, where and from whom to buy the raw materials needed, where and how to raise the funds necessary for the growth of the company abroad, and so on. The global approach to planning requires the making of current strategic decisions in all areas in the light of their present and future implications for the entire company and not just a part of it.

Impact of National Planning on a Multinational Company

A multinational company faces several unique problems, most of which were discussed in an earlier chapter. Therefore, the importance to a multinational company of designing and maintaining a formal global comprehensive planning system assumes special significance. We shall now take a look at one important phenomenon that was dealt with before and that has a significant impact upon a multinational company.

In recent years, a great number of nations have formed national planning organizations in an attempt to develop overall plans for their economies. In the past, national plans have had very little influence upon international business activities because most countries were not sure that national planning would be of any value in obtaining their national objectives. But with the success of France and other countries in using the technique[1] and with the growing aspirations of the peoples of countries that are not yet industrialized to achieve rapid economic growth, it appears that centralized economic planning by national governments will be popular among many more nations.

National plans developed by central governments act as significant constraints to multinational companies as they develop their corporate plans. The move by national governments into the economic arena to implement policies for achieving full and stabilized employment and price stability and stimulating national industrial development has extended government influence beyond areas, such as taxes, tariffs, currency valuation, and credit, that are essentially financial in nature. National plans determine the preferred location of plants and their size, the sources of raw materials to be used, the distribution of finished goods, and quite often the price at which goods can be sold. A government may reward a company that builds a certain type of plant by offering it tariff protection, tax privileges, or low-interest government loans. It may retaliate against a company that does not conform by reducing its import quotas of essential raw materials, increasing tariffs, revoking licenses, and refusing to purchase (through government agencies) its products.

Thus, planners in multinational companies must give considerable attention to studying national plans of countries before determining the country in which to produce, the location of factories, and the products to be produced and in what quantities. Continuous monitoring of national plans is also essential because, if the plans change, it may be necessary for the multinational company to alter its product-market mix, make-or-buy decisions, and originally planned production levels. Because a change in operating plans in one country could have an impact upon the operations in another, a multinational company must constantly watch and plan the operations in all of its mutually dependent operating units, and that calls for global comprehensive planning by corporate management.

Multinational companies should perform long-range planning that takes into consideration all their foreign markets, because the national plans of many foreign countries are based on the planning inputs provided by companies in the respective countries. The assumption is that companies within an industry individually and as a group engage in planning and forecasting. A multinational company therefore must plan locally, at the subsidiary level, to provide the necessary input into the national plan for the industry in which it is operating if it is to protect its interests.

The need to monitor the host country's national plan becomes all the more urgent if the multinational company is a significant source of employment of human and material resources in the host country and also an important contributor to the country's foreign exchange earnings. A company in such a position should be very careful not to offend the host government through behavior that upsets the national plans. Any move by the company to curtail its exports or reduce its levels of production and thereby cause a reduction in employment levels is likely to be considered an unfriendly act by the host government. The host government could then retaliate by various means and even take the extreme measure of nationalizing or expropriating the company. Hence, a multinational company that plays a dominant role in the host country's economy must consider such constraints and make its global plans accordingly. The surveillance of each market and economy in which its products are produced and sold is required of a multinational company if it is to survive, prosper, and grow. And that calls for global comprehensive planning.

The Global Planning Process

Most executives I interviewed supported the view that the secret of success in managing a geographically diversified company lies in the principle that corporate management should reserve for itself the responsibility for strategic planning, for example, the formulation of the broad overall mission and the long-range objectives and policies of the company, and decentralize the responsibility for local planning operations to lower levels. If a company does not follow that principle and instead allows the lower units to formulate their plans without providing them first with an umbrella of strategic plans that combines them into a master corporate plan, then the end result will certainly be poor planning. That is because the various subsidiaries at lower levels do not have overall company missions, objectives, and policies as guidelines and therefore the result is most likely to be individual subsidiary plans inconsistent with each other and with the total company goals.

The following is a typical model of the global planning process, but a word of caution is necessary. Not all companies that I interviewed followed this model; and although some have a planning process that is very similar to it, others do not come close at all. The headquarters prepares the company's strategic plans, which include the mission, long-range objectives, policies, and strategies. The subsidiaries develop the medium- and short-range programs and plans, which include their own subobjectives, subpolicies, substrategies, goals, targets, procedures, tactical plans, and programs for their own operations based upon the strategic plans developed at the corporate level.

The subsidiary plans are then sent to the corporate headquarters for review, evaluation and modification if necessary. (Corporate headquarters could, of course, require that the subsidiary medium-range programs and plans be reviewed before the subsidiaries are allowed to formulate short-range plans.) Subsidiary managers are given the opportunity to present their own viewpoints and to justify their plans, but the final decisions are made at the top management level. The individual subsidiary plans are then combined into one master plan for the entire company. An attempt is made at the corporate level to match the various subsidiary plans and remove any conflicts or inconsistencies.

The master plan is constantly monitored and flexibly implemented. Care is taken to consider major changes in the political-economic-legal environment at the subsidiary level that may require changes in the original master plan. In this way, the corporate headquarters, with its global viewpoint, can make sure that each subsidiary is following the aims of the company and is contributing to the performance of the entire company in the most efficient way possible.

Headquarters must first establish the strategic plan of the company, because it is impossible for any one subsidiary or group of subsidiaries to possess a global viewpoint. Decisions concerning long-range marketing strategies, deployment of key personnel, investment of corporate resources, location of production facilities, and organization must be made at the headquarters in light of the global alternative opportunities available to the company. As Clee and Scipio said: [2]

> Strategic planning, coordination, and control can only be carried out properly at corporate headquarters. These responsibilities can never in fact be decentralized, because decisions of strategic nature (e.g., selecting the countries or businesses to enter, allocating corporate funds, planning the logistics flow of goods from producing points to markets, and programming any research and development projects) necessarily involve the corporation as a whole and must be made by persons in a position to view the total enterprise.

> Responsibility for "local" planning and operations must be decentralized to the level of a practical span of control—that is, top management must fix responsibility and commensurate authority down the line for achieving corporate-approved objectives within the framework of guidelines (e.g., policies, strategic plans, and resources to be provided) emanating from headquarters.

Unique Planning Problems of a Multinational Company

A multinational company faces unique planning problems in implementing the global planning process, which we shall now briefly consider under three groups: finance, production, and marketing. It must be remembered, however, that the specific problems are all interrelated and must be considered from a total systems viewpoint.

Finance

Headquarters management in multinational companies always faces the problem of setting realistic goals, especially financial goals, for subsidiaries abroad. The problem arises because what may be realistic financial goals of return on investments, earnings per share, or whatever for a domestic subsidiary may not be applicable to a foreign subsidiary. The financial objectives have to be modified in the latter case for several reasons.

Inflation and currency devaluation are problems that a multinational company has to face in the various countries in which it operates. A foreign subsidiary could be very successful in terms of the local currency but sustain a net loss due to devaluation. Most companies borrow heavily in the local financial markets to hedge against such losses, but it is almost impossible to completely eliminate them. It is very difficult to use the return-on-investment criterion to evaluate a subsidiary operating in a country with an unstable currency. The problem arises in determining what is meant by "return." Is it local-currency return or dollar return? And what exchange rate should be used? Should it be rate at the end of the month during which the profit was earned, or should it be the current rate applied to all profits earned up to now? It is also necessary to determine what is meant by "investment." Does investment constitute original, current, or remittance dollar value?

All multinational companies do establish some sort of ground rules to handle these problems, but in spite of all their efforts at arriving at some measure of return on investment to evaluate their foreign subsidiaries, the figures do not help much in comparing the performance of one subsidiary with that of another. Here the example used the return on investment as a measure of comparison, but similar problems arise when attempts are made to compute other financial ratios as well.

Production

Production and logistical planning presents one of the most difficult tasks faced by the corporate planner in a multinational company. Forecasting the economic environment poses a quite different, but equally difficult, problem. As C. Wickham Skinner said:[3]

> Rapid changes, such as those occurring in Europe over the past five years, make forecasting difficult. An economic "cost-mix" which differs from that used in the United States requires a new rationale for decisions about equipment, process, make or buy, and economic order quantities.

The corporate headquarters staff must judge plans and requests by different criteria for each country, taking into account not only the specific mix of costs but local quality and material procurement problems as well. Moreover, the factors involved must be considered not just for the present; they also must be estimated for the future.

Skinner is referring to a company that is headquartered in the United States. Obviously, a company headquartered in a foreign country, say Switzerland, will face similar problems if the economic cost-mix in the foreign country differs from that in Switzerland.

In addition to the traditional controls over exports and imports, governments have now extended their controls in several other ways that have had effects on inventories and flow of raw materials, goods in process, and finished products within and between nations. They include barter exchanges with other countries (this is most prevalent among countries with soft currencies and foreign exchange problems), bilateral and multilateral trade agreements that accord special concessions such as bigger quotas and lower tariffs to goods emanating from countries that have signed the agreements, and area economic development schemes. Moreover, if the government is a dominant buyer in a national market, then it can and does have a significant effect upon the subsidiary's inventory levels and flow of materials and products. This the government does through its decisions as to the timing of its procurement commitments, the quantity of the products it purchases, and the suppliers it chooses to buy from.[1]

As was pointed out earlier, national governments are now playing an increasingly active role in influencing the multinational company with regard to the size, products, and location of its foreign subsidiaries. Management of a foreign subsidiary under such circumstances has to be extremely careful to insure that its production plans do not call for activities such as huge layoffs or transfer of production to a subsidiary in another country if such behavior could cause economic hardship to the host country's economy.

Marketing

Multinational companies face many unique problems in planning marketing. A comprehensive list of all the obstacles on an international scale would be quite extensive, and therefore only the most important planning problems will be examined here.

Absence of adequate data. In the United States, with its relatively homogeneous market, data pertaining to market characteristics, technology, consumption patterns and trends, and other relevant and significant aspects of the environment affecting the business can be obtained with little effort from the private and public sectors of the economy. That, however, is not true of most of the markets of the world. The development of this type of information about consumer trends is almost impossible to obtain even in many advanced countries. To further complicate strategic marketing planning, the experience a multinational company gains in one part of the world or in one market area is often of no value in other market areas. One example is the Singer Company experience. Singer found that most markets prefer light sewing machines except for certain African markets which prefer heavy machines, and that in France it is impossible to sell a particular model of a specific product. In Switzerland, on the other hand, no other model is acceptable.

Consumer preferences. Many multinational companies have found that consumer preferences are so different from one market to another that a very successful product in one market may not sell at all in another. Here are two examples:

When Campbell Soup tried to sell its U.S. tomato soup formulation to the British, it discovered, after considerable losses, that the English prefer a more bitter taste. Another U.S. company spent several million dollars in an unsuccessful effort to capture the British cake mix market with U.S.-style fancy frosting and cake mixes only to discover that Britons consume their cake at teatime and that the cake they prefer is dry, spongy, and suitable to be picked up with the left hand while the right manages a cup of tea.

Philip Morris attempted to take advantage of U.S. television advertising campaigns which have a sizable Canadian audience in border areas. The Canadian cigarette market is a Virginia or straight tobacco market in contrast to the U.S. market, which is a blended tobacco market. Philip Morris officials decided to ignore market research evidence, which indicated that Canadians would not accept a blended cigarette, and went ahead with programs which achieved retail distribution of U.S. blended brands in the Canadian border areas served by U.S. television. Unfortunately, the Canadian preference for the straight cigarette remained unchanged. American-style cigarettes sold up to the border but no further. Philip Morris had to withdraw its U.S. brands.[5]

Advertising. Preparing advertising copy in international markets can be a problem. There are several weaknesses in a standardized copy approach owing to the diversity of language, media, and government regulations. There are also differences in special demands, nationality of customers, culture, and living standards. Copy, no matter how well written, cannot be literally translated for use in another country. Advertising must be tailored to individual markets.

Translating advertising copy is difficult because not only do languages change at national borders but there may be several languages used in one country and local peculiarities as well. For example, in Switzerland an advertiser must use at least three languages. German is spoken by 73 percent of the population; French is spoken by 21 percent; Italian by 5 percent; and the remaining 1 percent speaks Romanish. Different versions of the same language also complicate matters; for example, Spanish spoken in Mexico is not the same as Spanish spoken in Argentina, nor is Spanish spoken in Chile the same as that spoken in Venezuela. Similarly, French spoken in France is not the same as that spoken in Belgium.

Because of these problems, it is essential, in preparing advertising copy, to have an understanding of the history, cultural characteristics, and nature of the country and its people. A poor research job could lead to some embarrassing problems, as some companies experienced:

> Copywriters for General Motors found out that "Body by Fisher" came out "Corpse by Fisher" in Flemish. "Schweppes Tonic Water" was speedily dehydrated to "Schweppes Tonia" in Italy, where "it water" idiomatically indicates a bathroom. In Brazil, one United States airline proudly advertised the swank "rendezvous lounges" on its jets and learned belatedly that "rendezvous" in Portuguese means a room hired for assignations. Africa is an account executive's nightmare. Native words acceptable in one city are obscenities fifty miles away, and that old advertising catchword "magic" has doubtful value; to Africans the word is linked with a mythical devil named Tokoloshe, who gets young girls pregnant.[6]

Being able to find a good medium for international advertising also poses many planning problems. For example, some media are nonexistent in certain countries. No commercial radio or television exists in France, Belgium, and the Netherlands. In those countries and in many others throughout the world, radio and television are nationalized and hence are not available for advertising.

The newspaper can be a good medium to use in foreign countries, but it usually does not have the mass circulation that the American newspapers have. For example, India has over 1,000 newspapers, but only one has a readership of over 200,000 in a country of over 500 million people. In comparison, *The New York Times* has a circulation of over 680,000.

Another problem is that media data are often difficult to obtain in foreign countries. Even in advanced countries like West Germany and

France, rate information does not include circulation figures and marketing data.

Culture. Another major marketing planning problem is the different cultures in foreign markets. Cultural problems create not only marketing planning problems but also planning problems in all the different aspects of overseas trade. Examples of conflicts caused by the collision of different cultures are abundant.[7] Any firm that operates in a foreign country must recognize that strong cultural differences do exist in all countries and that the success of the firm could hinge on its ability to adopt or make concessions to them. For example:

> Princess Housewares, Inc., a large U.S. appliance manufacturer, introduced a line of electrical housewares in the German market. The company's brand name was well known and highly regarded in the United States, but relatively unknown in Germany; and the brand had a definite "American" sound. The company discovered that the American association was a real drawback among German consumers. According to a survey, fewer than 40 percent of German individuals felt "confident" about electrical products made in the United States, compared with 91% who were "confident" of German-made products.[8]

But perhaps the real danger of different cultural factors is that of using what James A. Lee calls the self-reference criterion (SRC), which is the unconscious reference to one's own cultural values in dealing with overseas problems and situations. Lee holds that the use of the SRC instead of a more rational systematic approach to analyze differences and problems based on "cultural analysis" is the root cause of most international business problems. For example:

> The managers of a joint-venture tobacco company in an Asian country were warned that their proposed new locally named (a token adaptation) and manufactured filtered cigarettes would fail. Filters had not yet been introduced here. Nevertheless, the resident Western managers, along with local executives whose SRC was dominantly Western because of their social class and education, puffed smugly on their own U.S. filtered cigarettes while the product flopped, leaving the company with idle equipment and unrecovered setup and launch costs.
>
> The basic reason for the prediction of failure was a difference in fear of death—especially from cancer of the lungs. A life expectancy of 29 years in that Asian country does not place many people in the lung cancer age bracket. There is not the general cultural value of sanitation, the literacy rate, or a *Reader's Digest* type of magazine to motivate them to give up unfiltered cigarettes.

The Western-oriented tobacco company's management missed these two critical factors because of the operation of that perfectly normal human mechanism. *The SRC.*[9]

Although the marketing planning problems described are the major ones that a multinational company generally faces, it must be realized that there are many other marketing planning problems that must be considered by the management of any multinational company. For instance, a multinational company must consider the climate of the country, its economic development stage, marketing institutions, legal restrictions, and so on. Those problems, however, tend to be more of the operations type, and therefore we shall not go into them.

Common Mistakes in Global Planning

Planners in multinational companies and especially in companies that have been quite successful in developing comprehensive business plans for their domestic operations tend to make three mistakes in planning their global operations.[10]

Overcentralization in Detailed Programming

There is a tendency on the part of planners to formulate detailed programs of action for the company's entire overseas operations. That is a very difficult task in light of the planning problems discussed earlier in this chapter. Although detailed programming of operations of domestic subsidiaries is feasible because of the uniformity of legal, political, economic, cultural, and social factors, it becomes quite unbearable when attempted on an international scale. And planners who do succeed in formulating detailed programs of action for the domestic operations of the company soon find themselves disillusioned when they do not enjoy equal success on an international scale. The ultimate victim is global planning.

Planning on a Regional Basis

Plans developed on a regional basis often succeed, but the number of failures is equally great. Planners have a tendency to group countries that have similar cultural heritages into one planning region. That is often a mistake because, as was pointed out earlier in this chapter, although two countries may be culturally similar, they might be quite dissimilar politically and economically. Because of those differences, strategies that may be successful in one country may be unsuited for the other. For example, Argentina and Bolivia have similar cultural heritages, but are quite different in their political orientation and levels of economic development; yet they are almost always grouped into the same region by multinational companies. Another example is that of Australia and Canada, which are in different hemispheres and almost always placed into different regions; yet they are very similar politically and culturally.

Thus, although on the surface there may appear to be considerable similarity between countries in the same geographic area, more often than not there is a great amount of political and economic disparity between them. Hence, plans made for groups of countries situated in geographic proximity to each other often fail because they do not take into account some of the factors that to a great extent determine the ultimate success or failure of whatever strategy, be it production, marketing, or personnel.

Failure to Sense Political Trends Abroad

We discussed earlier in this chapter the impact of national planning by foreign governments on the plans of subsidiaries abroad. Changes in national plans that call for an imposition of fresh tariffs or quotas on goods imported by the subsidiary may have a significant effect on the business logistics of the entire multinational company, especially if there is inter-subsidiary transfer and exchange of components and/or finished products. Corporate executives often consider it a waste of time to discuss at length local politics with their subsidiary heads or key managers of their operations abroad. That is a mistake, because political trends abroad are often quite volatile and plans for the long-range future become meaningless when the political assumptions that were made in formulating them are no longer valid.

Preparing for Global Planning

Too many companies have inaugurated planning systems with haste and have failed. It is better to postpone the use of corporate planning than to introduce it and watch it fail, because then it becomes twice as difficult to start the planning process again. That is true of corporate planning on a domestic as well as a global scale. It is very important for a multinational company that it make plans for global planning. That means first of all, that there should be a proper climate for planning in the organization. Global planning should be acceptable from the start to those who would be expected to indulge in it, and that includes key personnel at the headquarters and subsidiary levels. The chief executive must get involved in the planning process and not delegate the task to staff groups; it is too important an activity to be delegated. Only by getting personally involved can the chief executive set an example for those at lower levels and help everyone in the company realize that global planning is an important activity that all should be involved in.

A planning format should be developed for the use of subsidiaries abroad, and necessary adaptations in it should be made for the differences in local conditions and subsidiary characteristics. The planning steps and their timing must be determined and communicated to the operating personnel at the headquarters and subsidiary levels. Who is to do what, when, where, and how has to be clarified, which means that global planning has to be adequately organized and staffed. Finally, what types of plans will be developed at which levels must be clarified. Questions such as who will be responsible for planning of new products and whether the activity will be performed locally, regionally, or at the corporate level must be answered beforehand. By careful preplanning of global planning, premature failures that many companies experience in that activity can be avoided. At all times it must be kept in mind that global planning is not easy, and therefore care must be taken not to expect too much from it too soon. To develop a sound and effective global planning system requires a commitment to global planning and a lot of hard work. A high level of tolerance for frustration is a personal requirement of all those involved, and especially the chief executive.

Planning Strategies in Selected Areas

Production

Decisions on location of new plants, expansion of capacity of existing plants, closing or reduction of production in certain plants, and shifting of production from one product to another by using the same plant facility are centralized at the top management level of the multinational company. Proposals do originate at the subsidiary, product division, or regional level, but they are evaluated and accepted, modified or rejected at the top management level. Here are a few examples:

Strategic plans and strategic decisions are made at the head office. The operational plans are made within each subsidiary. Proposals are often made by the subsidiaries for setting up a new plant which are approved or disapproved at the head office. Investment decisions are centralized. Planning of a new plant works both ways—proposals are generated by the head office as well as by the individual subsidiaries abroad. *The East Asiatic Company Ltd., Copenhagen, Denmark*

The company believes that the factories abroad which are subsidiaries legally should not be looked upon as independent units but as factories with businesses managed by the respective product divisions from the headquarters. In other words, planning for the entire product group should be integrated and centralized. There should be decentralization of operations but centralization of planning and policymaking. Plans of each division must be coordinated, and the Board of Directors must assign the priorities. This applies when a decision has to be made as to where in the world should the company build the plant. *Farbenfabriken Bayer AG, Leverkusen, West Germany*

This decision [where in the world to build the plant] is taken by the Special Committee. The recommendation for building a new plant may come from the regional or product managements, but the ultimate decision can only be made by the Special Committee because it is only at this level that an overall company-wide perspective is available. *Unilever Ltd., London*

Plant is built wherever there is an opportunity on an entirely pragmatic basis. Each operating company in light of its forecasts submits plans to the headquarters. The aggregation of these plans may itself suggest new or different plans. A top management statement is formulated which includes the group objectives for some years ahead, and these provide a broad, flexible framework within which operating companies prepare their subsequent plans. Thus, the "forward look" for the group as a whole is built up from the plans of operating units plus overall Group considerations. *Royal Dutch/Shell Group, London*

The company has a corporate business development plan which extends five years into the future, which is developed following a thorough product divisions' analysis. The product divisions prepare their own five-year plan using the corporate goals as guidelines. Conferences between the top brass of the company and each divisional head help the top brass to understand divisional plans, which are then approved or modified as required. The divisional plans are integrated into a corporate development plan for the whole company.

The decision as to where in the world to build the plant is made by corporate management as part of the corporate development plan. The initiative comes either from corporate management or from the product divisions, but the final decision is made at the top with the help of the corporate planning staff group. *Landis and Gyr AG, Zug, Switzerland*

The initiative for new projects rests with three authorities. (1) The overseas company might decide that it wants to build a fertilizer or polyethylene plant and make such a proposal to the overseas policy group for its region. (2) A U.K. manufacturing division might want to set up a plant in a country where it has a good export business. The reason might be to protect its business from, let us say, a Japanese firm setting up a plant there. (3) Territorial directors might suggest places to set up a new plant. The decisions are made in the appropriate overseas policy, or control group, and referred up the ladder to the board for approval. A special subcommittee of the board, called the policy and plans committee, consisting of the three deputy chairmen, assists the board in formulating major policies and programs. The company planning department, whose function it is to carry out planning studies assigned by the policy and plans committee or by directors, helps the policy and plans committee by providing it with company-wide studies and information. *Imperial Chemical Industries Ltd., London*

The proposal that a new plant be established abroad could come from the head office in London or from one of the overseas subsidiary companies. But the final decision is made in London. For example, the Thailand project, which led to the formation of The Metal Box Company of Thailand Limited, was worked on by The Metal Box Company of Malaysia Limited, but the final decision was taken at the head office in London. Ideas of this sort are generated at all levels, but they have to be acceptable to the executive committee and the board of The Metal Box Company Overseas Limited. *The Metal Box Company Overseas Limited, London*

From the examples given, we see a trend among multinational companies toward a bottom-up approach as far as the flow of new ideas and information is concerned and a top-down approach in evaluating and deciding upon the ideas and proposals generated from below. Multinational companies need the two approaches in their decision-making and planning process because their geographically far-flung operations cannot be managed otherwise. A huge and unmanageable number of staff specialists would be required at the headquarters level if the generation of ideas and proposals were to be wholly centralized. At the same time, strategic decisions, like setting up new plants, must be centralized because it is only at the top management level that the overall bird's-eye-view of the total company operations in the varied social-economic-political environments is available. Individual subsidiaries just do not have such a perspective. Top management at the headquarters alone is in the position to make a comparative cost-benefit analysis of the various alternatives available and, based upon such an analysis, to decide upon a course of action that is optimal in light of the overall company's objectives.

It must be mentioned that daily production planning is still decentralized and in the hands of the subsidiary heads. But even that activity is getting more and more centralized as companies are beginning to split up the production process and distribute it among subsidiaries in different countries to take advantage of tax and labor economies. As a result, the location of coordinative authority is being raised above the subsidiary level. For example, a multinational company might have one subsidiary in Hong Kong manufacturing components and another in Bombay assembling them and the final product might be sold in France by a subsidiary there. In that case, coordination of the production function—in particular, production scheduling—of the Hong Kong and Bombay subsidiaries might be the responsibility of a regional manager handling the Asia and Far East region. Thus authority over the production function would not be entirely in the hands of subsidiary heads but centralized one level above.

Product

Some companies, such as Schweizerische Aluminium AG (Alusuisse), of Switzerland, permit their subsidiaries to develop and market their own products without prior permission of the parent company. Mr. Wohnlich, general manager of Schweizerische Aluminium, said: "Subsidiaries can launch new products without previously checking with the parent company as long as the product is in the aluminium industry and does not need new investment." But Schweizerische Aluminium happens to be an extremely decentralized company as far as subsidiary operations are concerned. The company operates under the philosophy of giving the subsidiaries maximum freedom in running their own affairs as long as they consistently present reasonable profits to the parent company. Top management controls the subsidiaries by getting from them monthly balance sheets. But that is not true of most multinational companies.

Product-oriented as well as market-oriented multinational companies control the product mix of their subsidiaries; but product-oriented companies keep a much tighter rein over the subsidiaries, and product modifications to suit local conditions are slight. The attempt in product-oriented companies is to obtain a degree of standardization of products sufficient to reduce design and production costs. A proportionately greater amount of unique technical know-how is generally used in products offered by product-oriented companies than is used by market-oriented companies; therefore, an effort is made by such companies to exploit and market the unique technology and know-how to the fullest extent. Product planning in such companies is highly centralized. New product development almost always takes place with the guidance and under the supervision of the parent company.

In market-oriented companies, the parent company plans the general product categories to be marketed at home and abroad and the company's subsidiaries abroad develop products to suit the local tastes. For example, Campbell Soup Company, which is a highly market-oriented company, has products that fall into three groups: canned foods, frozen foods, and bakery products. The subsidiaries of Campbell Soup abroad operate quite independently and do not need close liaison with the domestic plants. But the control of quality is very strictly maintained by flying in samples from plants abroad to the quality control department of the parent company at Camden, New Jersey. Although quality control is centralized, the company's plants abroad do develop products to suit the local tastes. To illustrate, soups to suit local tastes have been developed and marketed by subsidiaries in England, Sweden, Mexico, and Australia.

By and large the trend in multinational companies is toward an increasing degree of centralization of product planning and away from the free-rein approach used by some companies, a practice referred to earlier. That is a result of the general movement toward the integration of the total operations of subsidiaries in order to benefit the total multinational company and not just parts of it. The headquarters of a multinational company serve both as receiver and transmitter of information generated in the company's worldwide field of operations. A product that happens to be successful in Canada could be equally successful in Australia, or a product that has gained consumer acceptance in Portugal might gain similar acceptance in Brazil. Such information is received at the headquarters from all parts of the world. And because experience with and knowledge of comparative world environments, which are required to make sound decisions that are in the total company's interest, are best available at the parent company level, product planning is a function that is getting increasingly centralized.

Research and Development

All companies interviewed have one thing in common: they all give centralized direction to the R&D activity conducted by the company. The objectives, policies, and programs that define the general scope of the activity performed within the total company framework are defined by the parent company. The reason is that only the top management of the parent company can (1) take the global viewpoint and determine meaningful objectives for research, (2) evaluate the company's long-term technological threats and opportunities, (3) study the company's overall strengths and weaknesses in the major functional fields, (4) develop an overall business strategy into which research is integrated, (5) develop a system for the evaluation of research projects in light of company goals and objectives, and (6) organize research and operations for the fullest transfer of technology from research to operations.

But various organizational patterns are used by companies for conducting research and development. For example, market-oriented companies that market a few standardized products throughout the world, but who also have some of their basic products modified or adapted to local tastes and preferences, use a procedure whereby R&D of products that are standardized and marketed throughout the world is centralized in laboratories located in the parent company. Such companies have small research laboratories within separate plants that are permitted to develop products for the local market after the prior approval of the parent company. Campbell Soup Company fits into that pattern. It has a large R&D laboratory at Camden, New Jersey, that conducts R&D of products, such as certain kinds of soups, that are marketed all over the world. Each subsidiary abroad has its own technology and research department that is free to develop products for the local market. Such products are first submitted for approval to the product committee of the parent company, which consists of senior officers of the company.

Another pattern is the one similar to that used by a Swiss chemical company:

> Each product division has its own research programs which it plans and controls. Each division has a few large research centers where basic research is conducted. Applied research is carried out in a decentralized manner in the various subsidiaries.

Some companies have centralized both basic and applied research in the parent company. The product divisions, not the subsidiaries abroad, conduct R&D. In some cases that is the result of a deliberate policy on the part of the parent company, but a few companies said that it was arrived at not by choice but by circumstances in their subsidiaries abroad, which were not yet sophisticated enough to do their own developmental research.

A Swiss chemicals and pharmaceuticals company has spread its basic research into three countries: Switzerland, the United Kingdom, and the United States. I was told that the decision was taken by top management because (1) basic research in Switzerland alone makes the company very vulnerable in the event of a foreign takeover of the country and (2) the company needs the scientific imports, fresh outlook, talent, and approaches from countries that are scientifically advanced. It is for the latter reason that a research center was established in the United States. A research center was established in the United Kingdom to take advantage of British ingenuity and creativity at a comparatively lower cost. Applied research is decentralized within each product division. Process development is mostly centralized within the production department of the parent company, although some process development is carried out within the product divisions.

Many European companies are now planning to establish basic research centers in more than one country in order to tap the technical and scientific expertise that exists in different parts of the world. For example, one European company conducts almost all its basic research in pharmaceuticals, pesticides, and plastics in sophisticated laboratories in Switzerland, India, the United States, and the United Kingdom. Dyestuffs and photochemicals research is conducted at home only. Developmental research in the company is conducted in the various plants around the globe, which accounts for the fact that 10 percent of the company's personnel around the world are engaged in research.

Certain large multinational companies have research activities that are centralized but do not have one large research facility conducting all research. For example, Unilever has more than a dozen research centers throughout the world, as well as smaller centers in West Africa, the Congo, and the Solomon Islands. But research at each of those centers is concentrated on a group of products only, and results are shared by the entire Unilever organization. The research center at Cheshire, United Kingdom, is concerned with detergents, chemicals, and timber; the center at Bedfordshire is concerned with the scientific problems of food preservation, animal nutrition; and so on.

To sum up, regardless of the organizational arrangements used, R&D is an activity that is conducted under the close scrutiny of the parent company. When R&D programs abroad are established, they are coordinated carefully with those of the parent.

Purchasing

Quite a few companies interviewed said that the purchasing of major raw materials and components is centralized in the parent company. But many companies said that the purchasing function is decentralized and is performed at the subsidiary level. Here are a few examples of centralized purchasing:

> We have a central purchasing department. On things that we buy in large amounts, we coordinate our purchases on a worldwide basis. For the thousands of things that you have to buy in a plant, each of our companies [subsidiaries] has its own purchasing department and they buy locally.
> *Hercules Inc., Wilmington, Delaware*

All major raw materials and components are the subject of central buying negotiation and, where appropriate, contracts are entered for the supply of these materials for the company as a whole. *The Metal Box Company Overseas Limited, London*

Crude oil is bought in big deals and they are ones which individual operating companies could not make. Hence the big deals are centralized. If there are small purchases, then they are made by individual operating companies. In such cases, since the operating companies are autonomous companies, they are free to make their small purchases from another Shell company or from somebody else outside the group. *Royal Dutch/Shell Group, London*

The company buys from numerous suppliers abroad. The purchasing office in the production department gives service and advice to the company's purchasing offices abroad, but the decisions are taken centrally. This way the company can compare prices and get the best price on its raw materials purchases. *A chemicals and pharmaceuticals company in Europe*

As was mentioned earlier, some companies interviewed said that purchasing of raw materials and components was left to the subsidiaries by the parent company. Here are a few examples:

The nature of the products and their raw materials force the company to decentralize purchasing. All of Campbell's plants are near the source of supply of raw materials and water. *Campbell Soup Company, Camden, New Jersey*

Purchasing of raw materials is decentralized. Each subsidiary has its own purchasing department. This is true for all Nestlé's businesses. *Nestlé Alimentana S.A., Vevey, Switzerland*

There are purchasing departments within each division. There is a small central purchasing department in the headquarters only for the reason that it is practical and economical to create certain purchasing agreements centrally. *Atlas Copco AB, Nacka, Sweden*

Purchase of raw materials is decentralized within each overseas company. In certain cases ICI has been able to negotiate a worldwide contract, and the scale of buying enables the company to get concessional prices which become available to overseas companies. This is done wherever it is practicable, but a great deal of purchasing is done by each overseas company. In the United Kingdom there is a central purchasing organization for all the operating divisions which buys centrally when there is an economic case for doing so. Centralized buying is done only when there is an advantage. *Imperial Chemical Industries Ltd., London*

The preceding examples indicate that, whenever possible, multinational companies prefer to centralize their purchasing in order to get economies of bulk buying. The parent company generally negotiates with several suppliers and finally agrees to buy specified amounts of raw materials at a certain price. Once the price and terms are agreed upon, the subsidiaries often order what they need directly from the supplier and pay the negotiated price. Thus, common purchasing gives the subsidiaries the advantages of a lower price plus better deliveries and quality, which they could not have obtained had they gone about negotiating their purchases independently. The movement in multinational companies is clearly toward an integration of the purchasing activities of subsidiaries.

Marketing

Earlier in this chapter we examined several unique marketing problems that multinational companies face. In view of those problems, is it possible for a multinational company to plan global marketing strategies at the corporate level? Or is the task impossible because of the differences between nations? Should marketing strategies be formulated by local managements in each country? Most companies interviewed said that they recognized the differences that exist between nations and admitted that a uniform global marketing strategy is not practical. But they added that the great increase in international travel by tourists and businessmen and the tremendous flow of communications between nations via radio, newspapers, magazines, and television within the last two decades are bringing peoples within major regions of the world closer together in terms of their tastes and preferences. Therefore, although a single standardized marketing strategy is not yet practical for the whole world, it is now possible to have some parts of the marketing strategy standardized within major regions of the world.

Multinational companies have been quite successful in using common advertising messages and brand names. For example, Nestlé used very successfully the basic theme of "New Nescafé with fresh-ground aroma" throughout Europe, the United States, and Australia. More and more companies are also moving toward the use of the same brand name for the same product in different countries within a region. Problems arose for Unilever when it marketed a detergent called Radion in Germany and marketed a similar detergent under a different brand name in Austria. German newspapers and television are popular in Austria. Housewives who were exposed to Radion advertisements in German media could not get Radion in Austria, and Unilever suffered a loss of sales of the product in Austria even though it was actually marketed there, but under a different brand name. On the other hand, Unilever's Lux and Lifebuoy soaps can be bought in India, Australia, the United States, and elsewhere throughout the world.

Common advertising themes have been used quite successfully by other multinational companies than Nestlé. For example, Esso's "Put a tiger in your tank" slogan was used quite effectively not only in the United States but also in Europe and Asia. Similarly, I saw Pan American's advertisement, "Pan Am makes the going great," which was seen extensively on American television, on a movie screen in Copenhagen. I could not understand the words because they were spoken in Danish, but the rest seemed quite familiar. I was told by one executive that such standardization is very beneficial to a multinational company in terms of reduced costs and greater effectiveness in marketing, because the added cost of producing separate advertisements for each market could run into millions of dollars.

One note of warning is in order at this point. What I meant to point out earlier was that multinational companies are attempting whenever and wherever possible to standardize portions of their marketing strategies. A single global marketing strategy for the entire world market is impractical because of the differences between peoples in different parts of the world. But what we are witnessing now is a phenomenon, due to rapid transportation and communication between nations, that is slowly removing the diversity between markets in a given region, for example, Europe. And that is allowing multinational companies to standardize parts of their marketing strategies not on a global, but on a regional basis. The goal of a marketing strategy is to not only maximize sales but also reduce costs, and standardization allows the multinational company to reduce costs.

Financing of Subsidiaries

What policies are generally followed by companies in financing their operations abroad? How do they finance a new project or the expansion of an operating subsidiary? A company has various alternative methods of financing at its disposal. I was interested in whether the companies interviewed had any preference in the methods they used. The replies showed that different companies do have different policies and preferences, which makes the formulation of generalizations quite difficult. But if some generalizations are to be made, then I believe that the most favored methods of financing subsidiaries abroad are local borrowing from banks and financial institutions and retained earnings. The next most favored method involves loans from the parent company to the subsidiary abroad. At this point a few examples are appropriate.

Working capital financing is preferred through local borrowing. The fixed capital requirements are loaned from the head office, although retained earnings are used when they are available. An East Asiatic Finance Company has been established in Luxemburg, for tax purposes, which makes loans to the subsidiaries if local borrowing is not feasible or is expensive. But as far as possible, the company favors the use of local borrowing. *The East Asiatic Company Ltd., Copenhagen, Denmark*

Finance companies located in places that give distinct tax advantages have been used by other companies as a means of financing their subsidiaries abroad. Bayer AG, of Germany, has a wholly owned holding company, called Bayer Foreign Investments Ltd., in Toronto, Canada, for tax purposes. That company holds all the American and a great many of the European subsidiaries and also shares in affiliates. It does not hold any of the Asian subsidiaries of Bayer. Bayer Foreign Investments Ltd. has the advantage of owning considerable assets, and it can therefore go to American bankers and obtain huge loans. Bayer uses Bayer Foreign Investments Ltd. for making loans to subsidiaries or affiliates that need the money. It uses other methods of financing as well, however, and it chooses the one that is most profitable under the circumstances. Unilever has a finance company located in Curaçao for tax purposes; it is a subsidiary of Unilever N.V., the Dutch arm of the Unilever organization, and it is used by the company to inject money into an overseas subsidiary whenever the parent company has to do the financing.

Some Swiss companies have a policy of encouraging local borrowing by subsidiaries for their short-term requirements only. One company has the policy of having a central cash fund in Switzerland because it feels that the Swiss economy is an excellent place to keep money. It uses the fund to allocate money strategically to its subsidiaries at home and abroad. The company officials said that Swiss money is the cheapest in terms of cost of borrowing, and they therefore supply long-term loans to subsidiaries abroad from Switzerland. The company policy is to keep retained earnings by subsidiaries abroad at the bare minimum.

Sulzer Brothers Ltd., of Switzerland, has a policy of financing the subsidiaries abroad by using local sources if there is an exchange risk and danger of devaluation of the local currency. If taxes on corporate income are too high in the country concerned, then funds are transferred to Switzerland, where taxes are lower, and loans are made from Switzerland. Although the most advantageous method for the company is used, the preference is clearly for financing subsidiaries abroad through retained earnings or local borrowing. Brazil is one example of a country, among many others, in which Sulzer does not make any loans from Switzerland because of the recurring devaluation of the Brazilian currency.

Nestlé Alimentana S.A., of Switzerland, has subsidiaries abroad that are usually able to meet their own short-term financial requirements to a certain extent through internal cash flow and depreciation funds. If a certain subsidiary cannot finance itself, then the parent holding company loans it money or has it borrow the money from a local bank in the host country. The parent company then guarantees the loan. If the capital requirements are more substantial and permanent, then the parent company subscribes more capital and raises its equity in the subsidiary.

The financial strength of Nestlé is unique. It has very little medium- or long-term debt. That helps, because it has never asked stockholders or lenders to finance its acquisitions or new ventures. The company has substantial reserves for expansion, diversification, and future risks. All capital expenditures since 1964 have been self-financed. The company holds high amounts of cash as a precautionary measure. The precautions are justified, according to Nestlé's managing director, Pierre Liotard-Vogt, because Nestlé has a small home base and operations worldwide that are subject to risks such as currency devaluations and exchange controls.

Companies such as Imperial Chemical Industries, Metal Box, Pirelli, and others that do not insist upon 100 percent control of their subsidiaries abroad often finance the long-term capital requirements of their subsidiaries either by inviting the local investors to subscribe to a minority of the equity through a fresh issue of stock or by sale of a portion of the subsidiary's stock. In case of an on-going joint venture, local partners are often asked to put more capital in the local venture. If the local partner can contribute, then the parent company contributes an amount equal to the local partner's contribution. If the local partner cannot contribute, then the parent company alone puts in the required amount and thereby increases its percent of ownership of the subsidiary concerned.

Although there might be exceptions, American multinational companies engaged in manufacturing use the following pattern of financing their overseas operations. The first preference is to use retained earnings; the second is to borrow locally. If they are unable to do that, some firms such as General Foods Corporation use local borrowing with parent guarantee. If that is not feasible, then the last resort is a loan from the parent company. Companies such as Scott Paper that do permit joint ventures abroad ask their partners for additional capital input if the joint venture needs financial help. There is very little direct loaning by Scott to the foreign subsidiaries. There are some companies—Ingersoll-Rand is an example—that resist methods such as a Euro-dollar loan, a loan from the parent company, or intercompany financing in the sense of extension of credit and so on. The OFDI regulations on foreign direct investments abroad by American companies have also contributed toward heavy local borrowings by American companies in Europe.

REFERENCES

1. W. P. Brass, "Economic Planning, European Style," *Harvard Business Review*, September–October 1963, p. 109.

2. Gilbert H. Clee and Alfred di Scipio, "Creating a World Enterprise," *Harvard Business Review*, November–December 1959, p. 81.

3. C. Wickham Skinner, "Management of International Production," *Harvard Business Review*, September–October 1964, p. 128.

4. Robert E. McGarrah, "Logistics for the International Manufacturer," *Harvard Business Review*, March–April 1966, p. 161.

5. Warren J. Keegan, "Multinational Product Planning: Strategic Alternatives," *Journal of Marketing*, January 1969, p. 58.

6. *Time*, September 20, 1963, p. 93.

7. Edward T. Hall, "The Silent Language of Overseas Business," *Harvard Business Review*, May–June 1960, p. 87, and Dudley L. Miller, "The Honorable Picnic: Doing Business in Japan," *Harvard Business Review*, November –December 1961, p. 79.

8. Robert D. Buzzell, "Can You Standardize Multinational Marketing," *Harvard Business Review*, November–December 1968, pp. 110–111.

9. James A. Lee, "Cultural Analysis in Overseas Operations," *Harvard Business Review*, March–April 1966, p. 107.

10. Millard H. Pryor, Jr., "Planning in a Worldwide Business," *Harvard Business Review*, January–February 1965, pp. 130–131.

6

Ownership Strategies

MULTINATIONAL companies have to select ownership strategies that enable them not only to realize their full potential through integrated global planning but also to satisfy the wishes of host country nationals and/or governments to have "a piece of the action" as well. The joint venture is one method of sharing ownership of the subsidiary abroad with host country nationals and/or governments. Another method is to open up the equity of the multinational parent company to worldwide ownership.

In this chapter we shall look at the attitudes of multinational companies toward joint ventures and worldwide sharing of ownership of the parent company, the various forms of joint ventures and methods of worldwide ownership used by the parent company, and factors that determine to a certain extent the attitudes of multinational companies toward the two methods of sharing ownership with foreign nationals.

Definition of Joint Venture

A joint venture is a subsidiary that is owned by two or more partners, one of which is the parent multinational company. The other partner could be either the host country government, one or more foreign and/or local firms, or the general public.

Company Attitudes Toward Joint Ventures

Companies interviewed have different attitudes toward joint ventures abroad. Some companies said that they would not establish a subsidiary abroad unless it was wholly owned. But a great majority of the companies interviewed said that although they prefer to have 100 percent ownership of subsidiaries abroad, at least in the beginning of a new venture until it becomes profitable, that is not always possible. Under such circumstances they are willing to have less than 100 percent control. Some companies said that although they are willing to share ownership of their subsidiaries abroad with local parties, under no circumstances would they accept less than 50 percent of the ownership. Others indicated that they might accept a less than 50 percent ownership, but only if they owned a majority of the equity of the subsidiary, which is feasible when there are more than two partners.

Another group of companies said that they would be willing to own a minority of the equity of a subsidiary provided they had the control of its management. Some companies said that although they would prefer to have 100 percent, or at least a majority ownership of a foreign subsidiary, they would accept a minority interest without even the managerial control if circumstances required that they do so. But a company faced with the latter choice often insists that the production of the jointly owned subsidiary be marketed worldwide through its wholly owned sales company or global sales network.

There are various factors that have a bearing upon a company's willingness or hesitancy to accept joint ventures abroad. In the following pages we shall examine them.

Management Philosophy

If the management philosophies of the partners engaged in a joint venture are incompatible in areas such as risk taking, R&D, and dividend policies, problems arise very quickly. For that reason, many companies prefer to have 100 percent ownership of their operations abroad.

> We find that our concept of management . . . is very often diametrically opposite the management philosophy of our partners. We have had some sad experiences along those lines. We got along on a personal or human relations basis marvelously well. But when it came to basic management philosophy, we were talking two different languages. If you have 100 percent control, you make the decision, right or wrong. You do not have to go to time-consuming and elaborate education processes of trying to convince the other partner. *Johns-Manville Corporation, New York*

Technological and Production Characteristics

A company that produces different components of its products in different countries needs flexibility in production scheduling and control over pricing procedures. It has to take into account in its production planning process tariff barriers, import restrictions, taxation, and production costs in each country if it is to optimize the entire production line. In doing so, it might have to suboptimize the operations of subsidiaries in some countries. If local partners are involved in countries whose plants have to be suboptimized, problems could arise because the local partner most probably would object to policies and programs that adversely affect a subsidiary in which he has a vested interest. Such companies are most likely to avoid joint ventures.

Companies that spend huge sums of money on research and development are also likely to avoid joint ventures. That is because most research-oriented firms find that, even though they are paid with equity and/or royalties for unique products or processes, adequate compensation is seldom negotiated because of disagreements between the parties as to what amounts to adequate compensation. But if they do accept local participation, it is only under the condition that they be given control of the joint venture. One pharmaceuticals company interviewed had this to say about joint ventures:

> Joint ventures do have their advantages—they certainly do not solve all problems. They have their advantages as regards personnel, marketing policy, promotion relations with local authorities, distribution, or cooperation with charitable organizations. But they could have their problems if joint ventures are not a genuine partnership but merely a capital participation agreement. Both parties should contribute to the venture in terms of know-how, experience, and responsibility. Only then will there exist a fruitful relationship between the foreign and domestic partners. Unfortunately, viable partners are not easy to find and very often they already have ties with competitors, which creates more problems.
>
> Where local participation is insisted on, the company strives to obtain a majority holding in order to retain control over the newly established company. We, like many other pharmaceuticals companies, base our success upon our specialized scientific knowledge obtained through expenditure of a considerable amount of time and money on research. Like many research-oriented companies, we are not too inclined to turn over our scientific knowledge, technology, and experience to a joint venture which we cannot control. We are all the more concerned about obtaining control of a subsidiary abroad because of the delicate nature of the production process used in the manufacture of our products. A small

mistake in the process could affect human lives adversely and consequently tarnish our reputation, which has been carefully developed over several decades.

When the company is compelled to accept a minority partnership, it still tries to keep its control over the management of the subsidiary. This it does by means of a management agreement under the terms of which we bear the responsibility for the overall conduct of the business, inclusive of production, despite the minority participation. This procedure has been adopted in Mexico, where local interests—which include private parties and the Mexican government—own 60 percent of one of the companies. This agreement has worked quite satisfactorily even though we entered into it with some uncertainty at first. We fully realize that nationalistic fervor in the developing countries will make it increasingly difficult to construct wholly owned production centers. The trend toward local participation is growing from year to year, and we are making efforts to come to terms with it.

Companies that have developed a unique production process and/or trademark and brand name are quite unwilling to enter into joint ventures whose management they cannot control. For example, Solvay et Cie, the Belgian chemical giant, insists on a 100 percent ownership in subsidiaries in which a Solvay specialty is involved such as the Solvay process for making soda ash and electrolytic cell with diaphragm. The company does not go with its specialty into countries that insist upon local participation.

Similarly Pirelli, the Italian tire and cable maker, gives first preference to 100 percent control of the subsidiaries abroad. The company finds it much easier to operate abroad with complete ownership when the Pirelli name, trademarks, and technical assistance are involved. That is not a rigid rule, because there are instances when the company has accepted less than complete ownership of a subsidiary abroad owing to economic and political realities. But in almost all cases the company will not give its name, trademarks, or techniques unless it has at least 51 percent ownership of the subsidiary abroad. (There is one exception in Mexico where the company is producing electric cables. There Pirelli and Anaconda each own 33 percent of the stock ownership of the subsidiary, and the rest is in Mexican hands.) Another example is that of Unilever, the giant British/Dutch manufacturer. Unilever prefers to own 100 percent equity in its subsidiaries abroad, but that is not always feasible. Since the 1950s, Unilever has shown its willingness to enter into local financial partnerships for founding or expanding enterprises. The local financial partner could be a bank, as it is in Turkey, the local government or government agency, as it is in Kenya and Pakistan, or private shareholders, as it is in India. The company reputation is built upon branded quality products, which means that Unilever has to retain managerial control over the subsidiaries abroad. The company insists upon the right to control financial expenditures and management appointments. It has to have that right; otherwise it would become merely an investment trust.

AB SKF, of Goteborg, Sweden, a maker of ball bearings, is proud of its name and the fact that the SKF trademark stands for excellence. The company's executives said that, originally, the policy was to have 100 percent owned subsidiaries abroad but that the policy has somewhat changed and now the company tackles matters of ownership of subsidiaries abroad on an ad hoc basis. In the example of the company's subsidiary in India, 40 percent of the equity is in public hands and 60 percent is held by the parent company. SKF in the last few years has formed a joint venture in Yugoslavia. The subsidiary in Iran is a joint venture with SKF in a minority position. But under no circumstances will SKF accept a minority position in a joint venture unless it can have control over the technical process and, to some extent, management of any subsidiary that wishes to use the SKF trademark or otherwise sail under the SKF flag. I asked one of the executives of SKF how and why the company attempts to obtain managerial control, and he answered:

> That differs from country to country and situation to situation. It can happen that through negotiations we get the right to have majority on the board, for example. It can also happen that certain decisions are taken by a qualified majority or that the day-to-day management is vested in the managing director, whom we have the right to nominate. The important thing for us is that we can live up to a certain standard of quality. We do not like to endanger the reputation of our biggest asset, maybe the biggest one we have, the SKF trademark and what is behind it.

Market Characteristics

A company whose products have a worldwide market prefers to have the flexibility of supplying the market by production in plants that are, from the company's viewpoint, strategically located. The parent company takes into account the capacity, costs of production in each marketplace, and so on, with the objective of maximizing its total gains and minimizing its total costs. In doing so, the company might have to suboptimize the operations in one or more of its plants if it is in the interest of the overall multinational company.

Such a company would be severely constrained if it had a joint venture in a subsidiary that was asked to take a cut in production, or market share, or whatever, in the interest of the total multinational company. That is because the partner in the joint venture could not care less about the multinational company. All that he is likely to be interested in is the local subsidiary first and foremost.

The local partner would, in fact, object to any actions taken by the parent multinational company that would limit the sales of the joint venture. An executive of Atlas Copco AB said that his company does not allow host country nationals to own any part of the company's subsidiaries abroad because "we feel that the control of the company and its integration with the other Atlas Copco group companies is best served by having the absolute ownership." But Atlas Copco has made two exceptions to its rule, and they are its subsidiaries in Italy and South Africa. In both countries, the company was forced by the respective governments of the two countries to call in local shareholders or face the abrogation of import licenses available to the subsidiaries.

Pierre Liotard-Vogt, the managing director of Nestlé Alimentana S.A., had this to say about his company's policy toward joint ventures:

> Nestlé's general policy is to keep 100 percent of its subsidiaries wherever feasible. Exceptions occur, such as when an existing company is acquired by Nestlé, but in that case management would attempt to buy as many shares of the newly acquired company as possible in an effort to obtain ultimate control. In other exceptional cases Nestlé satisfies itself with a minority participation for investment purposes, such as Libby, McNeill and Libby, the Chicago canning company, where Nestlé has held approximately a one-third interest for the past few years. Nestlé's preference for full control accounts for its reluctance to achieve take-overs and mergers by way of exchange of shares. Nestlé prefers to get 100 percent of its subsidiaries because it permits top management to plan and control for the entire group on a global basis and without minority shareholders' conflict of interests. "Blackmail is very easy for small shareholders."

Nationalistic Pressures

Some countries do not permit wholly foreign-owned subsidiaries to operate in their markets. The only way a multinational company can penetrate the markets in those countries is through joint ventures. The possibility of establishing a wholly owned subisidary in India, Japan, or Mexico is extremely remote. (Exceptions are made at times when the host country badly needs the technical know-how or product that the multinational company is best able to provide.) Again, there are certain industries, which the host country governments call essential industries, that a foreign company can enter only through some form of collaboration with local parties. Some multinational companies that, at one time, refused to accept anything less than 100 percent ownership of their subsidiaries, especially in the developing countries, are now realizing that they either have to change their policy or lose the markets to a competitor.

Some companies have even gone so far as to pull out of a country when the host country insisted on local participation as in the case of Ford and General Motors in India. If the local market is big and there is a possibility of profitable operations, such companies do weigh the advantages against the disadvantages of a joint venture and very often decide to be flexible in their policy toward joint ventures. It was reported recently that Ford is establishing a factory in India in collaboration with an Indian firm—Escorts Ltd.—to manufacture Ford model 3000, 50-horsepower tractors. The factory was scheduled to begin operations in 1971 to produce 6,000 tractors annually. Ford will contribute 40 percent of the equity; the rest will be provided by Indians. A large part of the equipment will be locally produced, and the plant will be manned by Indian personnel with the exception of one American expert. To begin with, the plant will have 50 percent imported content, but within three years that will be reduced to only 8 percent with the Indian content at 92 percent.[1]

In some countries, multinational companies are compelled to share ownership with local parties or face the possibility of seeing their wholly owned subsidiary nationalized by the government. For example, The Metal Box Company Overseas Limited, of the United Kingdom, had this to say about nationalistic pressures in Tanzania, East Africa, and how it handled them:

> The company initially in developing an overseas subsidiary prefers to have 100 percent ownership. This enables it to have complete freedom during the initial years. Once the company is established, it looks to introducing some local participation but prefers to have a majority ownership of the overseas subsidiary's shares. When majority holding is impossible, the company is receptive—if the conditions indicate that this is the last available alternative—to owning only 50 percent of the overseas subsidiary's shares, as is the case now in Tanzania. But in the latter case the company does institute certain safeguards as in the case of the Tanzania subsidiary in which the company has a majority representation on the subsidiary's board of directors. Actually, in Tanzania the company, through negotiations with the host government, prevented an outright nationalization of the subsidiary by the host government. There Metal Box is sharing ownership with the host government, but it retains management control of the company through a management agreement which was negotiated with the host government. It also maintains a majority on the board of directors and thus keeps the company as a subsidiary. The company recognizes that conditions in many parts of the world are arising where it no

longer becomes possible to have 100 percent conrol, or even majority control. As a matter of fact, the company tries to introduce local capital in the overseas subsidiaries as soon as it is practical to do so.

Sometimes a multinational company is forced to share ownership of its subsidiary abroad because the subsidiary's major buyer is a nationalized industry. For example, Sulzer, the Swiss manufacturer of diesel engines among other things, was compelled to keep only 50 percent ownership of its French subsidiary because, according to French law, the subsidiary had to be French-owned in order to qualify as a supplier of diesel engines and other products to the nationalized French industry, navy, and armed forces.

Host governments often give better treatment to subsidiaries that have local equity participation. Some executives interviewed said that the local partner is a good man at times in contacting key government officials in order to obtain concessions on issues such as foreign exchange, import permits, and government contracts. Some companies may face sudden difficulties in obtaining import permits for essential raw material imports or equipment for plant expansion if they resist sharing ownership with local nationals. In such markets, joint ventures are almost a must in the interest of smooth subsidiary operations.

The rise of nationalism and its attack on the foreign subsidiary of a multinational company is by no means restricted to the developing areas of the world. The press and business communities in Canada, the United Kingdom, and Australia and France and other European countries have raised the banner against the wholly owned subsidiaries of foreign multinational companies. Evidence of this is in the now famous book *The American Challenge* by Jean-Jacques Servan-Schreiber, which dramatizes the dilemma created for Europe by American direct investments in high-technology sectors of that continent. The presence of a local partner or of public participation in a local subsidiary of a multinational company may help to lessen the nationalistic attacks on the local subsidiary.

Financial Characteristics

A shortage of funds to support the establishment of expansion of subsidiaries abroad often forces multinational companies to open up the ownership of their subsidiaries to local shareholders. That was one reason for local participation given by European companies interviewed, and many European companies have taken American companies on as their partners for that very reason when they have set up subsidiaries in the United States.

Multinational companies are particularly reluctant to invest cash in countries that have high rates of inflation and/or currency instability. In countries such as Brazil and India, companies try to tap the local market by entering into joint venture agreements under which they provide machinery, know-how, and technical assistance but no capital in exchange for a certain percent of the equity of the newly formed subsidiary. To protect their ownership position, companies include in the agreement a clause that, in effect, says that the value of their investment will be raised in accordance with the exchange rate.

Governmental constraints on the outflow of funds also force multinational companies to use joint ventures as a means of penetrating foreign markets. In such cases the local partner becomes the major source of capital needed to set up the joint venture and the multinational company's contribution comes in the form of equipment and know-how. Several British companies interviewed said that the rigid foreign exchange controls imposed by the British government were leaving them short of funds for direct investments abroad and therefore the best route that they could take for setting up subsidiaries abroad or for expansion of existing subsidiaries was that of inviting local businessmen or the public to share in the ownership of the subsidiaries.

Expertise Offered by Foreign Partner

Some multinational companies interviewed said that, theoretically, a company collaborates with a foreign partner if it needs any of the three factors—know-how, finance, and management—that the foreign partner may be able to provide. If a multinational company has all three of those factors, it does not need a foreign partner unless it is forced, in one way or another by factors discussed earlier in this chapter, to take a partner locally. European and American companies, particularly those that have flexible policies regarding ownership of foreign subsidiaries, are reluctant to bring in a local partner if they know their way around in a country. But if they do not, then they are more than eager to form a joint venture with a local partner provided he brings the expertise they need. Often the expertise is in the form of local marketing and knowledge of local marketing conditions, or it may consist of contacts with key officials in the government, which are particularly important in the developing countries. American Cyanamid Company, for example, has and wants partners in foreign countries, but it will accept a foreign partner only if he has some expertise to contribute. The company feels that it is much better off without a local partner if he has nothing to contribute but money. Hercules Inc. feels similarly about the local partner it would like to have. If he is better equipped than Hercules to deal with the government and has local marketing expertise, then Hercules would be favorably inclined to supply the technical know-how and join hands with him in forming a subsidiary.

In the more advanced countries, joint ventures may be especially useful because the local partner may be able to bring with him his local marketing and service organization, know-how, patents, a trained labor force, or competent management. That is what European companies are generally looking for when they form joint ventures with American companies. Not all European companies are weak in those areas in Europe, but they do lack that strength in the American market. Many American companies are forming joint ventures with European companies that are strong in R&D, marketing channels, and distribution and service organizations in Europe.

Advantages of Joint Ventures with Local Partners

Companies interviewed mentioned several advantages of joint ventures with local partners. Some were obliquely mentioned earlier in this chapter, and the more important ones will be considered here.

The local subsidiary is much more comfortable in the local environment if there is local participation. It finds it much easier to obtain the necessary permits and licenses for imports, plant expansion, water and electrical supply, and so on.

Some companies said that in certain developing countries there was a select group of business concerns that had obtained permits, no longer granted by the government, to produce the same products as the multinational company produced. Collaboration with such business concerns, therefore, furnished the multinational company with permits that they could otherwise never have obtained.

Often the government is a very big buyer of certain goods with the stipulation that it will not buy them from a foreign-owned company. A joint venture with local participation stands a much better chance of being considered a local company, and that, in turn, enhances the chances of selling to the host government.

Companies that spend huge amounts of money on R&D and which have developed unique technology and know-how are reluctant to enter into joint ventures. But if they are short of funds or are blocked by foreign governments from entering the foreign markets with wholly owned subsidiaries, they must find ways to locate markets that would pay for the R&D expenditures and still reduce their capital investments and risk. Many companies have been able to form joint ventures by getting equity in a newly formed subsidiary not through capital expenditures but through an exchange of their technology and know-how. The local partner might be able to provide trained personnel and experienced management for the joint venture. That becomes quite important for the profitability and success of the subsidiary, particularly in countries where both of those necessities are in short supply.

Many companies collaborate with a local firm that is capable of providing the joint venture with a steady supply of essential raw materials of the right quality. That factor becomes crucial in a developing country whose government has cut off all imports of that particular raw material and given a license for its production to a local firm.

The local partner might provide the joint venture with essential services such as important top-level contacts with the government. Foreign companies that want to set up joint ventures in India, for example, prefer to collaborate with one of the four biggest family-owned industrial and commercial groups in India: Birla, Dalmia, Tata, or Sarabhai. All four have been staunch supporters of the ruling Congress Party for the last four decades and have donated millions of rupees to it. Naturally, there are many at top-level positions in the government who repay those family concerns with special favors.

Joint ventures with local partners have advantages. At times, companies consider it advisable to form a joint venture in a foreign country, even though a wholly owned subsidiary could be formed, because of the advantages of a joint venture discussed here. But a joint venture is not without its own drawbacks and they will be considered in the following paragraphs.

Disadvantages of Joint Ventures with Local Partners

Several disadvantages of joint ventures were explained to me by the companies interviewed. The host government might at first allow a multinational company to form a joint venture with a local company in order to import the foreign company's technology, know-how, patents, and technical expertise. To lure the foreign company, the host government may grant special concessions such as permits to import essential equipment and raw materials or protection from competition from local or foreign companies through a nonissuance of licenses. But after a few years, the host government may begin to pressure the local subsidiary to export a certain amount of its output in order to earn foreign exchange for the country or face a cut in its essential raw materials imports.

One multinational company that was faced with that problem found it very difficult to meet the local government's demand because the products produced by the joint venture subsidiary were so high in cost that they were not competitive in the world's markets. The company finally solved the dilemma by embarking on an entirely unrelated venture. It began to export locally produced staples and thus earned foreign exchange for the host country. That satisfied the host government.

Many foreign companies enter a protected market in a country through the joint venture route while knowing very well that the products produced there will not be competitive in world markets but that the protected market is big enough to justify the move. The host government permits the foreign company to enter with the objective of import substitution and conservation of foreign exchange. Conflicts arise when the objective of the host government gets switched from that of import substitution and foreign exchange conservation to exports and foreign exchange earnings.

Conflicts between the foreign multinational company and the local partner occur when the multinational company attempts to integrate the joint venture subsidiary's operations with its own and with those of its other subsidiaries. Here again there could be a conflict between the objectives of the two partners. A multinational company is interested in taking actions locally that would benefit the total enterprise, but the local partner is interested only in how well the subsidiary in which he has a direct stake serves his own interests. The multinational company may want to reinvest earnings and forego dividends for a few years if the tax rates at home are high, but the local partner may ask for immediate dividends. He might be more interested in high current returns than in growth through ploughing back of profits.

Problems may also arise when a multinational company has the option to fill an order abroad from a wholly owned subsidiary or from a joint venture subsidiary. By supplying the customer from the joint venture subsidiary, the company would, in effect, be penalizing itself because part of the profits would go to the local partner, and it would, under those circumstances, naturally prefer to fill the order from its wholly owned subsidiary. The local partner in the joint venture subsidiary would not be likely to welcome that course of action, and conflicts could arise as a result.

What constitutes an acceptable degree of risk could be a source of conflict. A multinational company, because of its diversified operations in various countries and strong financial position, can take much bigger risks in one of its operations; for it knows that any losses taken in one subsidiary can be offset by gains in another. But a local partner might not be in the same boat and would therefore be unwilling to take the risky course of action. Severe problems could arise if the joint venture contract does not give the parties the right of first refusal on the other's equity or contain a provision to liquidate the company if insurmountable problems should arise. If no provision existed, the local partner could sell out to an undesirable investor.

Conflicts between the partners could arise if the local partner desired to sell the subsidiary's products in markets abroad that are already being supplied by another subsidiary of the multinational company. Price competition between the two subsidiaries could only hurt the multinational parent.

If there is intersubsidiary buying of components and raw materials, problems often arise in determining the prices to be charged for items bought or sold by subsidiaries from each other. The multinational company is more interested in using intersubsidiary transfer pricing to maximize its long-range aggregate profits, and not those of one subsidiary or another. The local partner in a joint venture obviously will not accept that objective and is therefore most likely to charge that the joint venture is being milked by high prices for items bought from another subsidiary and cheated by low prices on items sold by it to other subsidiaries. He is likely to charge too that all this is being done not in his own interest, but in the interest of the multinational company.

Thus, there are many disadvantages in using the joint venture with local partners as a route to markets abroad. A multinational company that is contemplating joint ventures abroad should, therefore, weigh the advantages against the disadvantages before deciding. It should take a good inventory of its strengths and weaknesses, opportunities and problems, values, and long-range objectives, and, based upon the inventory, evaluate the advantages and disadvantages of joint ventures abroad.

Coping with Joint Venture Conflicts and Problems

Multinational companies can cope with the problems arising out of joint ventures or, at least, minimize them by proper preplanning. It goes without saying that a great number of problems can be foreseen and the source of conflicts ironed out before the collaboration agreement is reached. The parties can get together in a series of conferences and at least make each other aware of their goals and objectives and how the joint venture could help in achieving them.

Multinational companies prefer to have control over the management of the joint venture primarily because they do not wish to have the joint venture upset their overall integrated plans covering all subsidiaries. They prefer to have a majority ownership of the joint venture, and in most countries that gives them management control as well. But in some countries a simple majority ownership of the equity does not give the company control over the joint venture. In such countries, companies try to get as much equity as is required for effective control. If that is not feasible because of local laws or whatever, then multinational companies try to negotiate a management contract under which the local partner (or partners, if ownership is shared with the public) gives the right of managerial control of the subsidiary to the multinational company even though it has a 50–50 or less ownership of the subsidiary's equity. That is a technique used by many companies that have joint ventures in developing countries. For example, Metal Box Company Overseas, the United Kingdom concern, is sharing ownership of a subsidiary in Tanzania with the host government. But Metal Box retains control of the subsidiary through a management contract that gives it a majority on the board of directors of the joint venture. Some companies negotiate the right to name the managing director and/or the technical director of the subsidiary.

If all these methods of controlling the management of the joint venture fail, then multinational companies try to negotiate a contract that provides that all output of the subsidiary or, at least, the portion that is exported, be marketed worldwide by a marketing company that is wholly owned by the multinational company. There are several variations of this basic theme. At times the local partner asks for a minor or even a substantial minority ownership in the marketing company. That technique has been especially useful in Japan, where it is impossible for a foreign company to obtain a majority control of the equity of a subsidiary.

Some multinational companies prefer to form joint ventures with banks or insurance companies as partners because they consider their stake in the joint venture more or less an investment and do not show much desire to participate in the management of the subsidiary.

Not all the companies interviewed said that they had problems with joint ventures. There are companies who enter a foreign market solely to meet the local demand and have no intention of integrating the joint venture's operations with the rest of their subsidiaries. Such companies have a thorough understanding of that objective with the local partner and the host government in order to avoid demands for exports from those parties in the future. Such companies have found the joint venture route to markets abroad fairly smooth.

Parent Company Ownership Strategy

Advantages of Worldwide Ownership of Parent Company

Top management executives of numerous multinational companies are now coming to grips with the fact that a multinational company cannot evolve into a world enterprise or realize its full potential as a powerful instrument of regional and eventually global economic integration, and efficient allocation of resources between nations, unless the ownership of the parent company is dispersed globally. They have come to realize that giving host country nationals ownership in the local subsidiary has helped the multinational company to minimize problems arising from host country nationalism, but that strategy has not helped the multinational company as a whole to achieve its overall mission and promise.

Direct local participation in the ownership of the local subsidiary may have advantages over participation in the ownership of the parent company for companies that do not plan to integrate the operations of the total enterprise, that is, companies that do not plan on a global basis. But in the case of a multinational company that hopes to integrate its worldwide operations, direct local ownership participation in the subsidiaries abroad, and the fragmentation of ownership interest that occurs as a result, is inconsistent with its objective of optimizing the total multinational business system. The need for unified ownership is greatest in those companies in which there is a close business relationship between the parent company and its subsidiaries as well as between the subsidiaries themselves. The need for unified ownership is often compelling when the multinational company must make decisions that are not only consistent with world market trends but also consistent with the trends in each of the domestic markets it serves.

In a very thought-provoking article, George W. Ball, former Under Secretary of State of the United States, had this to say about the need for multinational companies to become world enterprises:

> The obvious drawback of local ownership interests is that they necessarily think in national and not in world terms. Thus they are likely to impress their narrowly focused views on vital policies having to do with prices, dividends, employment, the use of plant facilities in one country rather than another, even to the source of component materials. . . . Once the central management of a global company is restricted to the divergent interests of national partners, it loses its ability to pursue the true logic of the global economy. . . .
>
> We might do well to approach the problem at a different level, not by nationalizing local subsidiaries but by internationalizing or perhaps more accurately denationalizing the parent. . . . The company must in fact become international. This means among other things that share ownership in the parent must be spread throughout the world.[2]

The local shareholder is also the one to gain, for he now has a stake in the entire multinational company and not merely in one part of it located in his own country. He benefits not only from the local subsidiary's operations but also from the stabilizing effect of the global operations of the multinational company, which irons out any short-term ups and downs in any one subsidiary.

Employees of local subsidiaries who own shares of the parent company are more likely to show greater loyalty to the parent company and be more willing to accept and effectively implement decisions that benefit the multinational company as a whole, even though the local subsidiary may suffer in the short run. IBM makes parent stock available to its employees abroad as well as those in the United States at the same discount rate. Thus, IBM's employees abroad are not treated as second-class citizens. That helps to improve employee morale and loyalty throughout the world. Few companies have followed IBM's example, but I believe that an increasing number of companies will do so in the near future.

Not all companies interviewed had their shares listed on foreign stock exchanges. Those that did, had their shares listed on one or more of the major stock exchanges of the world; the favorites being New York, London, Zurich, Paris, Amsterdam, and Brussels. Companies that were eager to take advantage of worldwide trading and ownership of the parent company shares said that they are not successful in reaching that goal because there are still several obstacles that thwart their efforts. Table 4 shows companies listed on two or more foreign stock exchanges.

Barriers to Multinational Ownership of Parent

None of the American companies said that they would object if a substantial number of the parent company shares were held by foreigners; they would welcome foreign participation. Few companies, however, had listed their stock on the major stock exchanges of the world. Others said that foreigners were welcome to buy the company shares in the New York Stock Exchange; yet, of the American companies interviewed, none had more than 3 percent foreign ownership in the parent. United States tax laws, such as the interest equalization tax, discriminate against the foreign investor and are partly responsible for the small foreign ownership of American companies.

European companies interviewed, especially in countries such as Sweden and Switzerland, have devised ways of spreading, to a certain extent, the ownership of the parent company among foreigners without diluting national control in any way. Swiss companies use mainly two kinds of shares: nominal and bearer. Some companies use participation certificates, also know as participative shares, in addition to the nominal and bearer shares. Although they have different values, both nominal and

Table 4. Companies listed on two or more foreign stock exchanges.

Company	American	Amsterdam	Brussels	Frankfurt	London	Canadian*	New York	Paris	Union S.A.
AKZO (Netherlands)				✓				✓	
Alcan Aluminium (Canada)				✓			✓	✓	✓
Aluminum Co. of America (U.S.)			✓	✓					
AT&T (U.S.)			✓	✓				✓	
British Leyland Motor (U.K.)				✓					✓
Consolidated Gold Fields (U.K.)								✓	✓
De Beers (South Africa)			✓					✓	
Dow Chemical Intl. (U.S.)		✓	✓						
Dunlop (U.K.)	✓			✓					✓
Du Pont (U.S.)		✓	✓	✓				✓	
Eastman Kodak (U.S.)		✓	✓	✓				✓	
Electric & Musical Industry (U.K.)				✓			✓		
Farbenfabriken Bayer (W. Germany)					✓			✓	
Farbwerke Hoechst (W. Germany)					✓			✓	
Ford Motor (U.S.)		✓	✓	✓				✓	
General Electric (U.S.)		✓	✓	✓				✓	
General Motors (U.S.)		✓	✓	✓				✓	
Goodyear (U.S.)		✓	✓	✓				✓	
ICI (U.K.)	✓			✓					
IBM (U.S.)		✓	✓					✓	
International Nickel (Canada)				✓			✓	✓	
IT&T (U.S.)		✓	✓	✓					
L M Ericsson (Sweden)				✓	✓			✓	
Montecatini Edison (Italy)				✓	✓				
Olivetti (Italy)				✓				✓	
Petrofina (Belgium)						✓		✓	
Royal Dutch/Shell Group (Netherlands, U.K.)				✓	✓		✓	✓	
Schlumberger (Netherlands, Antilles)							✓	✓	
Snia Viscosa (Italy)				✓	✓				
Standard Oil (N.J.) (U.S.)		✓	✓	✓				✓	
U.S. Steel (U.S.)		✓	✓	✓					
Unilever (U.K., Netherlands)				✓	✓		✓	✓	
Union Carbide Intl. (U.S.)		✓	✓						
Volkswagenwerk (W. Germany)					✓				✓
Westinghouse Electric Intl. (U.S.)		✓	✓						
National Biscuit (U.S.)		✓						✓	
Kennecott Copper (U.S.)		✓	✓					✓	
Socony Mobil Oil (U.S.)		✓						✓	
Merck (U.S.)		✓						✓	
Monsanto Company (U.S.)		✓						✓	
Procter and Gamble (U.S.)		✓						✓	
Gillette (U.S.)		✓						✓	
Philip Morris (U.S.)		✓						✓	

*Montreal-Toronto.

bearer shares have one vote each. The bearer shares are traded at the Zurich Stock Exchange and can be bought by anybody, including foreigners.

Technically the nominal shares can also be bought by foreigners, but the owners have to be registered. The directors of a Swiss company have the right to refuse to register any person or group to whom they do not want to give voting rights. Nominal shares, therefore, allow management to stop any group or person it wishes, domestic or foreign, from capturing the management control of the company. Many Swiss companies give a quota of nominal shares to Swiss banks, who may sell them to foreigners, but the management of Swiss companies makes sure that only a small number of foreigners own nominal shares.

Swiss companies also use participative shares to raise capital. The shares do not have any voting rights, but they can be bought by a national of any country. Another measure used by management to keep management control and ownership in Swiss hands is to insure that the number of bearer shares and participative shares does not exceed a certain percent of the total number of nominal shares. For example, Nestlé Alimentana S.A. has about 67 percent of the total company shares in the form of nominal shares; the rest are bearer shares.

Swiss companies introduced nominal shares in the 1930s to prevent Germany from taking over Swiss industry. Chemicals, pharmaceuticals, and engineering companies in Switzerland were especially in danger of being absorbed by giant German companies. That, plus the desire to stay neutral in World War II, motivated Swiss companies to introduce nominal shares. It appears that the trend in the future will be for Swiss companies to make use of participative shares to raise required capital, which would disperse ownership, but not management control abroad.

Swedish law does not permit any company that is owned more than 20 percent by foreigners to own land or do business in Sweden without special permission from the government, but companies can list their shares on foreign stock exchanges. One company interviewed—SKF—has divided its shares into A shares and B shares. The A shares have one vote each, but B shares have only one-thousandth of a vote each and can be held by foreigners. In all other respects such as ownership, dividends, and profits, both classes of shares are treated equally. The company has obtained permission from the Swedish government to issue up to 49 percent of its total share capital in the form of B shares to foreign subjects. Residents of foreign countries are considered foreign subjects. Swedish subjects who are not residents of Sweden cannot hold A shares. About 44 percent of the total issued share capital of SKF is held by foreigners in the form of B shares. Because of the diluted voting rights under B shares, however, the company is controlled by Swedish stockholders only. SKF has been using B shares to acquire foreign companies without diluting the Swedish management control over the parent. In 1965 SKF acquired a two-thirds majority interest in an Italian company in exchange for B shares of the parent company.

There are institutional mechanisms in Belgium and Denmark that control the foreign ownership of national companies. According to Belgian law, control of a Belgian company cannot pass into foreign hands unless the transfer is approved by the government. Also, The Central Bank of Denmark has placed legal restrictions against foreigners owning stock of Danish companies. But in some instances foreigners did manage to obtain stocks in Danish companies through a stockbroker. Most companies in Denmark have now placed their own restrictions on the voting rights of shareholders which prevent any one group, foreign or domestic, from obtaining a dominating position in a company.

Thus we see that, in certain European countries, perhaps because of small size or because of a fear that large foreign groups such as banks or giant industrial firms will gain control of domestic industries and markets, techniques have been devised by companies to prevent foreign ownership and management control. My impression is that the attitude toward ownership varies among different countries. Some Swiss and Swedish companies, for example, are much more receptive than others to sharing ownership of the parent company with foreigners by using the nonvoting type of shares. As far as the management control of the parent companies was concerned, all agreed that it should be kept in national hands.

There are other barriers to multinational stock ownership of the parent company. In some countries such as the United Kingdom, India, and the Scandinavian ones, foreign exchange controls prevent or severely restrict foreign stock purchases by residents. Shareholders in European companies seldom have the legal right to examine the company's financial statements, nor are the company disclosure practices and financial reporting adequate. A prospective investor can only guess about the real earning capacity or profitability of a company in which he might consider investing.

Perhaps the major barrier to multinational ownership of multinational companies, however, is that the investment habit has not yet taken hold in other countries as it has in the United States. Very little effort is made by brokers to induce the public to buy stocks. In some countries, particuarly Switzerland, the shares are so high in par value that only the rich can afford to buy them. Many other kinds of barriers to multinational stock ownership of multinational companies exist, but I agree with Donald M. Kendall, president and chief executive officer of PepsiCo Inc., that "perhaps the best way to surmount these difficulties is to simply go ahead and establish a sound base of multinational stock ownership wherever it can be done without paying too much penalty."[3] Mr. Kendall suggests that multinational companies should list their shares on local exchanges around the world because "a good stock often creates its own demand regardless of nationality. Such blue chips as General Motors, General Electric, Eastman Kodak, and others are actively traded on European exchanges."[4] That is especially true in the European Common Market, where economic integration is proceeding at a rapid pace and consequently merging the member countries into one economic unit. I particularly like Mr. Kendall's thought-provoking comment that:

> Multinational stock ownership could be given major impetus through some form of official recognition by such organizations as the International Monetary Fund, the World Bank, or the United Nations. One of these organizations, for example, could offer a worldwide incorporation facility and thus become a neutral site of incorporation.[5]

REFERENCES

1. Reported in *India News*, September 11, 1970, p. 2.

2. George W. Ball, "Cosmocorp: The Importance of Being Stateless," *Columbia Journal of World Business*, Vol. 2, No. 6 (November–December 1967), pp. 28ff.

3. In a speech delivered at The Sales Executive Club in New York on March 7, 1969.

4. Ibid.

5. Ibid.

Organizational Patterns for Worldwide Operations

ONE of the main purposes of the organization structure of a company is to facilitate coordination of company parts and activities and help the company achieve its objectives with a minimum of unsought consequences. There is no one best way in which a company with geographically dispersed operations in different parts of the world can organize itself. An organization structure that may be right for one company may not be suitable for another. A company should plan for an organization structure that will provide top management with three types of informational and knowledge inputs: functional, geographical, and product.

The nature of the business and the size and geographical spread of the company's operations abroad influence the choice of organization structure. Other factors are company history, management philosophy, availability of competent managers, and ownership policies.

Factors Influencing Organizational Patterns

History of the company. A company that has experienced growth from within is likely to have a greater degree of centralization in its organization structure than one that has grown mainly through acquisitions of existing companies. Also, a company that for a long time has been owned and controlled by a close-knit family clique is likely to be far more centralized in its operations than a company whose ownership, historically, has been in the hands of numerous stockholders.

Management philosophy. A company whose management has an authoritarian philosophy is likely to have a far more centralized functional organization structure than one whose philosophy is to delegate as much authority as is required to get the job done effectively. Companies that have grown big over the years under the close direction and control of a dominant chief executive are apt to find that the chief executive retains in his hands the same amount of authority as he did when the company was small. One company interviewed changed its organization structure, which was functionally organized and highly centralized, in favor of a decentralized product divisional structure soon after the retirement of the chief executive who had controlled the company for several years.

Availability of competent managers. Multinational companies, as was pointed out in an earlier chapter, have problems in staffing operations abroad with competent managers. It is difficult to find a manager who is not only competent but also shares top management's operational philosophy. Conflicts often arise between top management personnel at the parent company level and those at the subsidiary level because of disagreements on operational issues.

For example, what may be considered at the parent company level as an appropriate risk for the subsidiary to assume might not be acceptable to the subsidiary head. That often occurs because there is a significant difference in the propensities of the subsidiary head to take risks and those at the parent company level because of differences in respective viewpoints. The parent company very often can afford a loss of revenue in one subsidiary because another subsidiary in a different country can compensate for the loss by registering greater profits. But to a subsidiary head, any losses in his own operations might be unacceptable. An international company, faced with such disagreements, is likely to centralize decision-making authority—to make decisions that are in the interests of the overall enterprise and not just one part of it.

A worldwide company that cannot find competent managers to man the subsidiaries abroad also is forced to tighten its rein over its subsidiaries and decide centrally what should be done at the subsidiary level.

Nature of the business. Companies that market highly standardized products whose production process uses complex and advanced technology require a close liaison on technical matters between the parent company and the subsidiaries abroad. Such companies need worldwide product coordination; therefore, they are likely to be organized on a product basis.

The possibility of their using a product-based organization is still greater if the product lines are divergent and each major product line uses a different kind of promotional technique and marketing channel.

Companies whose products do not have those characteristics but do require great amounts of modification to suit local tastes are likely to use the geographical, or regional, form of organization. The likelihood of that organizational form being used is greatly increased if the products use similar promotional techniques and channels of distribution.

The size of the company's international operations compared with domestic operations, plus top management's attitude toward and plans for international operations, also have considerable influence on the type of organization structure adopted.

Location of operations. A company with operations located in a few countries that have characteristics similar to those of the home country does not need environmental inputs as much as a company that has substantial operations in several countries with significant environmental differences. The first kind of company may organize in a manner that takes into consideration the functional and product inputs required for effective coordination and control. The second kind must organize in a fashion that takes into account its need for not only functional and product inputs but also for environmental inputs from the different geographical locations. Thus, location of operations also affects the organization patterns used by companies.

Ownership policies. A company that has a policy of not allowing any joint ventures abroad and favors only wholly owned subsidiaries is apt to have a greater degree of centralization in decision making and planning than a company that permits joint ventures. This characteristic is most likely to be reflected in the type of organization structure it uses to coordinate its domestic and foreign operations.

Impact of regional economic blocs. A company is forced to reorganize if there is a change in the environmental conditions in the foreign markets in which it has operating subsidiaries. That was true of several companies interviewed in Europe that had subsidiaries in countries that later became members of either the EEC or EFTA economic blocs. Some companies have created new regional units for Europe to facilitate the integration of their subsidiaries; others have reshuffled their regional organizational setup to accommodate the new economic relationships between countries within the EEC and EFTA regions.

Organizational Patterns for Worldwide Coordination

There is no one way in which international companies organize their domestic and foreign activities. As was pointed out earlier in this chapter, the organization pattern adopted by a company is the result of a number of influencing factors; consequently, no two companies are likely to have similar organization structures. Yet it is possible to label a company as being organized on a functional basis, or, for that matter, on a product or geographic basis. One soon runs into problems because worldwide companies emphasize all three inputs—functional, product, and geographic. The degree of emphasis on one kind of input as opposed to another varies from one company to another. Some companies emphasize the functional and product input, but not the geographic, although the geographic input is reflected in the organization structure. Others emphasize the functional and geographic inputs.

There are several ways in which it is possible to design an organization structure to reflect the need for one or all of the three types of inputs. I have formulated eight discrete organizational patterns. In doing so, I realize that not only is it difficult to create such discrete organizational patterns but that placing the various organization structures of companies into one or the other of the discrete patterns is twice as difficult.

Pattern 1. Domestic operations are grouped into several product divisions. The operations abroad are handled by an international department.

Pattern 2. An international holding company incorporated at home or abroad handles the operations abroad.

Pattern 3. Only one of the several product divisions has worldwide responsibilities. Other operations abroad are handled by an international department.

Pattern 4. Product divisions have worldwide responsibilities.

Pattern 5. Product divisions have worldwide responsibilities. An international division assists the product divisions to coordinate their operations abroad.

Pattern 6. Subsidiaries at home and abroad report directly either to top management or regional management. Functional and/or product divisions have worldwide responsibilities and have strong functional authority over the subsidiaries abroad.

Pattern 7. Multiple roles and responsibilities are assigned by a top-management-level committee to its members to coordinate the company's diversified and geographically dispersed businesses.

Pattern 8. The world-oriented organization structure.

The rest of this chapter will be concerned with explaining these patterns in detail by the use of case examples of companies studied. One or more case examples exemplifying each pattern will be presented. Pertinent background information of companies such as history and organizational changes in the past will be presented if it has an impact upon current organization structures. Any organizational changes expected in the future will also be included.

Pattern 1

General Foods Corporation

The company, based in New York state, is a collection of acquisitions of companies in the food industry by the original nucleus company called the Postum Cereal Company, founded in 1896. The company acquired a flour mill, a gelatin dessert company, a chocolate company, and a coffee company in the late 1920s. It changed its name to General Foods Corporation in 1929. Numerous other acquisitions were made by the company, which was then organized on a product basis with functional departments at the corporate level.

Evolution of the international division and current organizational relationships. Just before World War II, the export activities of the various product divisions such as coffee and cereal were centralized under a new department called General Foods exports. The department consisted of only one person selling the company's products wherever he could throughout the world.

In 1947, General Foods acquired its first overseas business when it bought Alfred Bird and Sons, Ltd., of England. A commitment to become an international company was then made by General Foods. An international division was formed in the early 1950s to organize the company's exports plus Alfred Bird.

The organization chart of General Foods is presented in Exhibit 1. Like other divisions, General Foods International is a profit center. The head of General Foods International has two regional managers reporting to him, one for Europe and the other for Latin America and the Pacific. General Foods International has its own functional staff in areas such as finance, marketing, product development, and engineering. It is responsible for all activities of General Foods outside the United States and Canada. The international division is also responsible for the overseas sales of products of the domestic divisions, it sends product specifications to the appropriate domestic division and the product division quotes price. The international division then buys the product from the domestic division and sells it overseas. Also, the international division buys from the corporate staff specialized services, such as legal services, that it cannot provide through its own functional staff. All such transactions are carried out at arm's length.

Exhibit 1. Organization of General Foods Corporation

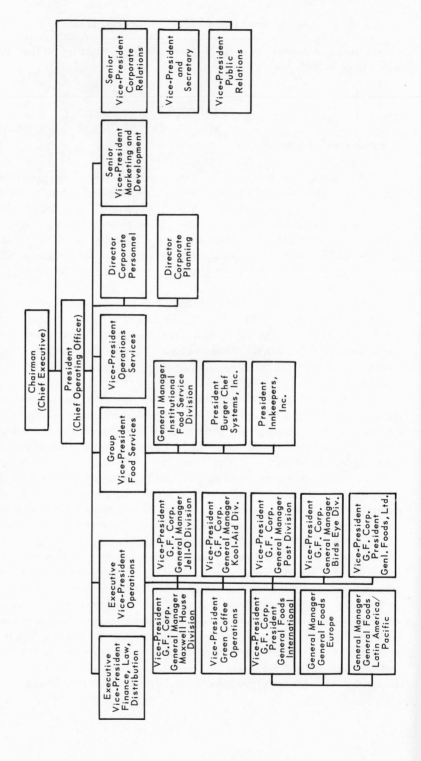

The company has thirty or more multiproduct plants in about eighteen different countries. The product lines are not widely divergent—all are food products. About 15 percent of the total company sales come from overseas sales. The domestic product divisions are not interdependent and do not operate on a worldwide basis; there is very little need for liaison between domestic and overseas subsidiaries. The food industry is basically not one of high capital intensity or great technological skills. General Foods does not have many patented products because most of its products do not require tremendous amounts of research to develop. But conditions in the food industry are changing—the company is involved in the process of freeze drying, which is capital intensive and does require high technical input. The company's products use the same channels of distribution: they are sold through food outlets. They are all distributed by similar marketing techniques, but each division has its own independent sales force.

Campbell Soup Company

The New Jersey-based company was founded over a hundred years ago and has been exporting its products to foreign markets for many decades. A number of its markets, however, could not be served economically from the United States, and other markets could not be served at all because of import restrictions, high tariffs, and other tariff and nontariff barriers. The company therefore turned to manufacturing locally in those markets where the demand for its products was growing and where the economic conditions appeared to be favorable. Foreign sales today account for 10 percent of the total sales of the company.

The company's first foreign venture was in Canada in 1931, and today it has five plants and mushroom and poultry farms in that country. In the past ten years, Campbell Soup Company has started operations in six other foreign locations; it now has plants in England, Mexico, Australia, France, Belgium, Canada, and the United States.

Evolution of the international division and current organizational relationships. The company began exporting before World War II, and an export department was established in 1946. Until 1957, the company did not have any production centers abroad except the Canadian plant.

The international division was created in 1957 to take charge of all the company's subsidiaries in Europe, Mexico, and Australia. Then, and until 1969, the company was functionally organized. The organization structure had the traditional functional heads and the international division head reporting to the president of the company. Plant managers reported to the vice-president of operations.

Product organization was introduced in 1969, and Exhibit 2 shows the current organization structure. The organizational details of the interna-

Exhibit 2. Organization of Campbell Soup Company

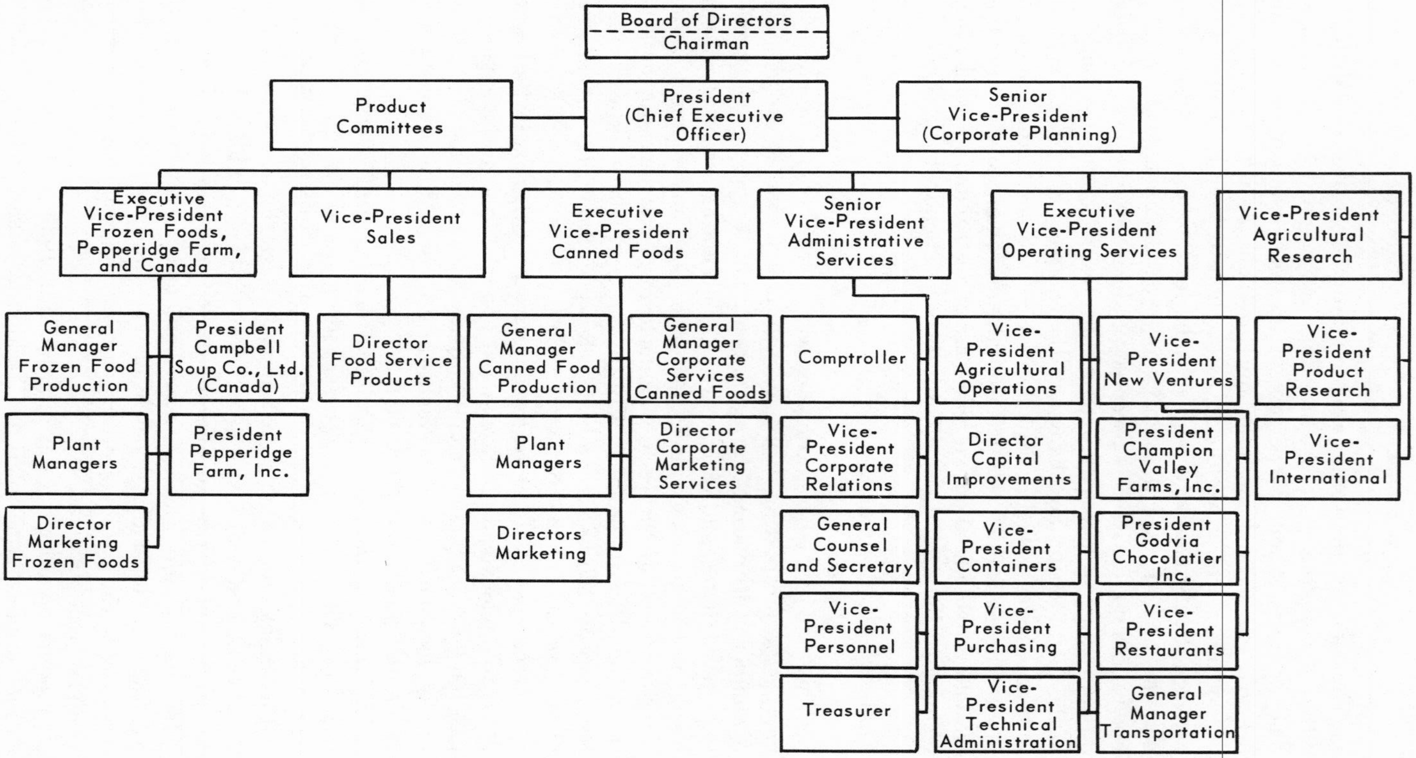

Exhibit 3. Organization of Campbell's Soups International

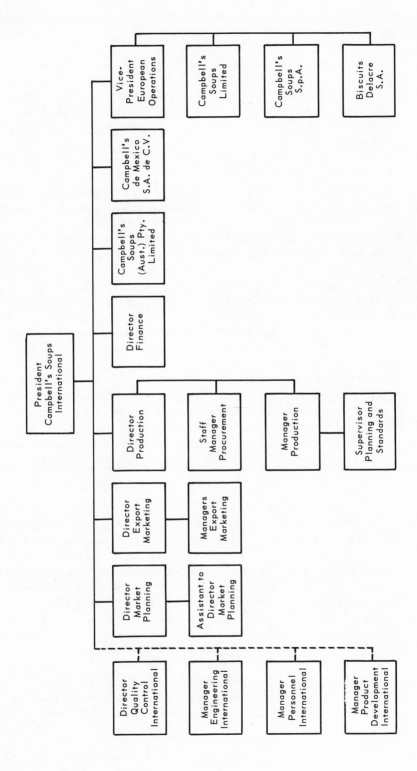

tional division, which is a profit center, are shown in Exhibit 3. The director of quality control, international, and the managers in charge of engineering, personnel, and product development, all international, are actually housed within the corresponding functional departments in the home office. They report to the head of the international division in a line authority relationship.

There is a very close liaison between the international division and the domestic product and staff divisions. The international division frequently solicits and obtains technical assistance from the domestic divisions. The president of Campbell's Soups International feels this is the best organizational design for the management and development of the international operations and that changing the organization in favor of one with product divisions having worldwide responsibility for their respective product lines "would be chaotic."

The company is highly market-oriented and does not have widely divergent product lines. Most of its products fall into three groups: canned foods, frozen foods, and bakery products. The major products are marketed through similar techniques and channels. Almost all are sold through the Campbell sales force; some, such as Pepperidge Farm products, are marketed through distributors and agents.

The plants abroad operate quite independently and do not need close liaison with the domestic plants. Quality control of products made in foreign plants is strictly implemented. Although quality control is centralized, the company's plants abroad do develop products to suit local tastes, as in England, Sweden, Mexico, and Australia. Those products are not marketed in the United States. The company is very much market-oriented.

Hercules, Inc.

A chemical business that is headquartered in Delaware and is organized according to pattern 1 is Hercules Inc. The organization chart of the company is shown in Exhibit 4. The company was formed in 1912, and it started with only one product: black powder. By the 1920s, it was manufacturing a diversified product line. The company's first exposure to foreign manufacturing occurred in the 1930s, when it began minor manufacturing operations in Great Britain. Selling organizations in Great Britain and in continental Europe were created, and exports of the company continued to grow and diversify as the company diversified.

Evolution of the international department and current organizational relationships. Prior to 1959, Hercules had six operating departments each of which was headed by a general manager who operated very independently. Three of the departments had plants overseas. Exports were handled by an export department that was strictly a service department. The three departments that had plants overseas were planning to expand their overseas operations. Rather than have each of the several departments of the company expanding overseas with no coordination of their activities, it was decided in 1959 to set up an international department, which was to be responsible for all overseas manufacturing and exports. Canada was excluded from the jurisdiction of that department because of its strong traditional ties with the domestic operating departments. The international department was given the same stature as any domestic operating department. It has operated that way since 1959.

Exhibit 4. Organization of Hercules Inc.

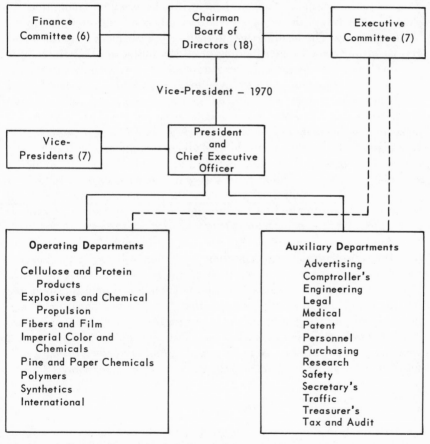

Today Hercules has eight operating departments including the international one, and each is headed by a general manager. Each operating department is a profit center. The general managers have the authority to run their "businesses" in the manner they see fit. Each operating department has its own functional organization and its own research budget. The operating departments, to the extent possible and practicable, use the auxiliary departments, which are service departments. The extent to which the operating departments make use of the auxiliary departments depends upon the nature of their respective businesses. The international department, for example, frequently calls upon the auxiliary departments for assistance on financial, fiscal, and legal matters. The vice-presidents do not have a line authority over the operating departments; they act in a staff capacity to the president. Most of them are on the executive committee.

All except two of the nineteen board members are full-time employees of the company. The head of the international department is on the board and has a fairly good understanding of all the businesses that Hercules is in, as well as the problems and strengths of all the operating departments.

The executive committee has seven members who are also members of the board of directors. The general managers report to the executive committee every 2 months on the general performance of their respective departments. In the fall of each year every general manager presents a 5-year plan of his department to the executive committee. The plan for the next year is presented in great detail, and it is the basis for obtaining approval of that year's budget. In this way, financial control, as well as general operational control, is exercised at the top management level. Each department is also limited on the amount of money it can spend without prior approval of top management.

The general manager of the international department has line authority over the subsidiaries abroad. Differences of opinion between the international department and any domestic department are resolved at the board level. As was mentioned earlier, the international department is responsible for all exports. Bookkeeping is such that the general managers of the domestic operating departments get credit for the profits from export sales. The international department keeps a certain percent of the profits as a commission that enables it to pay its expenses and provide a decent profit for the overseas sales companies to the extent that they are involved.

Scott Paper Company

A Pennsylvania-based company that is well known for its paper products but in recent years has diversified into other product lines is Scott Paper. The organization chart of the company is presented in Exhibit 5. In keeping with the current trend in large companies, Scott Paper operates

Exhibit 5. Organization of Scott Paper Company

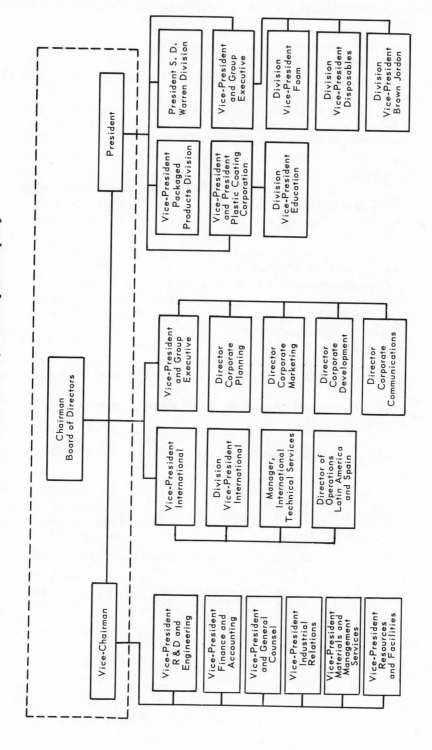

under the office-of-the-chairman concept. The "office" is composed of the chairman, vice-chairman, and president. The company is decentralized on a divisional basis. There are eight divisions, and each is a profit center: (1) packaged products division, (2) S. D. Warren Company division, (3) The Plastic Coating Corporation, (4) foam division, (5) education division, (6) disposables division, (7) Brown Jordon division, and (8) international division. Total company sales in 1969 were $731.5 millions. Most of the company's growth has been through acquisitions. Scott's worldwide operations are located in 17 countries.

Evolution of the international division. Scott Paper began exports in about 1930. In 1954–55 the company established three 50–50 joint ventures abroad. Those three affiliates were assigned to a vice-president as a collateral duty, for example, the vice-president was mainly responsible for another function or product group and was given the additional responsibility of looking after the affiliates.

The company added two more affiliates (joint ventures) in 1958–59, and at that time a marketing specialist was added to handle international marketing coordination and counseling. Three more affiliates were added in 1962–63, and at that time a technical specialist was an expert in the different engineering and technical aspects of papermaking. In 1963, a full-time vice-president for international operations was added, and at just about that time the company added two more affiliates. Two more techni-

Exhibit 6. Organization of the Scott Paper Company International Division

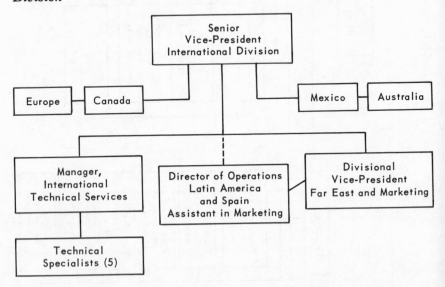

cal specialists were added in 1965, and two more marketing specialists were added in 1967. In 1969 a senior vice-president—a member of Scott's executive committee—was assigned the sole responsibility for international operations and the international division was made a profit center like some of the other product group profit centers.

The international division does not have its own comprehensive staff. Instead, it obtains assistance on a large number of issues such as taxes, legal matters, and technical matters from the staff services of the overall Scott Paper Company. International does not pay direct fees to the service (functional) departments for the services or advice received; instead, the international division is charged with a portion of the overhead expenses. The overhead contribution is supposed to pay for the services received. The organization chart of the international division is presented in Exhibit 6.

A divisional vice-president for the international division heads the marketing function for the entire division, and he is also responsible for operations in the Far East. A director of operations for Latin America and Spain reports to the divisional vice-president, as far as the marketing function is concerned, but also maintains a direct contact with the vice-president, international, in a line relationship. The divisional vice-president is again responsible for marketing in Europe, Canada, and Mexico. The vice-president, international, retains operations responsibility for Europe, Canada, Mexico, and Australia. The five technical specialists give assistance to all the regions.

Prior to 1969, when there were fewer affiliates, there were no regions. All the affiliates reported to the vice-president, international. Now there is geographic decentralization. Each geographic region is not a separate profit center, but there is some accounting on a geographical basis to evaluate each region.

Scott acquired The Plastic Coating Corporation in 1965 and the S. D. Warren Company in 1967. Each of these once-independent companies had its own international affiliates in Europe; now the two companies have been grouped under a separate Europe-based division. The international division of Scott Paper does not control that division. The reason is that the company feels that the products of those two divisions are distinctly different from the traditional Scott Paper products and no significant benefits would accrue from a consolidation.

Johns-Manville Corporation

In the opinion of a senior officer of the New York–based company, the Johns-Manville Corporation, like many other American companies,

"slipped unintentionally into international business." It was not a determined effort on the part of Johns-Manville to go international about
twenty years ago; it was more or less by opportunity or chance, partly
aided by compulsion because other people were beginning to think "international." The organization structure in use at that time is presented in
Exhibit 7. Each of the seven product divisions had its own production and
marketing operations and was run very independently as a separate business. Each division exported its own products to a limited extent. When
the exports of the divisions grew to between $1 and $2 million, an international division was created to handle them in a unified fashion. At approximately that time the company also began to enter into technical assistance
and know-how agreements abroad. The company gave its know-how to a
foreign company in return for a small minority shareholding in it. The
international division was given the status of an operating division during
the early 1960s, and it began to act in a small way as a complete business
with its own production, finance, and marketing organization.

There have been major changes in the international division since. In
the early 1960s Johns-Manville began to set up wholly owned manufacturing units abroad, mainly in Europe and more recently in Latin America.
The organization of the international division is presented in Exhibit 8.

The current organization structure of Johns-Manville is given in Exhibit
9. Depending upon the size of the divisions, each operating senior vice-
president is responsible for one or more product divisions. The activities of
the senior vice-presidents are coordinated in the "president's office." All
the senior vice-presidents and staff vice-presidents (marketing, production,
research) are members of the president's office. The international division
as well as the other product divisions are profit centers. The company has
selling or operating subsidiaries in 22 countries.

The Dunlop Company Limited

A United Kingdom–based company that is organized according to pattern 1 is the world-renowned Dunlop Company. In order to fully understand
the evolution of the current organization structure of Dunlop, it is important to know the three phases the company went through to reach the
stage it is in now.

The first phase of the company's history spanned the years 1889 to
1920; it could very well be described as a period of rapid diversification at
home and expansion overseas. The company became international very
early in its life. It all began in 1888 when John Boyd Dunlop, a Scottish
veterinary surgeon practicing in Ireland, invented the first practicable

Exhibit 7. Organization of Johns-Manville Corporation (1950)

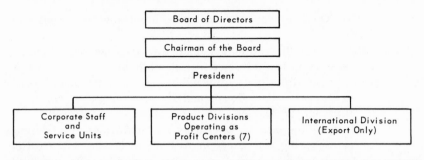

Exhibit 8. Organization of the Johns-Manville Corporation International Division

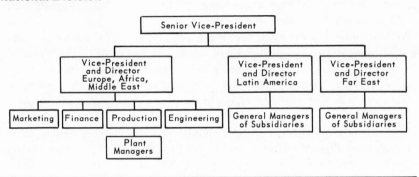

Exhibit 9. Current Organization of Johns-Manville Corporation

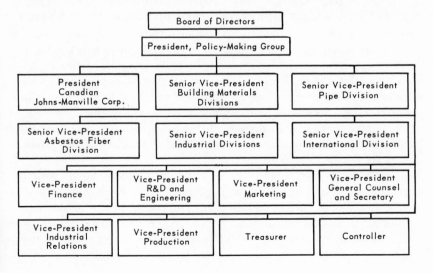

pneumatic tire. The rigid log wheel, centuries after its invention, could now be cushioned.

Soon after the invention of the pneumatic tire, the Pneumatic Tyre and Booth Cycle Agency Ltd. was formed in Ireland to develop the invention. The tires were made from material bought from existing rubber companies. Within a few years the company had acquired one of its own, Byrne Brothers of Birmingham. Dunlop's invention was received so well and so quickly too that, by the turn of the century, the company had established manufacturing or selling companies in Australia, Canada, France, Germany, and South Africa. A second factory was added in 1900 in the Birmingham area in Britain, and the company started manufacturing car tires. From that began the company's relationship with the motorcar industry. In the same year, the company's name of Dunlop Rubber Company Limited was adopted. It lasted until 1966.

The company soon faced tough competition from European and later from American tire companies, all of whom entered the European market. The car tire business did not develop in Britain as fast as on the Continent. Therefore, the company, in order to compete with the large American companies, was compelled to export to overseas markets or manufacture in them.

Realizing that wheels and tires should be thought of as a single unit, the company diversified horizontally and in 1906 acquired a wheel manufacturing firm in Britain. Attention was next directed to getting better control over rubber and textiles, which then were the predominant raw materials in tires. That led to a period of backward integration. The company's demand for natural rubber, which was the chief raw material in tires, was almost wholly met by supplies of wild Amazon rubber. Considerable difficulties in supply linked with an extremely volatile price situation led Dunlop to acquire rubber estates in Malaya. By the 1920s Dunlop was the largest single owner of plantations in Malaya. Quite dramatic is the fact that, although significant in their own right, the rubber estates were not intended to keep pace with the company's requirements so much as to ensure technical knowledge and control "from tree to product." It is interesting to note that today hardly any of that rubber is used in Dunlop tires, but it is vitally important in the manufacture of other company products such as Dunlopillo.

Further limited integration backward took place at home with the establishment of cotton mills to protect the supply of tire cord and other fabrics; but in this case, integration did not extend to the production of raw cotton, which continued to be bought in the open market. Today the mills produce rayon and nylon, which have wholly replaced cotton in tires.

Overseas activities continued to play an important role. Factories for the manufacture of tires were set up in Malaya and Nigeria in 1962 and more recently in Zambia and Trinidad.

Horizontal diversification at home brought on the manufacture of golf balls in 1908 and aircraft tires in 1910. So, by the end of World War I, the Dunlop organization had earned an international character with horizontal diversification and vertical integration at home and abroad.

The second phase of the company's history spanned the years 1921 to 1931; it could be identified as one in which Dunlop broadened its base of operations. The drastic fall in world trade in 1921 and collapse of raw material prices dealt Dunlop a drastic blow. A new board of directors took over. Decisions were soon taken to lessen the company's dependence on tires and broaden its base. Dunlop acquired, in 1925, an old established group of companies. The group manufactured, in addition to tires, footwear, cables, and clothing. It also manufactured a general range of industrial and other products, including hose, belting, and flooring.

The company disposed of the cable interests shortly after the acquisition and, much more recently, the clothing interests. Those products did not fit well into the company's long-term strategy. The products manufactured by the newly acquired group served as the nucleus of what in 1932 was to be the company's industrial and consumer groups. Further acquisitions involved the take-over of a firm that was a maker of cycle tires and rubber thread and another that manufactured wheels. The company extended its sports business through the acquisition of a racket factory. Tennis rackets and golf balls manufactured by Dunlop led to the formation of Dunlop Sports Company Ltd.

Then in 1929 there emerged from the laboratory an invention that ranks second in importance only to the pneumatic tire: Dunlopillo latex foam, made from rubber. The use of latex foam in mattresses and cushions revolutionized the standards of comfort and hygiene in homes, hospitals, and transport. The worldwide foam industry that emerged provided the second main support to the company's large plantations industry in Malaya.

The third phase of the company's history spanned the years 1932 to 1945. New factories were established, soon after the recovery from the slump of 1931, in India, South Africa, and Ireland, and manufacturing facilities were extended in Germany and France. At home, tire production spread to Scotland with the acquisition of the India Tyre and Rubber Company (now India Tyres Ltd.). As World War II drew nearer and the motorcar and aircraft industry continued to grow in size, the company's business grew with the increased demand for its tires and wheels. In the Dunlop aviation division production had diversified from tires to wheels to brakes to hydraulic or pneumatic operating systems for brakes to gun-firing mechanisms. The company had, in fact, become precision engineers working in exotic metals and alloys.

During the war years the company produced several products useful to the armed forces. Although it was a period of rapid growth, Dunlop could not devote enough attention to the development of synthetic rubber, a circumstance of which the company's American competitors were quick to take advantage. Dunlop's factories in Germany and France were largely destroyed, and a host of other projects had to be shelved. As a result, Dunlop emerged from the war in a commercially weaker position than its main competitors did.

After 1946 the company tackled the task of converting production and policy to peacetime competitive activity. New factories were established in Britain. Overseas, new plants were added in India, Canada, Japan, South Africa, France, and the United States. The company also set up new manufacturing facilities in New Zealand in 1946, Brazil in 1953, Malaysia in 1956, and Rhodesia in 1959. Further overseas expansion took place in the 1960s with tire factories started in Malaysia and Nigeria in 1962 and a cycle tire factory started in Uganda in 1964. Recently, tire factories have been established in Zambia and Trinidad.

A new research center was established in Britain with branches in Canada, Malaysia, Japan, Germany, and Ireland. Technically, the direction of these branches comes from the central research center in Britain, but it is Dunlop's philosophy to get the best collaboration among the different minds and approaches of several countries. Under the guidance of the research center, Dunlop in 1953 began work on the first British pilot plant for the manufacture of synthetic rubbers. Subsequently, Dunlop and other tire manufacturers formed a company to erect a large plant in Britain in 1958 for the production of general-purpose synthetic rubber.

Organization before World War II. Before World War II the company had been a highly centralized organization, as is shown in Exhibit 10. The structure was right for the company until the war, but afterward, several factors suggested that the company had to be decentralized. It had grown in size and complexity and had expanded overseas considerably; competition had become much more intense, and there was the need to improve its return on capital. The company realized that a geographically far-flung organization could not remain agile and ready to change and attack unless the decision-making authority was pushed down to levels at which available knowledge and experience were most likely to produce the proper decisions.

Current organizational relationships. The current organization structure is presented in Exhibit 11. Overall control of the company is vested in the main board. Under the chairman, the main board consists of eight

Exhibit 10. Organization of The Dunlop Company Ltd. to 1938

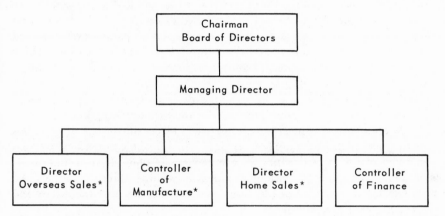

* These officials were not board directors.

Exhibit 11. Current Organization of The Dunlop Company Ltd.

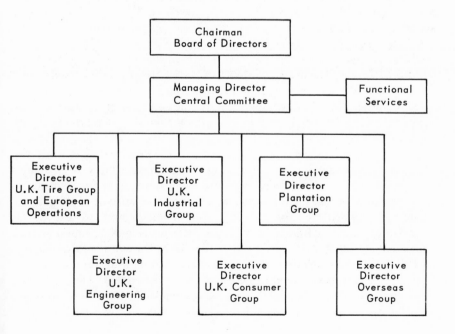

executive directors, normally headed by a managing director, and six to eight nonexecutive directors. The executive directors form a central committee that performs a useful role in coordination and communication and is a forum for discussing matters of group interest. These matters include new and revised group policies and procedures, even though the committee has no executive powers.

Reporting to the board through an executive director, who is responsible for one group of subsidiaries, are (1) four United Kingdom groups of subsidiaries, tire, engineering, industrial, and consumer, (2) an overseas group that comprises companies each of which is the counterpart overseas of some of the United Kingdom groups or is responsible for selling their products, and (3) a plantations group. An executive director may also be responsible for (4) a set of functional services that are essentially staff and specialist service departments.

The main board and the central committee are assisted in their work by functional services such as research, finance, marketing, and personnel. The task of the functional services at the center is to advise heads of Dunlop subsidiaries in Britain and overseas on particular problems and coordinate the work of similar departments at the subsidiary level. The working relationship between the functional services departments enables the main board to delegate authority to the subsidiaries without the fear of creating autonomous empires within the Dunlop group. The nonexecutive directors, who are well-known industrialists or financiers, bring the benefit of their independent judgment and expertise to bear on performance and policy and advise on specialized matters.

Each subsidiary prepares a three-year plan that it submits to the main board each year. The executive directors review the plans submitted by the various subsidiaries and make the necessary modifications after taking into consideration the overall company viewpoint and interests as discussed by the central committee. The aggregate plan is then considered by the main board.

Once a plan has been roughly discussed and approved, it is up to the subsidiary managements to implement it. Each subsidiary head enjoys considerable freedom in deciding the specific strategies or programs to be adopted to fulfill the planned goals and targets. The purpose of the plans is really to coordinate the efforts of the various domestic and overseas subsidiaries and efforts of functional staffs in order to have a minimum of conflicts among them and to insure that the entire Dunlop organization as a whole grows and prospers. Each subsidiary is responsible for showing a good profit and is expected to be financially independent. That is a measure used to motivate the subsidiary heads to make decisions and formulate plans based on ideas that will enhance their own unit's financial position.

Functional services help the subsidiaries improve their performance, and they are also involved in comparing the actual performance of the subsidiaries with "planned performance." When conflicts do arise between subsidiaries and cannot be resolved mutually by the subsidiaries concerned, then the executive directors serve as arbitrators. The central committee is kept fully informed about major matters in each subsidiary. The executive directors decide on such matters as major capital expenditures, senior appointments, and price policies. Matters that are even more important are referred to the main board.

Pattern 2

The Metal Box Company Limited

The Metal Box Company, based in the United Kingdom, is the result of the amalgamation of a number of different companies engaged mainly in package making. It all began as far back as 1799, or perhaps even earlier, when certain of the original companies that founded Metal Box were formed, but the most logical time at which to start the history of the growth of Metal Box is in 1921. In that year, the company was incorporated as a private limited company under the name of Allied Tin Box Makers Ltd. to amalgamate, by means of an exchange of shares, four old, established family concerns engaged in the tin box and paper printing trade. A few months after incorporation, the name of the company was changed to Metal Box and Printing Industries. Further subsidiary companies were acquired in 1924 and 1927. The parent company remained a holding company. The board consisted of one director, or sometimes two directors, from the boards of the subsidiaries, depending upon their size.

The 1920s. There was no head office—each subsidiary managed its own affairs and had its own board. Each had its own sales force. There was some attempt to coordinate the selling efforts of the different subsidiaries—for example, each circulated to the others a daily list of inquiries received—yet competition between subsidiaries was as keen as ever. Indeed, if one subsidiary saw on another subsidiary's list an inquiry that it liked, it went after it quickly. Soon there was some delay in entering inquiries received; and when they eventually appeared, it was with a note in the remarks column: "Order Booked."

In 1929, the American Can Company of New York—then the largest can maker in the United States and indeed the world—decided to start operations in the United Kingdom. It was mainly concerned with the manufacture by high-speed methods of food cans or open-top cans. It linked up with a firm in Liverpool and formed the British Can Company. The appearance on the scene of the British Can Company constituted a threat to the companies associated in Metal Box and Printing Industries and to other British firms engaged in tin box manufacture. One such firm was E. C. Barlows of Hackney. To fight the American invasion of the tin box industry, Barlows merged with Metal Box and Printing Industries.

Metal Box and Printing Industries then developed a strategy that ultimately led to its acquisition of British Can Company. It entered into negotiations with Continental Can Company, of New York, which happened to be the largest competitor of American Can Company. In 1930, it concluded an agreement with Continental under which it acquired, for a period of 15 years, exclusive rights in the United Kingdom to the use of Continental's high-speed machinery, methods, procedures, and patents. The strength of British Can Company, as was noted earlier, rested in its technology, which made use of high-speed machinery for the manufacture of food cans or open-top cans. Now Metal Box and Printing Industries had similar technology, acquired from the Continental Can Company.

Other companies now joined Metal Box and Printing Industries, and the name of the company was shortened to The Metal Box Company Limited. Also, Metal Box converted into a public company, and Robert Barlow became its first managing director in August 1930.

The 1930s. A factory equipped with machinery purchased from the Continental Can Company was built at Perry Wood. It was devoted solely to the manufacture of open-top cans for the canning industry, then still in its infancy.

The American-controlled British Can Company and The Metal Box Company engaged in violent competition. Metal Box apparently emerged victorious, because in 1931 it acquired control of British Can Company on terms settled by arbitration. The American Can Company withdrew from the scene.

Until then Metal Box was an organization made up of a loose federation of companies with strong conflicting personalities. The immediate task for the managing director, Mr. Barlow, was to integrate the several autonomous companies into one company. The first step toward the integration was taken with the establishment of a head office in London. Next, in 1931, the foundation of a central sales organization was laid. Sales representatives were organized on a regional basis, and each of the five regions was under the direction of an area sales manager. The sales representatives were expected to sell all the products of the company and not merely the products of one particular factory as in the past. Other central departments also were established: a central purchasing department, a central accounts department, and a central production department.

The individual factories still retained a great amount of their autonomy, but they lost their individual boards of directors. A general manager was appointed for each factory, and he reported directly to the managing director of The Metal Box Company. Though the subsidiary companies were abolished and converted into "branches" of The Metal Box Company, they still retained their names.

Many other companies merged with Metal Box, and by 1939 there were twenty factory units. The twenty general managers, along with the heads of the four central departments at the head office, reported to the managing director of The Metal Box Company. Also reporting to the managing director were the company's first ventures overseas, which included a factory in India and another in South Africa. Exhibit 12 shows the top management organization of the company until 1944.

Organizational changes in 1944. The company had now reached a stage in its development that required a drastic change in its organizational structure. Changes in the authority and responsibility relationships between the general managers and the heads of the central departments were necessary. The company in 1944 introduced functional authority relationships between the central department heads and the general managers heading the domestic and overseas factories.

The functional organization was introduced because the managing director needed functional staff assistance to help him manage the growing organization, which then consisted of twenty-two general managers, (twenty domestic and two overseas) heading the factories. There was also a need for the establishment of uniform policy controls throughout the organization. The general managers required specialized help in the operations of their factories, particularly in the introduction of modern methods, techniques, or procedures. Exhibit 13 shows the top management organization of the company from 1944 until further changes were introduced in it.

The introduction of group management. The company benefitted greatly by the introduction of the functional organization, and it also became increasingly diversified in its product lines. But the managing director still faced the problem of an unmanageable span of management; there were twenty domestic and two overseas general managers and four heads of functional departments reporting to him. Although the functional department heads relieved the managing director of many of his tasks, more factories were being added or new businesses being acquired. The company felt the need for further reorganization of its structure to further relieve the managing director of the problem of too many executives reporting to him.

Reorganization was also felt necessary to provide specialized attention and sales and technical services to the different product lines, which the

Exhibit 12. Organization of The Metal Box Company Limited to 1944

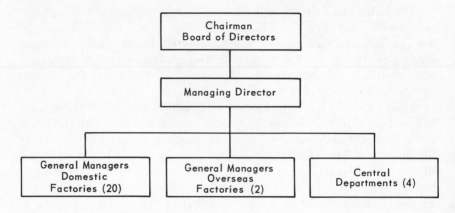

Exhibit 13. Organization of The Metal Box Company Limited from 1944 to Adoption of Current Structure

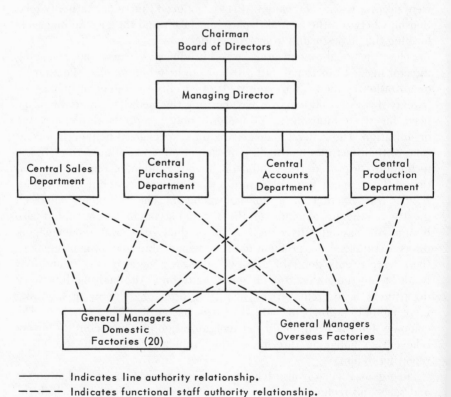

—————— Indicates line authority relationship.
— — — — Indicates functional staff authority relationship.

company had started producing as a result of its product diversification. Metal Box produced not only open-top cans but also plastic packaging, paper and board packaging, and all forms of general-line containers and closures. The company had greatly expanded its services to the canning industry; it now rented to its customers machines for closing cans and cartons. It was also engaged in the design and manufacture of auxiliary equipment for the canning industry such as driers and conveyers. Because of this diversification in the product lines produced, it became impossible for the central services departments (functional departments) to provide equally efficient and effective services to all the products. The company now had 38 domestic factories plus its overseas subsidiaries. It therefore instituted a group organization, and the operations of the company were divided into five domestic groups and one overseas company: (1) open-top cans, (2) general-line group, (3) paper group, (4) plastics group, (5) machinery-building group, and (6) The Metal Box Company Overseas Limited. The current organization structure of the company is given in Exhibit 14. An executive committee, consisting of eight executive directors, who are appointed by the board of directors, is responsible for the everyday operations of the company. Each of the central services departments has the responsibility for providing its specialized service to every operating group and the overseas company.

Each operating group now has its own functional staff such as sales and production. It is the duty of the group staff to insure that the services provided by the central services departments of the company are effectively used within the group. Each group, in effect, is a separate profit center. The group management has the overall responsibility for running that business within the general policies and constraints laid down by the board of Metal Box.

The overseas organization. The Metal Box Company's operations abroad first began in 1933 with the opening of a branch factory in India at Calcutta. Later in that year the company took a small interest in a company in South Africa, and it formed subsidiary companies in both countries. The company did not start any new operations abroad until 1947, when operations were started in what was then called Malaya. Factories were established soon afterward in East Africa. After that, Metal Box expanded into other parts of the world, and now the company has 10 operating subsidiaries and numerous other affiliates and correspondent companies throughout the world. The subsidiaries all together own and operate 33 factories in 13 countries.

Organization of overseas group. Soon after World War II, the company developed an interest in overseas operations. Therefore, a need was felt at the headquarters to have a group of management personnel specialized in

Exhibit 14. Current Organization of The Metal Box Company Limited

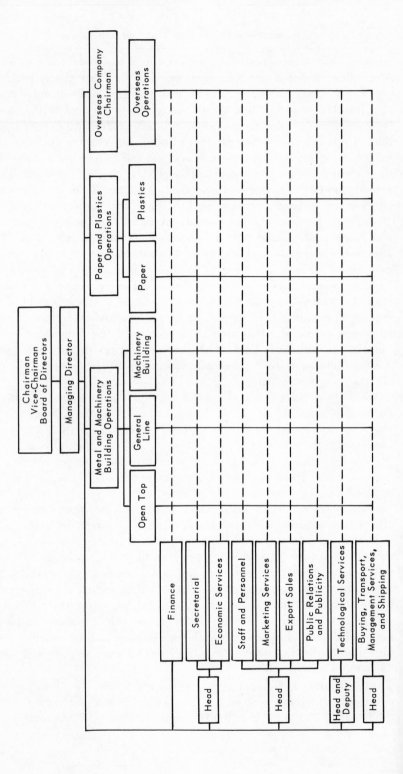

overseas activities who would also have the authority to deal appropriately with matters of major policy and finance that had an effect on the overseas operations.

The growth of the home organization and its responsibilities precluded the executive board members from giving sufficient time to overseas operations. Besides, the added threat at the time of the company being incorporated in the Steel Nationalization Plan influenced the company's decision to break off all the overseas activities from the domestic activities. Hence, the company put all of its overseas subsidiary companies into the hands of a subsidiary holding company and called it The Metal Box Company Overseas Limited.

The new company was formed on June 21, 1948, and in May 1950 it became an operating company. The parent company—The Metal Box Company Limited—held all the equity capital of the newly formed overseas holding company. The arrangement continues today.

The overseas company is one of the groups of the parent company and relies on the parent company's central services for a great deal of functional assistance in both technical and nontechnical matters. The organization structure of the overseas company is similar to that of the parent company; it is shown in Exhibit 15.

The overseas company is considerably decentralized. Subsidiary companies abroad are given a great deal of independence and sufficient authority "to run their own ship" provided they run their company affairs within the constraints imposed by major policy and finance, over which the overseas company head office in London keeps strict control.

A very close liaison between the head office and the overseas subsidiaries has been made possible through a group of territorial officers. They are all senior officers who have had considerable previous overseas experience and are free of the day-to-day responsibilities of running departments. Their duties are to keep in close touch with the senior executives in both the home company—The Metal Box Company Limited—and the overseas subsidiaries. The territorial officers are usually members of the local boards of the subsidiaries as well as of the executive committee of the overseas company.

Foreseeable organizational changes. Metal Box expects that custom barriers in Europe will drop even further and that the company will therefore have to look at Europe in a different way organizationally. A much stronger European international organization in the next 5 to 10 years is bound to come. The company does not anticipate abolition of The Metal Box Company Overseas Limited, because that structure keeps the parent company in touch with the overseas packaging companies and their needs. (Plants of Metal Box are located near the packaging plants.)

Exhibit 15. Organization of The Metal Box Company Overseas Limited

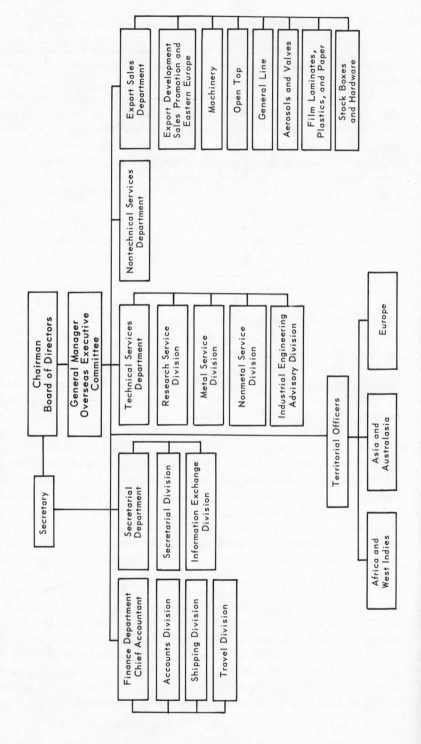

The Pirelli Group

Pirelli & Co. was founded in 1872 by Giovanni Battista Pirelli, who built a factory for the production of rubber products in Milan, the first of its kind in Italy. The original lines of production were in technical rubber goods and goods for household and medical uses. In 1879, production of insulated electric cables, including submarine cables, was started. This was followed in 1890 by the production of cycle tires and somewhat later of car tires.

By the turn of the century, the company had become highly successful and held a commanding share of the domestic market. A need was then felt to expand operations beyond Italy in order to spread the burden of the expenses of research and development. That led to the erection of a factory in Spain, in 1902, to be followed by factories in England, 1914; Argentina, 1917; Brazil, 1929; Belgium, 1936; Canada, 1953; Mexico, 1955; France, 1957; Greece and Turkey, 1960; and Peru, 1965.

Pirelli was originally established as Pirelli & Co., Societa Accomandita Semplice, which roughly corresponds to a limited partnership company. In 1883 that was changed to Societa in Accomandita per Azioni, which is somewhat similar to a joint stock company. The founder held control of the company during his lifetime. The company became a public company soon after 1921. The tightness of the Italian financial markets and the need to secure protection against political risks suggested the creation of a holding company that would have ready access to the international money markets. As a result, Pirelli & Co. was made a holding company, and Societa Italiana Pirelli (later Pirelli S.p.A.) was made responsible for all the industrial operations. In 1921, Société Internationale Pirelli, with headquarters in Brussels and later in Basle, was given the ownership of all the foreign subsidiaries. SIP thus became a holding company located in a neutral country—Switzerland—with an active capital market. The structure proved to be very useful during World War II.

The organization of the Pirelli group has changed to meet the changing needs of the markets as well as the changing economic and political complexion of the world. A recent example is the transfer of the ownership and control of all the company's operations in the European Common Market from SIP to Pirelli S.p.A. The change was made in order to present an integrated organization to the EEC.

Today the company has more than eighty plants in thirteen or more countries. More than half of its sales, which amount to $1 billion, come from abroad. The company employs more than 69,000 people, half of whom are employed abroad. Among tire companies, Pirelli is second largest outside the United States, Dunlop is first, and Michelin is third. Pirelli runs a close race with British Insulated Callender's Cables for the title of largest European producer of electric cable.

Present organization structure. The ownership pattern of the Pirelli group is as follows: Pirelli & Co., A.p.A. is a holding company. (The general partner nominates the chief executive subject to the approval of the other stockholders.) Pirelli & Co. owns 8 percent of the stock of Pirelli S.p.A. and 18 percent of SIP. In turn, SIP owns 12 percent of the stock of Pirelli S.p.A. Pirelli S.p.A. owns 40 percent of the stock in SIP's subsidiaries (outside the EEC). Despite the apparent complexity, the structure helps to spread the risk and makes financing easier. SIP enables the Pirelli group to tap the huge Swiss financial market.

The Pirelli group, as a whole, is now the sum total of two independent corporations of roughly equal size incorporated in two different countries. The Italian company—Pirelli S.p.A.—controls all subsidiaries in Italy and the EEC. The international holding company—Société Internationale Pirelli—controls all other foreign subsidiaries.

The managing committee. As a result of the financial arrangements mentioned, the chief executive officer of Pirelli S.p.A. is also the chief executive officer of Pirelli & Co., the parent holding company. In addition, he is a director of SIP, but not formally its chief executive. The global activities of the entire Pirelli group are handled by the managing committee. The committee consists of the chief executive officer of Pirelli & Co. and five other top executives, three of whom are top executives of Pirelli S.p.A. and two are the chief executives of SIP in Basle, Switzerland. This six-man management team sets the overall policy for the Pirelli group. Thus, coordination between the two corporations—Pirelli S.p.A. and SIP— is brought about by the group of top executives.

Organization of Pirelli S.p.A. A skeletal organization chart of Pirelli S.p.A. is presented in Exhibit 16. The three managing directors are members of the managing committee mentioned earlier. Two of them are directly responsible for the domestic and EEC subsidiaries and the third is in charge of the functional departments. The functional departments are not staff departments; in fact, they have strong functional authority over the domestic organization.

The subsidiaries of SIP receive assistance from the technical staff of Pirelli S.p.A. Basic research is conducted almost entirely by Pirelli S.p.A. and is made available to SIP for a price. Pirelli S.p.A. gives aid to SIP in fields such as design and supply of plants and machinery, production methods, and engineering. In this way, SIP does not have to maintain a separate technical staff—it obtains the help it needs from Pirelli S.p.A. staff but pays Pirelli S.p.A. through a set mechanism of intercorporate charges.

Exhibit 16. Organization of Pirelli S.p.A.

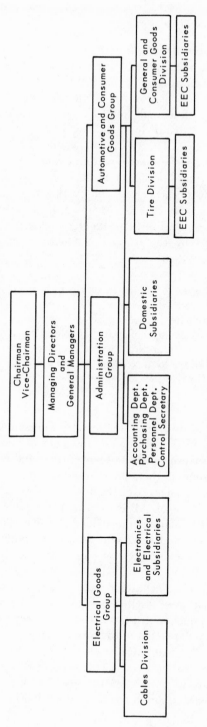

Exhibit 17. Organization of Pirelli SIP

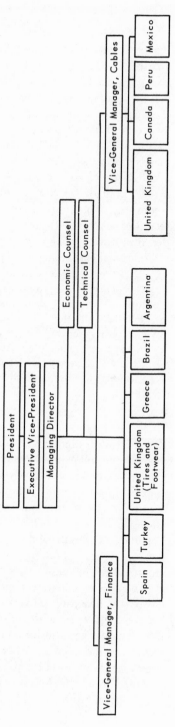

Organization of Société Internationale Pirelli (SIP). The legal head-quarters of SIP are located in Basle, Switzerland, where a small staff performs financial operations. The organization chart of SIP is presented in Exhibit 17. The managerial functions are performed by an executive vice-chairman and a managing director with a small staff. The group works in Switzerland, but it also maintains a staff office in Milan not far from the headquarters of the domestic company. The top management of SIP is mainly concerned with general and developmental planning and selection and transfer of key executives in the subsidiaries under its command. The overall policies for SIP, as mentioned earlier, are set by the managing committee. The subsidiaries also receive, as was also mentioned earlier, technical assistance from the Pirelli S.p.A. in Milan. Pirelli's philosophy of decentralization was well expressed by the company's chairman at an international conference in September 1965:

> The policy of our group is to delegate to foreign subsidiaries as much authority as is possible within the limits of the necessary unity of direction and the utilization of the same technique. . . . The fact of our foreign units being separate companies, set up in conformity with local laws, makes them virtually autonomous. . . . Our target is that they feel and act as being completely integrated in the local economy in such a way as to minimize, as far as possible, the fact that they are subsidiaries of foreign concerns.

The company has one or more subsidiaries in ten countries outside the EEC. The subsidiaries are engaged in the production and sales of one or more of the following products: electrical cables and wires, tires, and general rubber goods. In other words, some of them are uniproduct and others are multiproduct units. The general managers of the foreign subsidiaries report directly to the managing director of SIP located in Basle. General managers of a few subsidiaries that manufacture cables (Mexico, Peru, Canada, and Pirelli General of the United Kingdom) are an exception to the rule. They report to a vice-general manager for cables, who in turn reports to the managing director.

There is a separate reporting relationship for cable manufacturing companies because, unlike the situation in Pirelli S.p.A. in which the rubber products, tires, and cables are equal contributors to the total revenue, in SIP, cables account for more than 50 percent of the total revenue.

It was mentioned earlier that the SIP subsidiaries receive technical assistance from Pirelli S.p.A. The link between the two corporations is provided by the technical counsel on the staff of SIP. He is the one who maintains the flow of assistance from the Pirelli S.p.A. product divisions to the SIP subsidiaries. The principle is to solve technical and business problems at the local level as much as possible. If a problem is not resolved at that level, then assistance is sought from Pirelli S.p.A.

Pattern 3

American Cyanamid Company

American Cyanamid Company, headquartered in New Jersey, was founded more than 63 years ago. It has sales or manufacturing subsidiaries in more than 150 countries. Foreign sales of the company now account for 20 percent of total sales.

The pre-World War II organization of the company, presented in Exhibit 18, was strictly geared to the U.S. market; the company did not then pay much attention to operating abroad. The U.S. market was big enough to keep it engrossed with domestic operations alone.

Evolution of the international division. Soon after the war, the company established a patent department to exploit the company's technology abroad on a royalty basis. That phase lasted until 1959, when one of the divisions became internationally minded and formed an export department. It was copied by the other departments. Soon afterward, the company stopped its practice of "licensing for licensing's sake." It realized that it might face itself in the marketplace if it found that a foreign licensee was also trying to compete in a market in which it was interested.

The company found that its exports had become substantial by that time; therefore, it opened some sales distribution outlets abroad. Following that, it became involved in semimanufacture abroad. Gradually some of its divisions began to put plants abroad and do some fundamental manufacturing and selling either from intermediate products or from the ground up.

By 1968, the company decided to form an international division on the theory that management personnel in the United States who were running the business were too preoccupied with their problems of selling in the big U.S. market. Therefore, they could not devote the necessary time, effort, and patience to gain the expertise required to operate in many overseas markets. The subsidiaries abroad could not get the top-level management directions necessary from the export managers. Therefore, an international division of stature equal to that of the other product divisions was created. The current organization chart of the company is presented in Exhibit 19.

The evolution of the international division went through three phases. In the first phase there was a managing director who attempted to run the

Exhibit 18. Organization of American Cyanamid Company before World War II

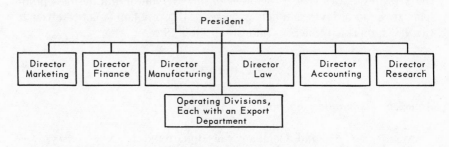

Exhibit 19. Current Organization of American Cyanamid Company

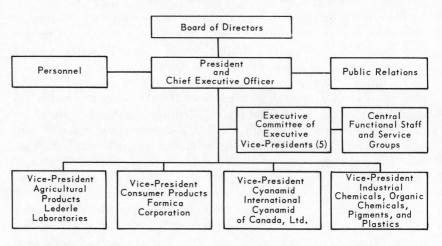

Exhibit 20. Organization of the American Cyanamid Company International Division

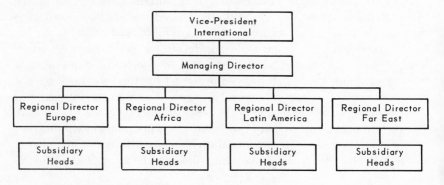

entire global operations through his office. He had subordinates specialized in a broad group of products. For example, there was a manager
appointed for pharmaceuticals whose responsibility was to oversee the division pharmaceuticals business abroad and help the subsidiaries in that
field. Similarly, there was a manager for agricultural products, who had
similar duties with respect to his product line. Problems arose, however,
because the subsidiaries abroad had a tendency to report to the division in
the United States whose products they mainly handled. That led to conflicts.

The second phase in the international division's evolution saw the abolition of the product specialists and further departmentalization of the
operations abroad on a regional basis. Four regions were formed: Far East,
Africa, Europe, and Latin America. That did not work because each of the
regions created its own staff and the managing director's staff at the headquarters was not abolished. All this proved to be uneconomical.

Now the international division is going through the third phase in its
evolution. The regional directors—some of whom were abroad—have been
brought back to the headquarters. The managing director has no staff as
such; it now consists of the regional directors. Now there are three regions:
Latin America, Europe-Africa, and Far East. Product inputs are introduced within each region; thus now there are product directors within
each region (for example, consumer, agricultural, pharmaceutical, chemical, etc.,) who assist subsidiaries in all aspects of their expertise. They have
downward dotted line authority relationships to the subsidiary heads and
report to the regional directors in line capacity. The current organization
chart of the international division is presented in Exhibit 20.

Another concept of refinement has been introduced into the regional
setup. To overcome the objection that there are no front-line people where
the opportunities are, "key subsidiary concept" has been introduced. It
works as follows: If the German subsidiary has a very strong manager, then
he, in addition to running the German operations, also supervises the
Austrian and Swiss subsidiaries, which use the German language. As a key
subsidiary, the German subsidiary takes care of the problems that might
arise in that area.

Organizational relationships between the consumer division and the
international division. The company recently removed women's hair products from the consumer division and made the consumer division operate
with a worldwide perspective and responsibility. Currently there are three
major product divisions; of the three, only the consumer division operates
on a global basis. The company is not yet sure whether this organizational
arrangement is a success or not; only time will tell if it is.

In return for a management fee, the consumer products division uses the manufacturing and staff services of both the parent company and the international division. In this way, a foreign subsidiary that produces consumer products, as well as pharmaceuticals, chemicals, and agricultural products, has one manager reporting to the subsidiary head, who is responsible for products other than consumer products. The manager who is responsible for consumer products reports directly in line relationship to the marketing director—international, of the consumer division, but he has only a dotted-line relationship with the subsidiary head. The subsidiary head has no responsibility for the consumer products. The consumer products division pays the international division for any services it obtains from the subsidiary.

Pattern 4

Atlas Copco AB

The rapid international development of Atlas Copco, based in Sweden, started after World War II. During the war, the company turnover was about $10 million, and now it is about $250 million. Presently, 88 percent of the total sales of the company is in the foreign markets, 45 percent of which is supplied by the company's non-Swedish operations. From 1947 to 1967, the company concentrated on building up a very powerful sales organization outside Sweden. To achieve its objective the company established wholly owned sales subsidiaries in most of the important sales areas of the world. It now has 36 selling companies in all the important countries.

Evolution of the organization structure. About ten years ago, top management felt it was time to reconsider the organization of the parent company. Until 1968, the parent company was functionally organized. Reporting to the president were three vice-presidents, each responsible for production, sales, or finance. There were also staffs such as personnel and public relations. Management of the company was in the hands of a group management committee. The marketing department was responsible for sales promotion at home and abroad. Similarly, the production department was responsible for production units at home and abroad. In 1958, consultants from the Stanford Research Institute were asked to review the organizational setup and make recommendations for the reorganization of the company without disturbing the sales organization outside Sweden. A proposal for a divisionalized organization was made by the consultants, but, for certain reasons, it was not implemented at that time. Management felt that it was too drastic a step.

The consultants had recommended that the company should create a number of divisions, each having its own functional staff for activities such as research and design, production, and marketing. That would make the parent company merely a group center supporting, analyzing, guiding, and controlling all divisions and selling companies abroad. During the last ten years, top management came to the conclusion that the suggestions had to be implemented to shorten the long lines of communication in the parent company between sales, production, and research and particularly between sales and production, which made coordination of the two departments quite a problem.

Since January 1, 1967, Atlas Copco has implemented a completely new organization based upon the advice given by the Stanford Research Institute. The current organization structure is shown in Exhibit 21. There are three wholly owned product divisions: The Atlas Copco MCT (MCT stands for Mining and Construction Technique), Atlas Copco Tools AB, which sells all kinds of pneumatic tools, and Atlas Copco Air Power N.V. in Belgium, which produces compressors and tools that the other divisions use. The first two divisions are located in Sweden. Each division has complete responsibility for product design, production, and sales promotion worldwide and therefore plans on a global basis. The production units of the divisions are wholly owned, except in Italy, which is 60 percent owned by Atlas Copco. They are located in various parts of Europe; Great Britain, Switzerland, Denmark, West Germany, Finland, Italy, and Sweden. The Atlas Copco Air Power activities are concentrated in one plant in Belgium.

The product divisions are complementary as far as their production and technical needs are concerned; they use advanced, complex, and capital-intensive technology. The product divisions need different methods of distribution because they are oriented toward different types of customers.

All 36 wholly owned sales companies in as many countries, the distributors in 80 countries where the company does not have sales companies, and a group for Eastern Europe sales are handled by an international sales company that also handles all domestic sales. If conflicts arise between the divisions, which are profit centers, and the international sales company, which is also a profit center, then they are resolved by a functional marketing unit. The job of the functional marketing unit is to develop policies and marketing methods, do market research for the sales companies, and arbitrate pricing and profit issues between the divisions and the sales companies. The functional marketing unit also reviews the performance of the sales companies, and so it has functional authority over some activities of both the product divisions and the international sales company.

Exhibit 21. Organization of Atlas Copco AB

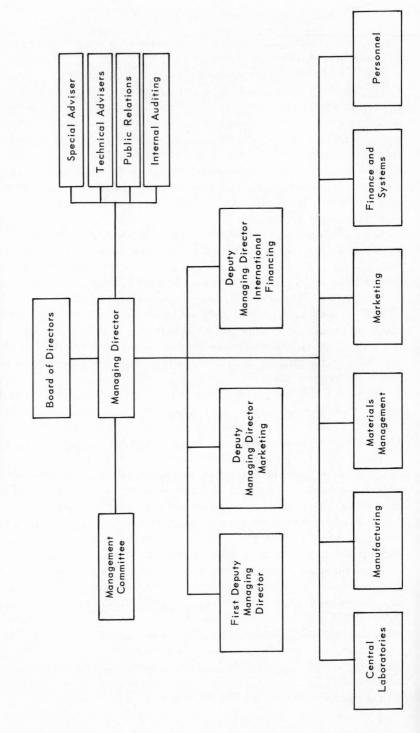

A Swiss Chemicals and Pharmaceuticals Company

This company, which prefers anonymity, acquired a Swiss company in early 1967. As a result it had to reorganize. The reorganization took effect on April 1, 1967, and led to the adoption of the following organization structure. At the top is the board of directors consisting of eleven members. The board of directors has delegated a number of its powers to a committee of the board consisting of the chairman and two vice-chairmen. Reporting to the committee of the board of directors is an executive committee consisting of five senior officers. The executive committee is responsible for the day-to-day operations of the company. All decisions that are beyond the jurisdiction of the executive committee are referred to the committee of the board for action.

The operations of the company are divisionalized along product lines. There are three divisions: pharmaceuticals, dyestuffs-chemicals, and agro-chemicals-dietetic products–miscellaneous. There is also a fourth department called administration, which is further subdivided into finances and documentation, personnel, legal, and engineering. The administration is a support-oriented department servicing the company as a whole.

The divisional heads and the head of administration are members of the executive committee, which is headed by a fifth member who happens to be the company's chairman and managing director.

Each of the product divisions has worldwide responsibility for its product line. It has its own functional staff such as R&D, marketing, production, and planning. Each staff group is in turn obliged to handle its function with a global perspective. The same kind of structure exists within each subsidiary.

Future organizational changes. The company believes that its structure, or at least some of its departments, should be revised from time to time. The frequency of such revisions may be every three to five years, or it might depend upon sales growth. One might make a case for reorganization every time the sales double. In any case, the company intends to modify its structure from time to time. For one thing, in the future the marketing function will be taken over entirely by the subsidiaries and the parent company will concentrate upon the most important marketing tasks such as product management at group level, market research for the group, central group advertising, and the training of top executives and specialists. The control of the subsidiaries by the center will also grow, and a decisive part will be played by short, medium, and long-range planning and budgeting. That will allow greater coordination among the company's various subsidiaries at home and abroad. There will be what is often called

Exhibit 22. Organization of a Swiss Chemicals and Pharmaceuticals Company

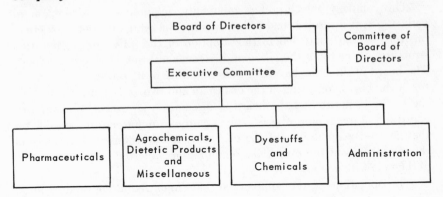

centralized control with decentralized responsibilities. Management by exception will be the guiding philosophy of top management.

The entire group has more than 39 subsidiaries, some wholly owned and others partly owned, operating in about 34 countries including Switzerland. An approximation of the current organization structure is presented in Exhibit 22.

Farbenfabriken Bayer AG

Bayer AG, based in Germany, is one of the biggest European chemical companies. It was founded in 1863 jointly by Friedrich Bayer, a dyestuff merchant, and Johann Friedrich Weskott, a dyer. The firm began with the manufacture of aniline dyestuffs. It suffered many setbacks during World Wars I and II, but today it is a giant that produces not only dyestuffs, but a variety of diversified products such as plastics, synthetic fibers, pharmaceuticals, and crop protection products. It has 56 production plants in more than 50 countries and sales agencies in almost every country in the world. It owes its growth to research, in which every sixth employee is engaged. The Bayer group employs 86,000 people, and 8,800 of them work in research and technical laboratories.

The original Bayer company founded in 1863 merged in 1925 with seven or eight German coal-tar dye manufacturers to form the I.G. Farbenindustrie AG. After the war, in 1946, the company was broken up by the Allies. Three major and a few smaller companies were formed after the split-up. The major companies were Hoechst, BASF, and what is today known as Farbenfabriken Bayer AG. Each of these three companies is now a large company by itself. This study will deal with Bayer AG alone.

I.G. Farbenindustrie AG lost all its sales organization abroad to confiscations in different countries during World War II and after. Consequently, Bayer, Hoechst, and BASF had to establish joint sales organizations in certain countries; in some other countries each company established its own independent sales organization. Export or import had to be through an agency established by the allied governments. That created problems. The problem eased after 1949, owing to the new economic policies of Dr. Erhard. From 1953 on, Bayer became a normal stock company that was allowed to freely export or import. Sales organization at that time consisted of five divisions: dyestuffs, pharmaceuticals, chemicals, pesticides, and synthetic fibres. Each division was coordinated with every other division and formed a unified sales organization in each country with the exception of pharmaceuticals, which bought pharmaceutical organizations abroad or established new ones. Presently, the sales organization abroad has one representative for pharmaceuticals and another for the other four divisions or one representative responsible for the sales of all five product groups.

The current organization structure is presented in Exhibit 23. One easily notices that it is dominated by committees. For each product group there is a committee responsible for production, sales, and R&D of its product group on a global basis.

Future organizational changes. There will be organizational changes in the near future. The product committees will be abolished, and in their place product divisions will appear. The number of divisions will be much smaller than the number of product committees at the moment. The product divisions will report to the board of directors. Each member of the board will be a specialist in one function, for example, finance, sales, R&D, or production. Product divisions will plan and control on a global basis. Divisional managers will be responsible for production and sales of their product group on a global basis. The present-day works managers enjoy considerable autonomy. The product committees of today can persuade the works managers to implement their advice but cannot force them to. That will change under the product divisions setup. The works managers will lose much of their authority over their respective factories, and they will, in effect, become merely coordinators. The various department heads in each factory will report directly to their respective product division heads. More than one man may be responsible for each product division.

Landis and Gyr AG

Over the last twenty years the Swiss-based Landis and Gyr AG company has progressed in size from a one-product division company to a

Exhibit 23. Organization of Bayer AG

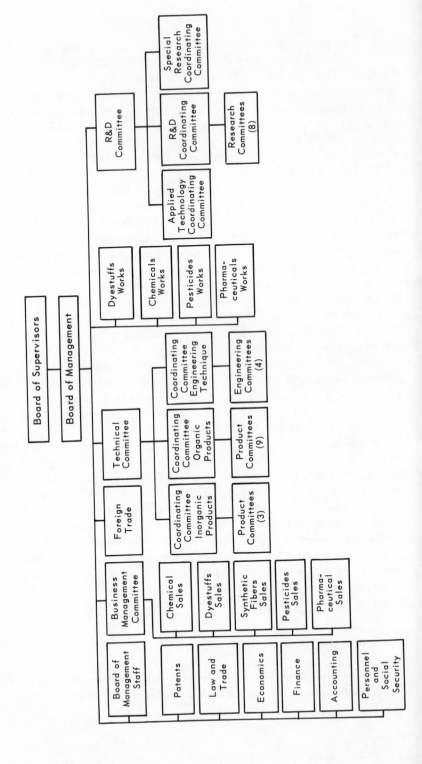

multiproduct corporation. Originally, the bread-and-butter product was electrical meters. That was, in fact, the only line produced by the company both at home and abroad. The public utilities in Switzerland and in other countries would not buy any product that was not produced within their own borders. At the same time, the norm for each country's public utility system was different, so Landis and Gyr was forced to produce meters at home and abroad.

Previously, the company had a strong headquarters unit with subsidiaries abroad reporting directly to the president. The functional managers at the headquarters had functional authority over their specialized areas within each subsidiary, but the subsidiaries themselves were very autonomous.

Over the years the company began adding new products to its product lines. The need was felt to pay closer attention to the different product groups, a need not met by the existing structure. Both the company and its markets were growing, and the growth characteristics of the different products were quite different as well. For all those reasons the company began reorganizing in 1961 and completed the process in 1969 with the organization structure shown in Exhibit 24.

There are two product groups—the public utilities group and the industrial group—and each comprises several divisions. There are in all eight divisions. The product divisions are profit centers that operate on a global basis. The subsidiaries abroad are multiproduct companies, some of which report to the public utilities group head. Others report to the industrials group head or the corporate business development group head. The product divisions are quite decentralized, but they operate within the framework of a central plan for the entire company. The overall management of the company is in the hands of a corporate management committee. The heads of finance and accounting, public utilities, industrials, and corporate business development groups, along with the president, are members of the corporate management committee, which formulates the company's goals, policies, and plans.

The company does not anticipate any major changes in its organization structure in the near future, although a lot of organizational relationships need to be defined. For example, the interrelationships between the product divisions and the multiproduct companies need clarification. Previously, and to a certain extent even now, the subsidiaries operated like separate kingdoms. The company hopes to change that and make the subsidiaries cooperate more closely with the product divisions by making the divisional managers more powerful.

Exhibit 24. Organization of Landis and Gyr AG

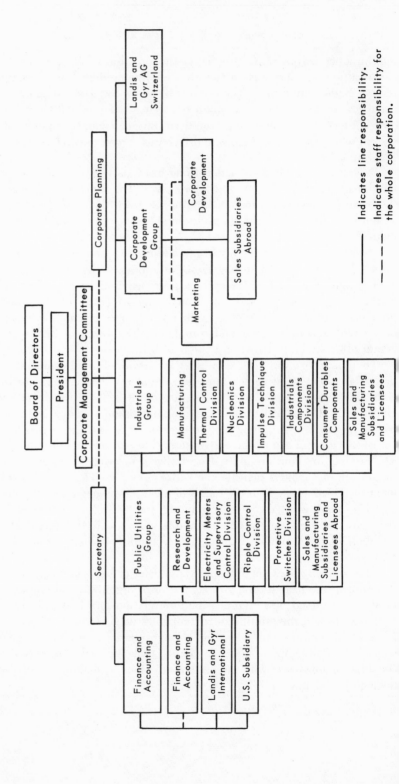

Board of Directors

President

Corporate Management Committee

Secretary

Corporate Planning

Public Utilities Group
- Research and Development
- Electricity Meters and Supervisory Control Division
- Ripple Control Division
- Protective Switches Division
- Sales and Manufacturing Subsidiaries and Licensees Abroad

Industrials Group
- Manufacturing
- Thermal Control Division
- Nucleonics Division
- Impulse Technique Division
- Industrials Components Division
- Consumer Durables Components
- Sales and Manufacturing Subsidiaries and Licensees

Finance and Accounting
- Finance and Accounting
- Landis and Gyr International
- U.S. Subsidiary

Corporate Development Group
- Marketing
- Corporate Development
- Sales Subsidiaries Abroad

Landis and Gyr AG Switzerland

———— Indicates line responsibility.

- - - - Indicates staff responsibility for the whole corporation.

A Diversified Swiss Chemicals and Pharmaceuticals Company

One of the most diversified of all the Swiss organic chemicals companies, which is more than a hundred years old, is also organized under pattern 4. The company, which wishes to remain anonymous, developed into a business of international scope after World War I. Today it is comprised of more than 60 manufacturing and sales companies in more than 36 countries in Asia, Africa, Europe, North and South America, and Australia. Most of them are multidivisional. At the present time the group employs about 31,000 workers and staff, of whom about a third work in Switzerland. At the head of this worldwide industrial body is the parent company, which is both a manufacturing and selling organization and an international holding company. The group is involved in the manufacture of agrochemicals, animal health products, dyes and pigments, electronic instruments, home products, pharmaceuticals, photochemicals, plastics, rare metals, and technical application products.

The company is organized on a divisional basis; see Exhibit 25 for the structure. There are six product divisions: (1) dyestuffs and textile applications, (2) pharmaceuticals, (3) synthetic resins and plastics, (4) pesticides, (5) cosmetics, and (6) photochemicals. The divisions operate on a worldwide basis as profit centers; they enjoy a considerable amount of freedom from corporate interference. Each division has its own functional organization that consists of R&D, marketing, production, planning, and auxiliary functions. The planning function is responsible for planning in all the functional areas within the divisions mentioned plus finance. Company management believes that the divisional concept is essential for the company's growth as a multinational enterprise. The divisions are responsible for the research, development, growth, and marketing of their product line throughout the world, and they almost operate like separate businesses subject, of course, to the financial and policy controls imposed by top management. Decentralization exists within the divisional structures as well, in that each function is further decentralized on a regional basis.

The company makes a basic distinction between the verticulated divisions and the central services. Cutting across this vertical structure with its component divisions are the central services, which function for the benefit of all divisions.

The general management committee. Coordination between the divisions and the central services is exercised by the general management committee, the membership of which includes the chairmen of the divisional managements and delegates of the central services. It is chaired as an independent duty by a member of the committee of the board.

Divisional matters as such do not come within the review of the general

Exhibit 25. Organization of a Diversified Swiss Chemicals and Pharmaceuticals Company

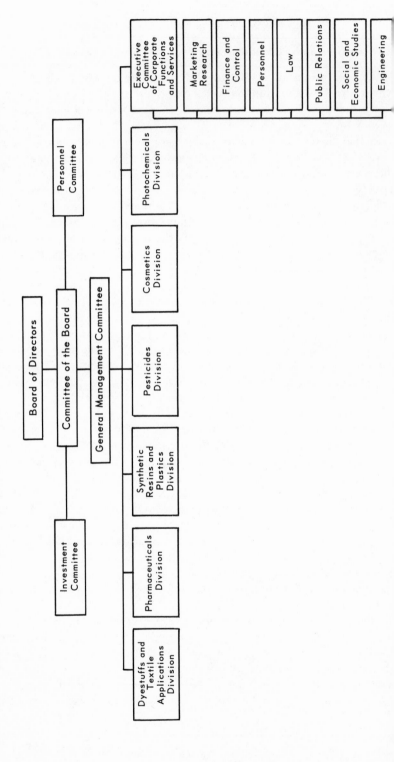

management committee. The burden of the committee assignment is the gearing of divisional operations to the means available for attaining corporate objectives as a whole, and, further, striking an appropriate balance whenever a consistent line is called for in working toward success. This pertains to finance, personnel, and investments, for example. For the rest, committee authority encompasses all matters of general importance to the organization, for which it either makes decisions or formulates explicit proposals for submission to the next higher authority, the committee of the board.

One of the crucial functions of the general management committee is to bring about meaningful coordination between the different divisions and service departments of the company. The divisional development plans are brought together in the form of a group development plan by the experts in the general management committee. The decisions taken by the general management committee are target-oriented and guided by the comprehensive group development plan.

The committee of the board. The committee of the board determines corporate policy and supervises the conduct of the company's overall business. The corporate policies are executed by the general management committee. Certain members of the committee of the board, in their capacity as delegates, are directly active in day-to-day affairs. To prevent the autonomy of the divisions from suffering, the duties and authority of the delegates are precisely defined.

Divisional managers report to the general management committee and through it to the committee of the board regarding their divisional long-term plans, which are approved by the general management committee. The liaison between divisions and the corporate functions at the top is executed by the divisional executive committee of each division, which is composed of the heads of the divisional functional departments, one of whom serves as the chairman. As was mentioned earlier, the chairman of each division is represented on the general management committee. Other members of the divisional executive committee or the chairman himself could be a member of either of the committees reporting to the committee of the board: the investment committee and the personnel committee.

Previously, the company had one division only with sales and product research on a divisional basis and all other functions at the corporate level. The functions that currently exist at the top of the divisional level were previously at the corporate level because the company had only one division. The company became multinational and multidivisional simultaneously, and decentralization was carried out geographically, divisionally, and within the divisional functions as well as on a regional basis. There are now regional managers at the corporate level looking after corporate policies and regional interests and problems.

The company's subsidiaries and affiliates abroad also enjoy considerable autonomy and freedom from interference by the parent company. But that does not mean that they are free to operate as they please without due regard to the overall group's interest. The necessary coordination is facilitated by the appointment of the parent company's representatives, from its divisions or central services, to be members of the board of its subsidiaries or affiliates.

The current organization structure enables the divisions to operate as profit centers but prevents any one division from getting out of control. Healthy competition between the divisions is encouraged. The committee structure at the corporate and central services level provides for decentralized performance by divisions within the centralized control exercised through the group development plan and corporate policies.

Pattern 5

Ingersoll-Rand Company

The Ingersoll-Rand Company, headquartered in New York, has been in business for over a hundred years. The first products produced by the company were unique in that they were developed by only a small number of companies in the world. The products had application in the mining industry, which is itself an international industry. Within a year or two of starting as a company, Ingersoll-Rand had begun to sell its products abroad and shortly thereafter to manufacture them in South Africa, Australia, and in various countries in South America and Europe. Prior to World War II, the company had about sixteen foreign subsidiaries. Presently, the company has more than twenty-seven foreign manufacturing or large sales subsidiaries.

Evolution of the organization structure. The structure of the company, before changes began to take place in about 1959, is presented in Exhibit 26. The company was functionally organized All the overseas subsidiary companies reported to a vice-president, international. The three United States plants, headed by a vice-president, reported directly to the president. The company was highly decentralized, and only the chairman and the president had a total view of it. The only department that could be identified as a profit center was the international one. It was also the only department that operated on a decentralized basis, and it had more autonomy than the other departments. Vice-presidents heading large

Exhibit 26. Organization of Ingersoll-Rand Company (1959)

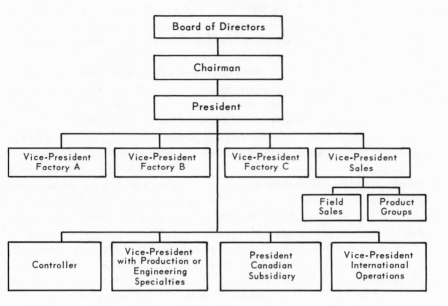

Exhibit 27. Current Organization of Ingersoll-Rand Company

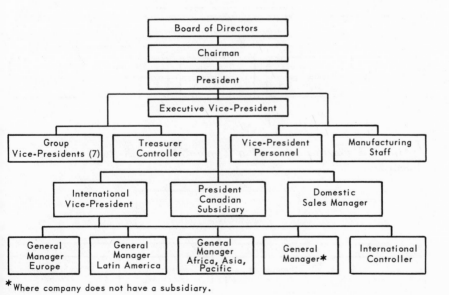

*Where company does not have a subsidiary.

plants were responsible for manufacturing, engineering, and other operations within their plants. The controller at the headquarters had a functional authority over finance. The product groups reporting to the sales vice-
president were responsible for setting prices and imposing them upon the
plants and the field sales force. They were also responsible for application engineering—most products made by the company were technical in
nature. The product groups were, in fact, liaison personnel, but they
were part of the organization reporting to the sales vice-president.

The organization structure of the company was in a flux from 1959 to
1964 when the management of the company was decentralized. The present organization structure is shown in Exhibit 27. There are seven product
groups: (1) the Torrington group, (2) compressors, (3) gas engine and
reciprocating process, commonly known as the gas process group, (4)
the tool group, (5) mining and construction, (6) pulp, plastic, and paper
machinery, and (7) pumps and condensers. Each product group comprises
three or four profit centers that are either divisions of the old Ingersoll-
Rand, or subsidiary companies that were later acquisitions. The structure
of a typical product group is shown in Exhibit 28. Each division or subsidiary
has functional staffs for engineering, marketing, and manufacturing, and a
controller. A skeletal organization chart of a typical division or subsidiary
is presented in Exhibit 29.

Exhibit 28. Organization of a Typical Ingersoll-Rand Group

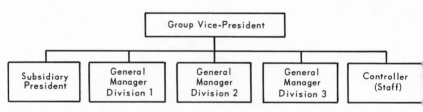

Exhibit 29. Organization of a Typical Ingersoll-Rand Division or Subsidiary

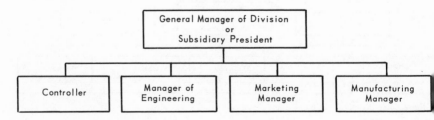

The international division is departmentalized on a regional basis, but now the international vice-president's role has changed. Every product division (or subsidiary) has a worldwide responsibility for a product line. The product divisions, individually or cumulatively as a product group, work through the international vice-president. The subsidiary heads abroad report to the appropriate regional head in the international division, but the product groups and division managers have the responsibility for integrating the foreign subsidiary operations through the international division.

The company is trying to disrupt the old idea of dealing with the foreign subsidiaries at arm's-length. It is the job of the international division to help the product profit centers to integrate their operations worldwide. Problems arise when subsidiaries abroad produce more than one product line, and it is in such situations that the international division's role as coordinator becomes of paramount importance. The international division has an overlapping responsibility in that it requires each product profit center to optimize its product line operations world-wide, and simultaneously, it requires each foreign subsidiary to do its best in each country. For example, if a certain product line is doing very well on the whole, but not in Europe, then the European regional manager is likely to complain about the situation. In that case the international division could bring pressure to bear upon the product division concerned to improve its operations in Europe.

Relationships between the international division and subsidiaries abroad. Subsidiaries abroad that are uniproduct or multiproduct but are locally oriented and principally concerned with furnishing products for the local market only are controlled to a very high degree by the international division. For example, the company has a plant in Mexico that makes six or seven different product lines, each in a small quantity. Because it would be impractical to have each of the product lines independently responsive to each of the product divisions, the international division handles them. The international division tries, however, to cater to the needs of the product divisions by giving the divisions a monthly report on the operations showing costs, sales volume, and associated expenses connected with each major product line. The international division accepts the advice and criticism from the product divisions and attempts to use it.

Another approach is taken in the case of a large plant established abroad with the objective of exporting the products from it to other countries. As an example, the company has one of its largest plants in England and has organized it as a division. The head and all employees of the division are employees of the international division. The organization in this division has been established along lines that facilitate management from the product divisions centered at the headquarters in the United States. The international division is in effect saying: "Here is your plant. We have created this element of the plant for you, Mr. Product Division. We are here to do what you want!" The international division is then very responsive to the subsidiary, especially with regard to things like scheduling. In fact, the subsidiaries get their scheduling from the product divisions. The British plant is scheduled from the United States product divisions. The international officer is responsible for coordinating the activities of plants abroad that might have to be responsive to not one but maybe three or four different product divisions.

Under the new organization Ingersoll-Rand has decentralized its operations considerably. However, at the same time it has attempted to have the product divisions integrate the operations abroad and at home to a much greater degree. Although the international division has, in strict organizational terms, line authority over the subsidiaries abroad and the product divisions have functional staff authority over their particular product line operations abroad, the authority relationships are quite blurred and the international division actually plays the role of a coordinator and liaison between the various product divisions or groups and the multiproduct subsidiaries abroad.

Pattern 6

Nestlé Alimentana S.A.

Nestlé Alimentana S.A. is Switzerland's largest business enterprise and Europe's second biggest food specialist behind Unilever. The Nestlé group employs more than 90,000 people in 208 factories and has 536 sales branches and depots throughout the world. The group has factories in 39 countries and sales branches and depots in more than 51 countries. Only 3 percent of the company's sales are in Switzerland; about 47 percent are in the rest of Europe, 30 percent in North and South America, and 20 percent in the rest of the world.

Nestlé did not start out as a Swiss company; it was international from the beginning, having been founded by two Americans and a German. The two Americans were Charles Page, United States consul in Zurich, and his brother George. They started Anglo-Swiss Condensed Milk Company in 1866. The German was Henri Nestlé of Frankfurt, who had invented dried-milk baby food in Vevey, Switzerland. The two concerns merged in 1905.

Nestlé basically remained a manufacturer of the same products until 1929, when it merged with a conglomerate of three Swiss chocolate manufacturers who had merged over the previous years. In 1947 Nestlé merged with the Alimentana Company, a well-known Swiss soups and seasoning goods manufacturer whose products were sold under the Maggi brand. In 1950 Nestlé bought Lamont Corliss & Co., an American chocolate company; in 1960 it acquired Crosse and Blackwell in England; and in 1962, it acquired Findus, a Scandinavian firm in the frozen food business. In that way, over the years, Nestlé has diversified out of its traditional market of milk products and into chocolate and instant coffee, culinary products, and frozen foods.

Nestlé's management system is the ultimate in decentralization. The fabulous glass palace on Lake Geneva in Vevey, the company's nerve center, houses 1,500 people, many of them trainees.

Evolution of the organization structure. The organization structure of today, presented in Exhibit 30, was adopted some five years ago. Before that time, the company had all its subsidiaries abroad and the finance, production, and marketing departments reporting to the office of the managing director.

Today the Nestlé world is divided into four geographical zones called

Exhibit 30. Organization of Nestlé Alimentana S.A.

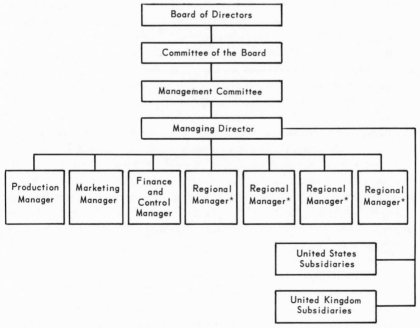

* Subsidiaries abroad report to the appropriate regional manager.

regions. Subsidiary companies report to a regional general manager. The regions are one of the two pillars of head-office organization; the second pillar is constituted by three functional divisions: production, marketing, and finance and control. The functional divisions are advisers to the regional managers as well as to the subsidiary heads. The four regional managers and three functional general managers report to the managing director. The United States and United Kingdom subsidiaries report to the managing director directly and not to a regional manager. A five-man committee, the committee of the board, consists of the chairman, two vice-chairmen, the managing director, and a fifth board member. It is responsible for the welfare of the Nestlé empire. Final decisions are made by the committee, although it is a fact that local subsidiaries abroad have considerable managerial freedom. The committee of the board meets once a month. Besides the committee, there is the management committee consisting of all the general managers and certain other top executives of the company. It also meets once a month.

Nestlé changed to a newer organization structure because of the need for better coordination and geographical inputs. The company's products have to be adapted to local tastes because tastes and consumption habits vary from one country to another. That is especially true of coffee and soups. Coordination between the far-flung producing and selling units had to be brought about at a lower level to facilitate decentralization of decision-making without loss of central policy control.

It should be mentioned that, for the 20 years before the reorganization in July 1968, the company was managed by two managing directors. The situation existed because one managing director could not effectively oversee all of the company's expanding operations. As the change-over to the geographical structure took effect, the dual command at the top was abolished, and presently the company has only one managing director.

Subsidiaries abroad are autonomously managed, although control is exercised by the regional managers. Subsidiary heads, who are usually local nationals, have discretion over their capital requirements and methods of management. Their chief contacts with headquarters are through a very elaborate budget system within which the marketing budgets play an important role, as it does in all consumer industries. The committee of the board generally has suggestions to make to the subsidiaries on their marketing budgets, but very rarely does the committee make fundamental changes in one of the budgets. With this management pattern Nestlé has been able to enjoy the mixture of local initiative with central direction.

Nestlé management does not foresee any further organizational changes in the near future. The only change that could come about—"we are thinking about it, but we do not expect to adopt it"—is the use of product divisions like Unilever. "It is too awkward to work with three pillars."

Alfa-Laval AB

Even at the beginning of this century, Alfa-Laval, based in Sweden, had a large international organization. The company manufactures three main product lines: farm machinery, separation equipment, and thermal or heat-transfer equipment. Total group sales equal $300 million, of which 85 percent is sales outside Sweden. The company has 15 factories in Sweden and 20 factories abroad in 14 countries. About 75 percent of the products produced in Sweden are exported. Foreign plants account for more than 50 percent of the company's total production volume. The bulk of the company's sales are channeled through its foreign subsidiaries; independent agents account for only 10 percent of the business. Approximately 65 percent of the 18,000 employees are employed abroad. The company does business in more than 100 countries.

Alfa-Laval sells equipment piece by piece, but it also sells complete installations (turn-key plants), complete dairies, plants for extracting protein in the fish industry and fat from what is left in slaughterhouses, and so on.

Old headquarters organization. Prior to 1965, the company's structure was horizontal. Subsidiary heads abroad reported to the company president, as presented in Exhibit 31. The main task of the three sales divisions was

Exhibit 31. Organization of Alfa-Laval AB to 1965

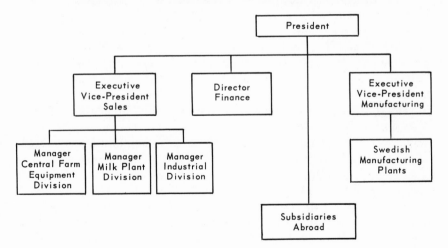

to support the sales in the subsidiaries, coordinate sales policies and product lines, produce advertising and sales promotion material, and help subsidiaries and agents with more difficult engineering problems.

The production department, headed by the executive vice-president of manufacturing, was responsible for manufacturing in Sweden. It was also responsible for coordinating the manufacturing activities in the subsidiaries abroad and advising the subsidiary heads abroad on manufacturing problems. The executive vice-president of manufacturing was also directly responsible for product development in all product areas.

The director of finance was responsible for the optimum utilization of capital resources. Subsidiaries sent all free money to the parent company, and the money was then reallocated to the subsidiaries as required. Borrowing for the whole group was coordinated by the finance director.

The president, the executive vice-presidents of manufacturing, and sales, and the financial director formed the top management of the group. In that structure there was no R&D, materials management, administration, or corporate planning on a worldwide basis. Each manufacturing unit at home and abroad did its own design and manufacture. There was no coordination among the units on a product line basis. R&D was localized in each plant. Each sales manager made sales and gave sales support to the product line to which he was assigned.

Current organization structure. The current organization structure is presented in Exhibit 32. The organization structure of the subsidiaries abroad remains the same as before, but the subsidiaries report directly to the group management of Alfa-Laval.

Three product divisions have been created at the headquarters. They have the responsibility for the development of their product line worldwide. The thermal and milk plant and separator divisions report to the president. The farm equipment division manager should report to the president, but at present he is under the direct command of the executive vice-president of marketing because of his special interest and expertise in that field.

The production manager has line authority for all domestic production operations and functional staff authority over production of subsidiaries abroad. There are four corporate vice-presidents—administration, finance, controller, and corporate planning—who have a centralizing effect and worldwide responsibilities. Regional expertise is provided by the four area supervisors reporting to the executive vice-president of marketing. The president and the two executive vice-presidents form the corporate group management that is responsible for the total company management. The corporate staff has worldwide responsibilities now. Alfa-Laval's new

Exhibit 32. Current Organization of Alfa-Laval AB

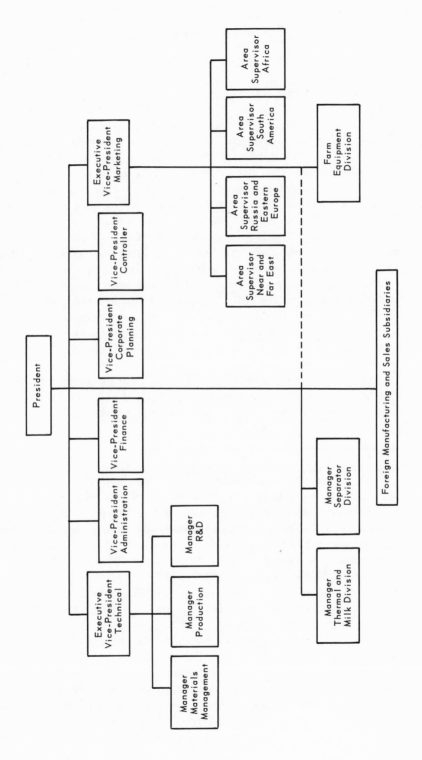

organization structure is a hybrid consisting of functional, product, and geographical inputs.

Future organizational changes expected. Changes in the company's current structure will take place in the future. There is a need for centralizing R&D and production even more than now. Presently, the subsidiaries abroad have control over their own sales and production. Neither the production manager nor the product divisions have line authority over production abroad. That has led to a suboptimization of the total group's production and sales system. Centralized production and sales for the whole group are necessary, and that might lead to functional production and sales managers at the top with worldwide responsibility for their functions.

The company intends to organize production and sales at home and abroad on a product or customer basis. If the grouping is done on a product basis, then the following groups will emerge: farm equipment, milk plants, thermal equipment, and separator group. The functional production and sales manager at the top will be responsible for the production and sales of each group on a worldwide basis. The functional managers will coordinate their functions at the top. If the grouping is done on a customer basis, then the following groups will emerge: food, chemicals, farm, milk products, marine.

The company's philosophy is to organize from the bottom up. It must first decide what kind of organization is required below and then provide for the necessary divisional and functional support at the top.

AB SKF

SKF, a Swedish-based company that has built its reputation as a manufacturer of ball bearings, is more than sixty years old. The SKF group has emerged from a factory that was built in Göteborg, Sweden, in the early 1900s. Today the company's sales amount to more than $800 million, approximately 95 percent of which are made outside the domestic market. The company has about 64,000 employees, only 20 percent of whom are employed in Sweden.

During the last 15 years the company's sales and the number of subsidiaries abroad have doubled. That alone had a lot to do with the company's decision to reorganize in 1965–66.

Evolution of the organization structure. The organization structure of the company until 1965 is given in Exhibit 33. The president, to that time, was responsible for the day-to-day operations of the manufacturing unit at home as well as for the long-range planning of the whole group, and he was extremely overburdened. There were also certain functions such as public relations, engineering and research, personnel and organization,

Exhibit 33. Organization of AB SKF to 1965

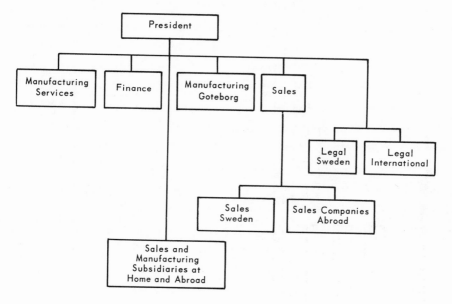

and marketing planning that were not performed effectively for the SKF group as a whole. Organizational changes were made to relieve the president of the day-to-day responsibilities of managing the domestic operations and to provide more effective functional services in areas just mentioned.

The current organization chart is given in Exhibit 34. The domestic operations have now been put on an equal basis with the operations abroad. Now each of the manufacturing subsidiaries at home and abroad is a profit center. There are now two product divisions as well: a steel division that is vertically integrated all the way from mining extraction to steel safes and the machine tool business. The product divisions and 18 manufacturing subsidiaries report directly to top management. The manufacturing subsidiaries operate in a very decentralized manner provided they operate within the corporate plans and policies formulated by top management. The various functional heads at the headquarters serve to coordinate their respective functional policies in the various subsidiaries abroad, which, before the reorganization, operated very much as autonomous units. The functional officers at the top thus have a centralizing effect on the overall operations of the SKF group. Top management is now mainly concerned with corporate planning and policy making in the various functional areas for the whole SKF group, and authority for day-to-day operations is delegated to the subsidiary heads.

Exhibit 34. Current Organization of AB SKF

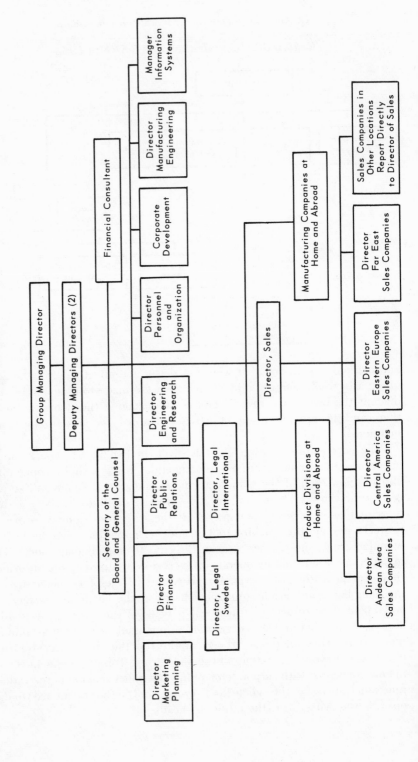

Any further reorganization that might take place would most likely be on a regional basis, possibly along the lines of the sales organization.

The East Asiatic Company Ltd.

The East Asiatic Company, based in Denmark, was established in March 1897. In its articles of association, its objectives were stated as being "to carry out trade, shipping and industry at home and abroad." The primary aim of the company, when it was founded, was to establish regular shipping connections between Denmark and the Far East. To meet that objective, the firm of Anderson and Company, which had started trading in Thailand 13 years earlier, was acquired. From the very beginning the company's strategy has been geared to the development of three interdependent and interrelated fields: shipping, trade, and industry.

During some periods of the company's history, it might have been more profitable to focus attention on the development of not all three but only one or two fields. In terms of the long-range growth of the company, however, it seems that the original strategy to develop all three fields has proved to be a sound one. At present, the East Asiatic Company is a multi-dimensional and diversified company that is equally well established in shipping, trade, and industry.

The growth and development of the company took place in three phases. The first, from the start of the company until World War I, was a period during which the company pursued its fundamental policy and strategy. The second, which covered the period between the two world wars, was one that saw rapid expansion of the company abroad. The expansion was centered in and around the countries of East Asia. During the third phase, which started after World War II and is still continuing, the company has grown in all respects—shipping, trade, and industry. The most significant growth has been in the industrial field not only in Asia but in all five of the continents.

At the founding of the company, three 6,000-ton steamships were ordered and put into commission on a regular route to the Far East. The fleet was soon increased with the development of, and to a great extent, supported by the substitution of, diesel power for steam in shipping. At present the company has a fleet of more than thirty-five dry-cargo motor-vessels and three tankers totaling more than 400,000 tons deadweight. Furthermore, the company and British Petroleum are joint owners of the I/S Nordic Tankships (partnership) with two turbine tankers totaling 71,260 tons deadweight. The company has been entrusted with the daily operations of those ships. It has also acquired an interest in a Danish tramp shipping company and has a 50 percent interest in 22 ships under the British flag.

The East Asiatic Company's worldwide industry activities started in a small way in Thailand and neighboring countries served by the company's ships. The company's trade soon extended to European countries. Timber, rice, spices, and other tropical products were shipped to the West, and Danish and other European consumer goods and industrial articles were shipped to the markets in the East. After World War II, many of the consumer goods and raw materials that formerly constituted the main exports yielded to proprietary articles and the products of more advanced industry, for example, machinery for rice and oil mills, diesel engines, automobiles and automobile accessories, printing machines, and Danish agricultural products and canned foods.

With the acquisition of Anderson and Company's business in Thailand, the company became interested in industry through operation of a sawmill, and interest in industrial activities has been pursued and expanded since. Presently the company has food-processing plants, coffee mills, flour mills, milk factories, pulp and sawmills, molding and plywood factories, plants for the manufacture of diesel engines, compressors, and ball bearings, shipyards, pharmaceuticals factories, coffee, rubber, and palm oil plantations, and textile and vegetable oil factories located in more than eighteen countries spread across all five continents.

Current organization structure. The head office in Copenhagen is the center of the company's organization, where all the threads are tied together. Administratively the company's activities are grouped into four line departments: shipping, trading, industrial, and timber. The company does not have an organization chart as such—top company executives said that the organization structure is too complicated to formulate— but an approximation is presented in Exhibit 35. Except for the industrial department, which was added in 1961 as a separate department, the organization structure presently in use is one that has existed ever since the inception of the company.

Some observations about the company's organization. The company is very much decentralized. The subsidiaries abroad report not to any one person at the head office, but really to the several managing directors shown in the chart. There is a lot of contact between the head office and subsidiaries abroad. The subsidiary managers have considerable authority over the subsidiaries abroad, but the subsidiary heads report in a line-authority relationship to the board of four managing directors at the top.

The company runs the various subsidiaries like a loose federation. The heads of subsidiaries abroad are Danes trained at the head office. They run their own ship while taking into account the company's overall policies and goals. There is no formalized comprehensive planning process or one corporate plan as such. Yet, the company as a whole does move in

Exhibit 35. Organization of The East Asiatic Company Ltd.

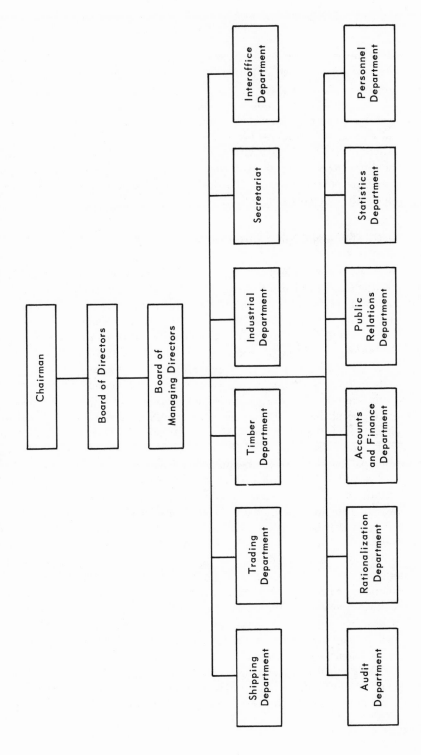

some unwritten but firm direction. A sort of information control through close personal contact is maintained by the head office over the subsidiaries abroad.

The company does not expect any organizational changes in the future. The current organization has evolved over the years and, as was pointed out earlier, the structure has not been formalized into an official organization chart. Working relationships between the various organizational members have evolved over time, and they are known to the various individuals in the company. The lack or absence of a chart does not seem to hinder the company's operations.

Swiss Aluminium Ltd. (Alusuisse)

Swiss Aluminium Ltd., formerly Aluminium-Industrie-Aktien-Gesellschaft, was founded on November 12, 1888, for the purpose of the industrial exploitation of the electrolytic production of aluminum. One year earlier at Neuhausen, the French inventor Heroult had successfully demonstrated the prototype of the electrolytic furnace that was to become the foundation of the first European aluminum reduction plant.

Swiss Aluminium Ltd. is a geographically widespread, vertically integrated organization embracing all aspects of the manufacturing processes of the aluminum industry. It is one of the most important light-metal producers of the world. The company has 38 wholly or partly owned principal manufacturing subsidiaries or affiliates in 17 countries excluding Switzerland. In Switzerland the company has 13 wholly or partly owned principal manufacturing subsidiaries or affiliates.

Current organizational relationships. Swiss Aluminium's plants and subsidiaries abroad and in Switzerland are controlled and directed from the headquarters in Zurich, where departments for each company activity and specialist and advisory groups are centered. The various activities of the company are research, bauxite, alumina, electric power, electrodes, virgin aluminum, semifinished products, foil, finished products, and plastics. The prime function of management is that of planning. The growth of the company with its numerous production plants and fabricating units requires long-term planning with regard to raw material supplies, provision of new energy sources, market analysis, profitability studies, the development of sites, the selection of capable personnel to manage departments and divisions, and the allocation of investment capital.

The company operates under the philosophy of giving maximum freedom to the subsidiaries in running their own affairs as long as they present reasonable profits to the parent company consistently. The current organization structure has existed for the last 75 years. There are twelve corporate vice-presidents who have functional authority over the subsidiaries at home and abroad. The subsidiary heads report to the group management called the board of management, which consists of the president and two general managers. The span of management of the group management is considerably wide, and this again forces decentralization of authority. The subsidiaries make their own policies regarding sales, advertising, new products, etc., as long as the products are in the aluminum field. Finance is centralized at the top, and new investment decisions are made at the top. Top management controls the subsidiaries by getting from them monthly balance sheets.

The company does not expect to have any drastic reorganization of its structure. If it grows further, it may group its subsidiaries abroad on a regional basis.

Pattern 7

Imperial Chemical Industries Ltd.

Imperial Chemical Industries, based in the United Kingdom, was formed in 1926 as a result of a merger of four leading British chemical concerns: Nobel Industries Ltd., British Dyestuffs Corporation, United Alkali Company, and Brunner Mond & Company. The four companies decided to merge to pool their resources in order to combat foreign competition that was threatening to drive British chemical manufacturers out of world markets. Foreign competition came primarily from I. G. Farben of Germany and the large-scale chemical organizations that had begun to grow in the United States.

Since 1926, the company has grown enormously to be the largest chemical company in Europe and the second largest chemical company in the world. It sells annually over $2,500 million worth of chemicals, fibers, plastics, paints, dyestuffs, pharmaceuticals, fertilizers, and crop protection products. More than half of the sales are made outside Britain from British exports and overseas manufacturing. ICI has manufacturing subsidiaries and affiliates in approximately 14 countries, and ICI selling companies or agents are located in nearly every country. A subsidiary company is one in which ICI owns more than half the equity capital. The term "associate" is used to describe a company in which ICI owns a significant part of the equity but not more than half. ICI has more than 325 subsidiary companies at home and abroad.

The ICI organization. The main ICI units in the United Kingdom are the eight manufacturing divisions: (1) agricultural, (2) dyestuffs, (3) heavy organic chemicals, (4) Mond division, (5) Nobel division, (6) paints, (7) pharmaceuticals, (8) plastics and ICI Fibres Ltd., the subsidiary company responsible for ICI's interest in the manufacture of man-made fiber. Another important unit is Imperial Metal Industries Ltd., a subsidiary company concerned with the manufacture of nonferrous metal and allied products, part of the capital of which is publicly owned.

Whenever practicable, subsidiary companies in the United Kingdom are grouped under whichever division is appropriate from the point of view of the products made. Similarly, the appropriate divisions look after ICI's interest in most associate companies in the United Kingdom.

The current ICI organization structure, presented in Exhibit 36, is as follows: The board of directors consists of 19 directors, of which 13 are executive directors and 6 are nonexecutive directors. The executive directors are full-time working directors who have generally spent all or most of their lives working for ICI. The 13 executive directors consist of the chairman, 3 deputy chairmen, and 9 other executive directors. The chairman and deputy chairmen devote a great part of their time to supervising the broad field of the company activities at home and abroad. Each of the 9 other executive directors has a number of more specific responsibilities.

The general direction and performance of the United Kingdom manu-

Exhibit 36. Organization of Imperial Chemical Industries Ltd.

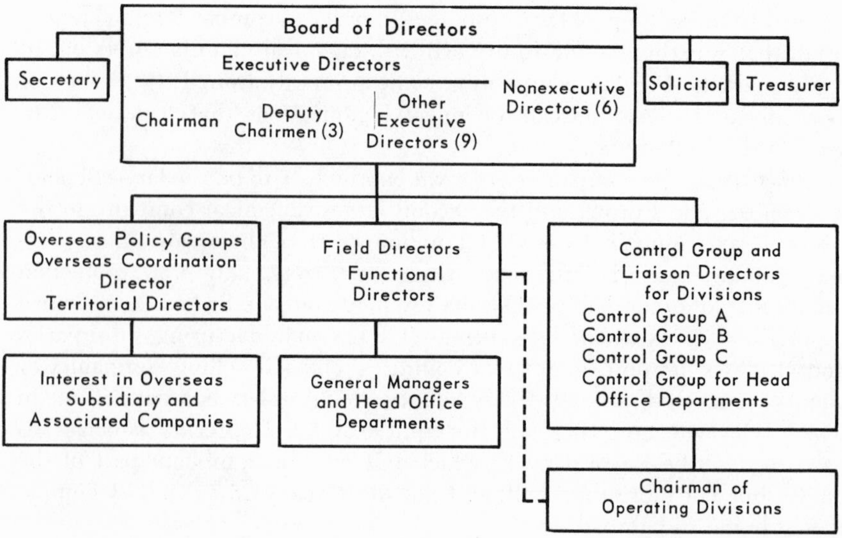

facturing divisions and the head-office departments are monitored by four control groups. Each control group has four members, all of whom are executive directors of the company. The chairman of each control group is a deputy chairman of the company. Each of the directors who serves on a control group is also the liaison director for a division. The division chairman runs his division within clearly defined responsibilities. He is left on his own and is held responsible for the profitable operations of his business. The control exercised by the control group is not a day-to-day control. The division runs its day-to-day business, but if it wants advice, the divisional chairman can get it from the liaison director, who keeps in constant contact with the division. The control group is really a subcommittee of the board of ICI, which meets with the divisions twice a year to discuss the divisional targets, performance, future plans, capital investments, and any other problems.

Seven executive directors, designated as territorial directors, are given the responsibility for looking after ICI's interests in particular overseas territories. One of them has the additional responsibility for coordinating overseas policy as a whole. Together with the other executive directors they serve on one or more of the eight overseas policy groups; four of them are presided over by a deputy chairman. On the whole, the overseas policy groups play a part that is similar to that of the control groups for the U.K. divisions; they cover the areas of the globe in which ICI has major manufacturing interests. Once a year the chairman of each major company overseas appears before his policy group and discusses all major aspects of his company's affairs as well as capital programs above certain limits of expenditure. The function of these policy groups is to supervise ICI's interests in and give policy guidance to the principal overseas companies in which ICI is a shareholder.

Apart from the big companies, there are a large number of small- and medium-size ICI companies abroad. The responsibility for monitoring and advising such companies falls upon the general manager, overseas, who reports to the overseas coordination director. The coordination director is asked to resolve any disagreements between companies that may arise. There are also eight directorships for functions that require central control or need coordinating throughout the company. In addition, there are three field directorships.

Executive directors in ICI wear several hats at the same time. For example, one deputy chairman is the chairman of an overseas policy group, a field director, and chairman of a control group. Another executive director is a territorial director, overseas coordination director, member of an overseas policy group, member of a control group, and liaison director for a division. Under this arrangement, each executive director is involved in the direction of the company's business, at the top management level, over a wide range of activities.

Evolution of current organization structure. ICI's business has evolved over the years; it has not progressed through a series of violent changes. Consequently, the company's organization structure did not undergo any drastic changes either, except for the minor modifications that always take place in a growing company. The major change that can be readily identified took place in 1966, when ICI created the overseas policy groups and territorial directors (discussed earlier). Until 1966, ICI had the functional directors, field directors, and control groups and liaison directors for the U.K. divisions, but there was no committee form of organization similar to the control groups to coordinate and oversee the activities of the numerous subsidiaries and affiliates abroad. All the subsidiaries and affiliates in Western Europe, except when ICI's interests were assigned to a U.K. division, reported to the chairman of the European council (created in 1960 following the emergence of the European Common Market). Subsidiaries in other parts of the world, again excepting the cases in which ICI's interests were assigned to a U.K. division, reported to the overseas controller. The European council was formed to make a detailed study of the desirability of large-scale manufacture in the Common Market and to coordinate ICI's activities in Western Europe. The council could not fulfill its promise because it encountered difficulty in pressing the European case, owing to the problems it faced in reconciling its views with those of the U.K. divisions traditionally responsible for their own exports. ICI (Europa) Ltd. replaced the European council in 1965. It is a new company responsible, jointly with the U.K. divisions concerned and with ICI Fibres Ltd., for planning the development as a whole for ICI's interests, other than metal interests, in Western Europe. Whereas the European council was advisory in nature, ICI (Europa) has executive authority over almost all of ICI's interests in Western Europe. The overseas controller and ICI (Europa) report to two functional executive directors.

Top management of ICI believed that the structure as described here did not give enough independence to the overseas subsidiaries and affiliates. Top management also felt the need for greater clarity in functional, product, and regional decision making and for improved methods of dealing with the large number of subsidiaries and affiliates abroad. From that need a new structure that is the one in use today was adopted in 1966. Under the new structure ICI (Europa) and all other major ICI subsidiaries, such as ICI America Inc., ICI (India) Private Ltd., and ICI of Australia and New Zealand Ltd., report to the appropriate overseas policy group. Details of the current structure have already been presented in this study.

ICI presently does not have product coordination worldwide in the totality. It has degrees of it and is moving toward more formalized product coordination in certain product lines, such as polyethylene, that will allow the global approach to be exercised. The precise form that will take has not yet been evolved. The organizational philosophy of ICI is to decentralize executive authority to the divisions in the United Kingdom and the subsidiaries abroad but to keep centralized the formulation of overall company policies and finance.

A Diversified Swiss Chemicals and Pharmaceuticals Company

The company was founded more than a hundred years ago. Since then it has progressed from trading in chemicals, dyes, and drugs via the manual processing of dyewoods to the large-scale production of natural and synthetic dyestuffs. The company's products were being sold in the industrialized countries of Europe as well as in Russia, the United States, Japan, India, China, the Philippines, and Indonesia, as early as the 1860s.

The company's first expansion abroad was in the late nineteenth century, when it established a small factory for the extraction of dyes in Russia, the first Swiss factory in Russia. World War I and the Russian Revolution put an end to that promising business venture.

The company's next attempt at expansion abroad was 10 years later, when it built a factory in Germany. Since then, production and sales centers have been established in several countries; today the company has more than 20 major works in 12 different countries. Moreover, during the last 30 years the company has progressed from what was largely a family enterprise producing dyes and textile chemicals into a worldwide organization with more than 12,000 shareholders. Today the company is engaged in the production and marketing worldwide of dyestuffs, industrial chemicals, pharmaceuticals, agricultural products, and consumer products. The company's domestic sales turnover is something over 50 million Swiss francs, whereas the worldwide turnover is much larger—over 2,300 million Swiss francs.

Evolution of the current organization structure. Until the end of 1967, the company was functionally organized. (See Exhibit 37.) The president and chairman of the executive committee was a man who, since 1939, had been guiding the destinies of the company and who was chiefly responsible for company growth and diversification. The organization consisted of four sales departments. Each was responsible for the sales of one of the four product groups, which then were dyes and textile chemicals, pharmaceuticals, industrial chemicals, and agricultural chemicals. Research was organized around product groups; consequently, there were four research departments. The production, legal, finance, and personnel departments

Exhibit 37. Organization of a Diversified Swiss Chemicals and Pharmaceuticals Company (to 1967)

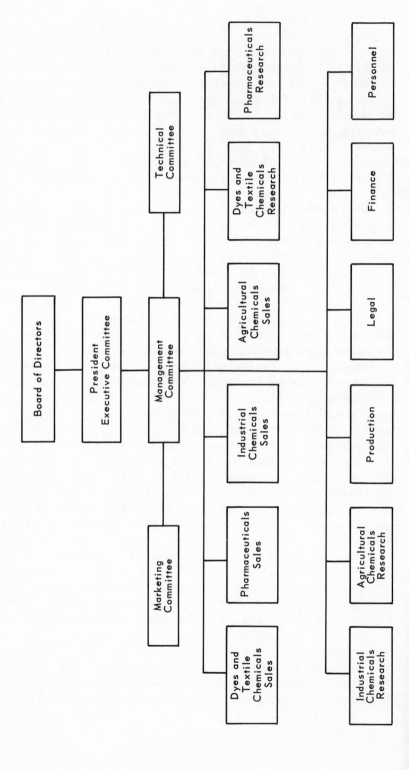

completed the departmentalization at the primary level. The company was managed by committees. Reporting to the executive board of directors was a seven-man executive committee consisting of senior officers of the company that met once a week and was responsible for formulating the company policies. Reporting to the executive committee was a management committee. The heads of the various functional departments formed the management committee. The management committee and its two subcommittees—the technical committee and marketing committee—were responsible for the actual execution of company policies. Subsidiaries abroad and at home reported directly to the management committee. The old structure had been able to manage the company's geographically far-flung operations because of the intimate regional knowledge of the company's president and the few senior officers.

Changes that took place in 1964 and 1965 triggered the reorganization of the company. In 1964, three members of the executive committee retired and were replaced by three members of the management committee, who belonged to the next generation. In 1965 the president appointed a younger man in his place as chairman of the executive committee. The new members of the executive committee asked the whole group to do a five- to ten-year projection of the probable development of the company's business. The study revealed that the organization in use since World War II was no longer adequate for the achievement of the aims of the company. That finding was not much of a surprise, since the functional structure was adopted at a time when the company was engaged primarily in the dye-stuffs business and had a large organization to handle the exports. It was obviously not suitable for a company that now was considerably diversified, whose sales had quadrupled over the last ten years, and that had worldwide sales, production, and research commitments. The company's products are sold in more than 150 countries. The economic, political, climatic, and other conditions in those markets varied considerably at times. The organization required both product and environmental inputs.

Purely product line or wholly regional structures were considered unsuitable. The company needed a structure that could identify individual spheres of product responsibility clearly, coordinate the far-flung production and marketing centers more effectively, and provide specialized as well as technical services to the entire group. To meet all those needs the company has now adopted a hybrid structure, presented in Exhibit 38, that has in it elements of product line, regional, and functional departmentalization.

Current organization structure. The new organization is headed by an executive committee. Members of the executive committee include the committee chairman and heads of the product and functional groups.

Some members of the executive committee are responsible for a product division and a function. Reporting to the executive committee are five product (business) divisions grouped on the basis of the type of product, five regional groups, and six functions.

The company's activities are divided into five "businesses": dyestuffs, industrial chemicals, pharmaceuticals, agricultural chemicals, and consumer products. Each product division is headed by a managing director who is fully responsible for research, business development, marketing, logistics, and planning for the results achieved by his business throughout the world. A product division is responsible for every important stage in the progress of a new product from research to point of sale with one exception: production. That belongs to the production department, which is a functional department but has line responsibility for manufacturing worldwide as well as for worldwide purchasing, engineering, chemical process development, and manufacturing planning. The link between the product division and production department is provided by the logistics department within each product division. The production department is also responsible for three "local" factories: two in Switzerland and one in Germany.

Exhibit 38. Current Organization of a Diversified Swiss Chemicals and Pharmaceuticals Company

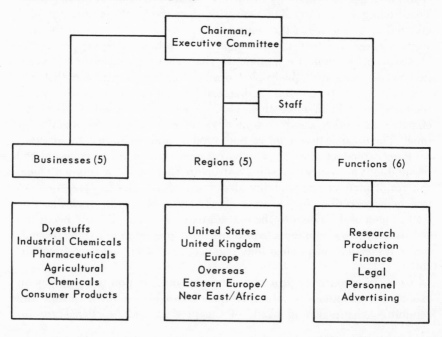

Chairman, Executive Committee

Staff

Businesses (5)

Regions (5)

Functions (6)

| Dyestuffs Industrial Chemicals Pharmaceuticals Agricultural Chemicals Consumer Products | United States United Kingdom Europe Overseas Eastern Europe/ Near East/Africa | Research Production Finance Legal Personnel Advertising |

There are six functions, namely, research, production, finance, legal, personnel, and advertising. Functional heads have specialized authority for the global coordination of their function. As was mentioned earlier, the production department has line authority and responsibility for worldwide production and related activities. The other five functions, however, have a functional authority relationship with the product divisions. Coordination between the product divisions and the functional departments is made easier because at times a product division and a functional department are headed by the same person. For example, the industrial chemicals division and production department are in the charge of one officer. Similarly, the pharmaceuticals division, the consumer products division, and the advertising department are all under another officer. The agricultural chemicals division and finance department are under a third officer.

The cornerstone of all these operations is research, which is an integral part of each product division (to keep it directly oriented to the needs of the market) but which also belongs to the central research function, which keeps a strict eye on all aspects of the company's research activities in all parts of the world. The central research department has within it two major subsidiary departments: basic research and central research. The activities of the basic research department are related to what is being done in the different product divisions or to areas that are entirely new fields to the company. Central research coordinates, plans, and provides services for research within the product divisions.

The geographical aspects of the company's activities are covered by five regional groupings: United States, United Kingdom, Europe, overseas, and Near East, Eastern Europe, and Africa. The regional managements are responsible for the development and growth of their own regions and companies within their regions. At present, strong managerial authority rests within product divisional hands. The regional head coordinates the plans of the five product divisions insofar as they affect his region. His job is to examine the financial feasibility of the divisional plans. He is a god-father to the subsidiaries within his region, whose viewpoints he presents to the executive committee. This indicates that, although the product divisional managements are responsible for planning on a global scale, the determination of the financial feasibility of the product divisional plans is in the hands of the regional heads. There is dual or multiple reporting at the subsidiary level abroad. Each subsidiary head reports to his regional head in line capacity as well as to the appropriate product division head in functional staff capacity. Most subsidiaries are multiproduct units, so they report to the appropriate regional head and product division heads. The regional heads form an important link between the executive committee and the subsidiaries abroad.

The regional heads are accountable for overall net profit and performance of subsidiaries within their regions. At the same time, the product divisions are responsible for profits of their respective product lines worldwide. The interdependence accounts for the close liaison necessary between the product divisions and the regional managements. Regional managements are also responsible for such activities as organization of subsidiaries, relations with governments, financial matters such as borrowings of subsidiaries, parent-subsidiary financial transactions, review of investment proposals for the region, and feeding information to the headquarters about regional characteristics.

Subsidiary heads abroad report directly to regional heads, who have the authority to hire or fire the subsidiary heads. Product managers within a subsidiary report directly to the appropriate product division head, and the product division head's approval is necessary to implement changes in product line or marketing techniques. The regional head is kept informed of any changes made.

The company has stationed the product, regional, and functional heads at the headquarters in Switzerland in order to facilitate the close coordination required between them, especially between the product and regional heads. The regional heads keep the product division heads informed about the status of their products within the regions, and any problems that occur are solved through mutual consultations. Coordination between the product, functional, and regional managements is brought about generally through informal contacts.

In the future, the company might bring about changes in the relationship between the regions and product divisions. Greater authority may be given to the regional heads than is given now. Production might be integrated within divisions; there is a separate production department. Another change that could take place is the grouping of the Swiss operations into a Swiss region. At this time, the Swiss operations are under the production department.

Pattern 8

Unilever

The name Unilever was adopted in 1929 when Lever Brothers merged with Margarine Union. To understand the Unilever of today, one must first examine the history of the company.

Unilever has business interests in over 60 countries in Europe, North and South America, the Middle East, Asia, Australia, and the Far East. It has two parent companies, Unilever N.V. in Rotterdam and Unilever Ltd. in London. The two companies have identical boards of directors, but each has its own stockholders. This is in accord with the equalization agreement between the two companies that has existed since 1929, when the two merged. The agreement provides for the payment of equivalent ordinary dividends to the stockholders of the two companies. For all practical purposes, the two companies act as one company—Unilever.

Unilever is engaged in the following businesses: margarine and other edible fats, other foods, toilet preparations, washing products, oil milling and animal foodstuffs, chemicals, African enterprises, and tropical plantations.

When Unilever was formed in 1929, Margarine Union was a group of companies based in the Netherlands. Its main interests were margarine and other edible fats, oil milling and animal foodstuffs, and ship companies. On its side, Lever Brothers Ltd. controlled companies throughout the world, especially in Europe, the United States, and the British colonies. Its main interests were soap, food, oil milling and animal foodstuffs, African plantations, and trading.

History of the events leading to the great merger.[1] Lever Brothers was founded in 1885 by W. H. Lever, later to become Lord Leverhulme. The firm began manufacturing and selling Sunlight soap in tablet form instead of a long bar. The new size and shape of soap proved to be very popular, and as a result the firm grew and expanded its operations to the Continent and other parts of the world. The British government asked Lever to enter the margarine industry during World War I to prevent the dependence of Britain upon foreign sources for its supply of edible fats. Lever sunk large amounts of capital into the new venture, and when the war ended, it stayed in the margarine business.

Margarine, a new kind of artificial butter, had been invented in 1869 by the French chemist Mége-Mouriés. By 1872 the rising standards of living throughout Europe had carried the demand for butter beyond the capacity of the contemporary sources of supply. Two of the biggest firms in Europe engaged in the butter trade were Van den Berghs and Jurgens, both domiciled in the Netherlands. In order to meet the increasing but unmet demand for butter, Van den Berghs and Jurgens purchased the rights for the production of margarine. They expanded their operations in the Continent, the British Isles, and in other parts of the world, and competition between them became quite intense. Both companies also diversified into soap manufacture, because the oils and fats that are the raw materials for making margarine are also the raw materials for making soap.

The three firms, Lever, Van den Berghs, and Jurgens, were forming new companies or acquiring existing ones, and in the process they were getting involved in new activities that could be conveniently carried on simultaneously with the manufacture of soap and margarine. Both soap and margarine can be manufactured on a large scale, and all three firms began to manufacture them in large quantities to meet the increasing demand. They also found themselves competing with each other for the raw materials.

The stage was now set for the eventual merger of the three firms into one company. The first step in the merger process was taken, in 1927, when Van den Berghs and Jurgens merged and formed the Margarine Union in England and the Margarine Unie in Holland. Two other firms—Hartogs, makers of margarine and active in the Netherlands, and Schichts, makers of margarine and soap who were active in central and eastern Europe from a seat in Czechoslovakia—merged with the newly formed Margarine Union and Margarine Unie.

Competition for the basic raw materials forced the two giants, Lever Brothers and Margarine Union, to merge in 1929. From the merger came two separate companies: Unilever Ltd. in England and Unilever N.V. in the Netherlands. Unilever N.V. took over Margarine Unie, and Unilever Ltd. took over Margarine Union and the ordinary shares of Lever Brothers. Two holding companies were formed: Unilever Ltd. with headquarters in London and Unilever N.V. with headquarters in Rotterdam.

Evolution of the Unilever organization.[2] From the very beginning Unilever has had two parent companies—Unilever Ltd. and Unilever N.V.—with identical boards of directors and constitutions. The directors delegated to a special committee, appointed by them, all powers of the Unilever board except those of great importance such as the power to declare a dividend and issue new capital. The Unilever board consisted of a maximum of 25 directors, each holding a managerial post in the company. The special committee included the chairman of Unilever Ltd., the chairman of Unilever N.V., and a vice-chairman of Unilever Ltd., and it was responsible for the conduct of the daily business of the company. The board never made any decisions without the participation of the special committee. The organization structure of Unilever in 1949 is presented in Exhibit 39.

The 1949 organization structure. The four management groups responsible for the conduct of business in The United Africa Company Ltd., the United Kingdom, continental Europe, and overseas (countries outside Europe) included some board members and representatives from the general management team. The advisory and service departments furnished advice and service to the central policy makers at the top and to the regional factory managements abroad.

Unilever faced a problem shared by many other large and geographi-

Exhibit 39. Organization of Unilever to 1949

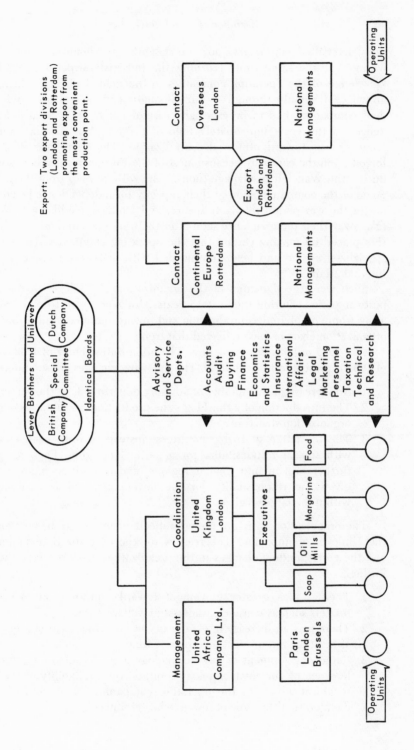

cally diversified companies: how much authority should be centralized without, at the same time, crushing the initiative, expertise, and local knowledge of the operating companies in the field. Unilever, which had grown centripetally through the amalgamation of several once-independent companies, had to be especially careful not to stifle local independence. In the years immediately following World War II, the trend in Unilever was toward utmost decentralization. The trend was in a way forced upon the company because most of the European subsidiaries were, during the War, left to manage their affairs with no help from the center. Some of the companies showed their capacity for independence by coming out of the war period relatively secure, and Unilever could not very well take away their independence soon after the war. The emphasis was therefore placed on making certain that the operating companies received the specialized advice and help they needed with little interference in their internal affairs.

Such were the dynamics of the organization of Unilever in the early postwar period. During the next 15 years, Unilever began to make moves away from complete decentralization and toward more centralization. The organization chart of 1965 reflected that trend.

The 1965 organization structure. The organization chart of Unilever as of 1965 is presented in Exhibit 40. The following changes are soon noted:

1. An increase in the number of advisory departments at the center.
2. The introduction of a third leg—the production coordinators—in the organization structure.
3. The formation of five committees, instead of four, each charged with special responsibility for a particular region. Each region is further broken into smaller regions, and committee members are given the responsibility for the development of the subregions within the larger region.

The organization structure merely reflected the recentralizing trend in the Unilever organization. The reasons for the centralization tendencies and the corresponding changes in the organization structure were the following:

1. There was a greater movement toward uniformity in personnel matters such as pensions, wages, and welfare services.
2. There was an increase in complexity of laws and fiscal matters such as taxation and international flow of funds.
3. Rapid development of new technology and the equally rapid obsolescence of current technology required the availability of the best technical advice to the operating companies. Economies of scale dictated that this type of resource be centralized.

Exhibit 40. Organization of Unilever to 1965

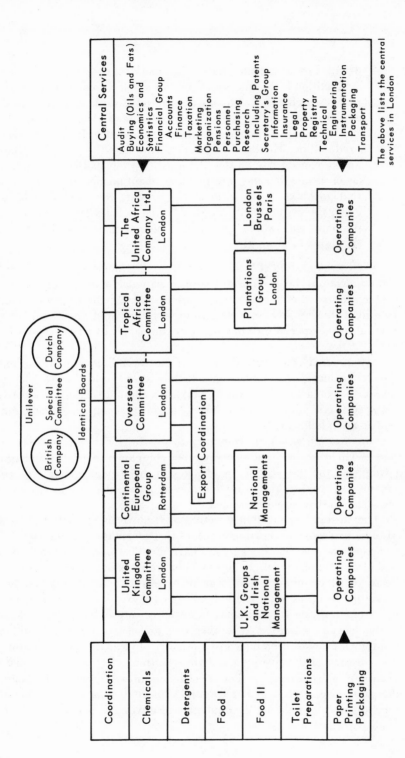

4. There was a growing battle for markets and, especially, severe competition from American companies that introduced the results of new research and technology deep into the world markets with drive and efficiency and capitalized on a few brand names. Unilever faced the American challenge by taking an analytical look at its existing product line. The basic idea was to eliminate the marginal products and to concentrate on the high-quality products that showed promise of success. The organizational mechanism created to help achieve that goal was in the form of the product coordinators, who were given the responsibility for developing policies and creative action programs that would expand the sales of their groups of products throughout the world.

The reorganization at Unilever was basically undertaken to improve the communications between the far-flung national managements and the center. Improved communications were essential if Unilever was to eliminate inefficiencies and cope effectively with the rising tide of competition from abroad, especially from American companies like Procter and Gamble.

The product coordinators represent the formalization of the "contact director" concept that existed immediately after World War II. The function of the contact director was to establish a communications link between the special committee and the several operating companies that required rejuvenation following the war.

Organization structure from 1967 to present.[3] The organization structure of Unilever, like that of many other companies, has been undergoing changes all the time; all of the changes in the structure after 1965 could not be discussed in this study. In the following paragraphs the current organization structure is examined.

The current organization structure of Unilever is presented in Exhibit 41. The two separate parent companies that make up Unilever, the British company and the Dutch company, have identical boards of directors that consist of 24 members each, all of whom are working members. Because a board of 24 members is too large to be effective in making day-to-day operating decisions, most of the board powers except those for making the most important decisions, mainly financial in nature, have been delegated to the special committee. It is, then, the job of the special committee to run the vast Unilever empire. For a number of years the special committee has consisted of the chairman and vice-chairman of Unilever Ltd. and the chairman of Unilever N.V. The special committee reports to the board of directors once a week. It is responsible for conferring with the board of directors and formulating the strategic objectives and policies for the total Unilever organization.

Exhibit 41. Current Organization of Unilever

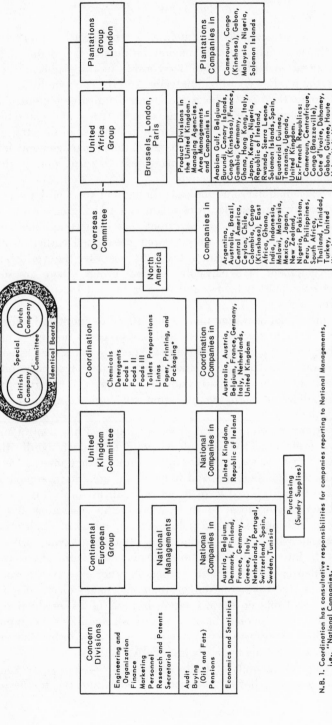

N.B. 1. Coordination has consultative responsibilities for companies reporting to National Managements, i.e., "National Companies."

2. United Kingdom Committee and National Managements in Austria, Belgium, France, Germany, Italy and Netherlands, and Australia have consultative responsibilities for those companies in their countries which are grouped under Coordination, i.e., "Coordination Companies."

* Paper, printing, and packaging has consultative responsibilities only.

With the strategic plans formulated by the special committee as guide-posts, the next managerial tier below formulates the medium- and short-range operational plans. This tier consists of three pillars: the regional groups, the product coordination teams, and the concern divisions.

The operations of Unilever are grouped into five regions: continental Europe; United Kingdom, overseas, united Africa, and plantations. Each region is in the charge of a management committee of directors and senior managers. Within the groups there are national managements for individual countries. Each national management in turn controls the various operating companies in the country.

Unilever manufactures and sells throughout the world a great number of products that are similar. A company can gain a great deal by standardizing its major products to the extent that local conditions permit such uniformity. For that and other reasons mentioned earlier, Unilever has appointed product coordination teams to look after the worldwide growth and development of a particular product group. There are seven such product coordination teams, and each is headed by a director or senior manager.

An individual operating unit cannot afford to maintain for itself experts in every field to furnish advice and assistance as needed. Unilever has therefore created a centralized core of experts in fields such as engineering and organization, finance, marketing, personnel, research and patents, insurance, taxation, transport, and information. The experts provide specialized advice to both the operating companies and the headquarters management.

The trend is certainly away from geographical line control and toward product group executive control. At present, product coordination teams have executive line responsibility in the United Kingdom, the Netherlands, Germany, France, Belgium, and Italy. The United States companies would also have been included were it not for antitrust problems. Coordinators have been placing most of their attention on marketing and research, global advertising and brand policies, and removal of duplication. Those are areas in which Unilever can bring about real savings without going against the interests of national managements and national governments.

As a matter of fact, if tariff barriers in other parts of the world fall, as they have in the Common Market, then one could expect a major effort on the part of Unilever toward rationalization of its production facilities within the new economic blocs. Under those conditions the importance of the product coordination teams would increase considerably and more countries would come under their executive authority.

The operating units of Unilever are still enjoying a great amount of freedom and are allowed to run their ship within the framework of the policies formulated by Unilever's board and the special committee. There is a policy of least interference in the affairs of the operating companies, and it is followed quite faithfully. Controls over the operating companies do exist in the form of (1) an annual operating plan of each unit, (2) capital expenditure control, and (3) selection and pay of top management of the operating unit. The controls are applied by the board through the special committee.

Royal Dutch/Shell

History up to 1907 merger. The two parent companies, The "Shell" Transport and Trading Company Limited and the Royal Dutch Petroleum Company, began as rival organizations toward the end of the last century. The oil industry was then about 30 years old; oil was discovered in Pennsylvania in 1859. Standard Oil was the leading and sole distributor of American oil on the world markets. American exports to Europe rose from 2 million gallons in 1863 to 700 million by 1890, but America had lost her monopoly by 1890. Russian oil from the Baku oil fields appeared in European markets by rail from Baku to Batum in 1883. By 1888, Russian oil was competing with Standard Oil in the Far Eastern markets. On all markets, kerosene was by far the most important product. Gasoline was burnt off as waste. That was the situation when Shell appeared on the scene.

Shell and Royal Dutch had independent beginnings. Shell had its origins in a small shop in the east end of London that was started in 1833 by Marcus Samuel, a dealer in antiques, curios, and shells. The trade in shells became so profitable that Samuel began to import shells in large quantities from the Far East, and from that he grew into a successful import and export business. In 1878 his son, also Marcus Samuel, took over the business and soon after handled a few consignments of cased kerosene as a sideline to his general business.

Samuel realized the economies and scope of bulk transport of kerosene during one of his visits to the East when, in 1890, he saw the first tankers, which were being operated in the Black Sea by the Nobel brothers. Samuel conceived his bold scheme for shipping Russian kerosene in tankers to the Eastern markets. He bought eight tankers, the first of which made her maiden voyage in 1892. He also established bulk storage facilities for oil at ports in the Far East. He contracted with a Russian group of producers and refiners, controlled by Rothschilds, for a long-term supply of kerosene.

By that time petroleum was being produced in the East Indies, now known as Indonesia. In 1890, N.V. Koninklijke Nederlandsche Maatschappij tot Explotatie van Petroleumbronnen in Nederlandsche-Indie, changed in 1949 to N.V. Koninklijke Nederlandsche Petroleum Maatschappij

(Royal Dutch Petroleum Company), was formed to develop an oil field in Sumatra, where, under the management of J. B. Aug. Kessler, a pipeline and a refinery at Pankalan Brandan came into operation in 1892. Kessler was joined by Henri Detering in 1896. Faced with the competition of Samuel's low transport costs for Russian oil because of the use of bulk carriers, Royal Dutch began the construction of tankers and bulk storage installations and set up its own sales organization.

Competition between the two companies became very intense, and each was also competing with Standard Oil. Samuel's reply to Royal Dutch was to obtain, in 1896, an option on a concession in Dutch Borneo, where he drilled successfully and later started a refinery at Balik Papan. His oil business became so extensive that in 1897 he formed a separate company to operate it and, as a connection with the older business, called it The "Shell" Transport and Trading Company Limited. The "Shell" Company continued to expand. The first motorcar was produced by Gottlieb Daimler in 1885, which meant that gasoline was becoming important. Also, Samuel was a firm believer in the future of fuel oil for shipping. His Borneo oil fields had little gasoline content, so he contracted for supplies from an independent producer in Sumatra. When oil was discovered in Texas in 1901, he contracted with J. M. Guffey Petroleum Co. to transport and distribute Texas oil, largely fuel oil, and so became the first oil company with worldwide sources of production. He was now well supplied with gasoline, kerosene, and fuel oil. Standard Oil was getting stiff competition from Shell and Royal Dutch in its Far Eastern markets. Determined to maintain its markets in the Far East, Standard made unsuccessful attempts to obtain control of both Shell and Royal Dutch.

First merger, 1903. Both Shell and Royal Dutch were actively competing with Standard. Both began to think about joining hands to fight Standard; moves toward cooperation between the two had been made periodically since 1892. Negotiations began again in the first years of the century and resulted, in 1903, in the establishment of The Asiatic Petroleum Company Limited with Rothschilds as a third partner. Asiatic Petroleum with Samuel as chairman and Detering as managing director combined the distributing resources and sales organizations of "Shell" Transport and Trading and Royal Dutch for all markets in the Far East and became selling agents throughout the world for East Indies (Indonesia) production. The marketing of other production remained separate.

The complete merger between the two companies was brought about for the following reasons:

1. Royal Dutch was rich in gasoline supplies; Shell was not.
2. The strength of Shell lay in fuel oil, for which demand was still far in the future.

3. Shell's source of supply in Texas began to fall off. In order to make good the loss of supply and to keep its four largest tankers employed, Shell began to ship kerosene from Rumania.
4. Heavy demand for gasoline in the United States made Standard dump large quantities of kerosene in Europe at very low prices and thereby cause heavy losses to its competitors, including Shell and Royal Dutch. Royal Dutch was not selling Rumanian kerosene, but it profited from the high gasoline prices.

Both Shell and Royal Dutch came to the conclusion that it was in their mutual interests to merge completely. The Royal Dutch/Shell Group was formed in 1907. By the agreement between the two companies, Royal Dutch and "Shell" Transport and Trading became purely holding companies with shares in the proportion 60 to 40 in two newly formed operating companies: The Anglo-Saxon Petroleum Company Ltd. in London and N.V. De Bataafse Petroleum Maatschaapij (BPM) at The Hague. The two operating companies were to manage the affairs of the entire group in association with the already existing Asiatic Petroleum Company (from which the Rothschilds had withdrawn in 1917).

The merger of the two companies proved to be very successful. Events since then have demonstrated that Samuel's faith in fuel oil was justified. The Royal Commission in 1912 recommended oil fuel for the British Navy.

A look at the history of the two companies shows that they reached the goal of complete vertical integration from opposite ends. Royal Dutch began as oil producers and refiners and later moved into transport and sales activities. Shell, on the other hand, began as merchants and shippers, and later moved into the area of exploration and refining of oil. Both realized that it is difficult for an oil company operating on a global scale to stop short of the complete range of operations.

The Royal Dutch/Shell Group grew by leaps and bounds during the years after 1907, and the growth is continuing even now. The group has oil fields, refineries, and marketing facilities all over the world. In 1928, Shell entered the chemical field with the foundation in the Netherlands of Mekog, a company for the production of nitrogenous fertilizers from coke oven gases. In 1929 Shell Chemical Company (which later became Shell Chemical Corporation) was formed in the United States. The company was the pioneer in the manufacture of chemicals based on oil and produced nitrogenous fertilizers from natural gas and synthetic solvents from refinery gases.

In 1938 Royal Dutch/Shell production had grown to almost 580,000 barrels daily out of a world total of 5,720,000, and the seagoing tanker fleet was made up of 180 vessels totaling 1.4 million deadweight tons.

The head offices of the Dutch companies were moved to Curaçao when

Holland was invaded by the Germans, but a nucleus staff was kept in London. Properties in the East were destroyed and access to Rumania was lost. The group lost 87 ships through enemy action.

Changes in group structure. In 1946 the name of the Asiatic Petroleum Company was changed to The Shell Petroleum Company Limited. In 1955 The Shell Petroleum Company took over the business of The Anglo-Saxon Petroleum Company and the number of parent operating companies was, in effect, reduced to two. In 1959, Shell Petroleum Company and Bataafse Petroleum Mij. became purely holding companies. Four new service companies were formed, two for the oil and two for the chemical side of the business. Of the four service companies, two were located in London and two in The Hague. Bataafse Internationale Petroleum Mij. N.V. and Bataafse Internationale Chemie Mij. N.V. (subsidiaries of BPM) were located in The Hague. Shell International Petroleum Company and Shell International Chemical Company (subsidiaries of Shell Petroleum) were located in London.

Position of the group today. Today the companies of the Royal Dutch/ Shell Group number several hundred that employ more than 172,000 employees and operate in more than 100 different countries. Some 40 nationalities are represented in the London service companies alone. The group has substantial stakes in oil and natural gas, chemicals, and shipping. It has a fleet of ocean tankers that range in size from 18,000 to 200,000 tons and total more than 22 million tons. It has production fields in 23 different countries from which come 75 different types of crude oil. It has 60 refineries that vary in capacity from 500 to 50,000 tons daily.

Current organization structure. The dominant organizational changes that the company had to undergo were described earlier in connection with the history of the company. The reasons for the changes were discussed earlier. The following paragraphs will deal with the current organization structure of the Royal Dutch/Shell Group presented in Exhibit 42.

The Royal Dutch/Shell Group is the name given to some 500 companies whose shares are owned directly, wholly, or in part by N.V. Koninklijke Nederlandsche Petroleum Maatschappij (Royal Dutch Petroleum Company) and The "Shell" Transport and Trading Company Limited. These two companies are known as the parent companies of the group. The "Shell" Transport and Trading Company is domiciled in the United Kingdom, whereas the Royal Dutch Petroleum Company is domiciled in the Netherlands. The two parent companies are quite separate. Each has its own board of directors, and none of the directors of one is also a director of the other. The parent companies are public companies whose shares are owned by hundreds of thousands of investors that include individual members of the public, insurance companies, insurance trusts, pension funds, and trade unions. Shareholders are located in the United Kingdom, the Netherlands, France, West Germany, the United States, and other countries. Each company is responsible to its shareholders. The shares are bought and sold on all the leading stock exchanges of Europe and in the United States. The parent companies do not themselves engage in oil or chemical operations; they act only as shareholders.

The two parent companies have joint ownership of two holding companies, namely, Shell Petroleum N.V. and The Shell Petroleum Company Limited. The shares of each are held in the proportion of 60 percent by

Exhibit 42. Organization of Royal Dutch/Shell Group

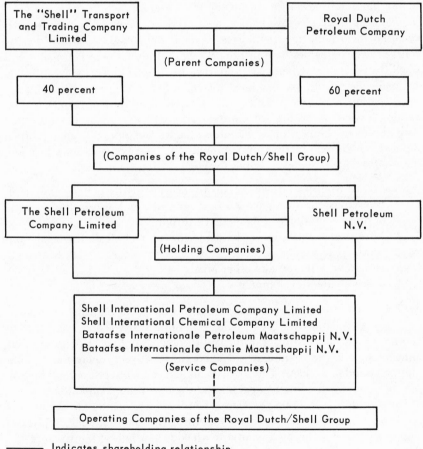

Indicates shareholding relationship.

Indicates advice and service.

Royal Dutch and 40 percent by "Shell" Transport and Trading Company. The holding companies in turn hold the shares, wholly or in part, of all the operating companies in the group.

Each of the operating companies carries on one or more of the activities of the oil, gas, and chemical industries from research and exploration to selling oil and chemical products to the customer. The activities of these operating companies are interdependent and, taken together, cover the whole range of the business. Although many operating companies are concerned with only one activity, such as marketing, other companies perform most of the operations. This represents an integration of the wide range of oil industry activities within a single company. There are also some auxiliary companies concerned with activities such as the administration of pension funds or the ownership of real estate.

The role of service companies. Some form of central business focus is essential for a large group such as Royal Dutch/Shell. It is provided by four service companies, two in London (Shell International Petroleum and Shell International Chemical) and two in The Hague (Bataafse Internationale Petroleum and Bataafse Internationale Chemie). Although they are separate corporate entities and located in different countries, the various service companies work organizationally as a single central office with almost no duplication of activities except for minor ones such as office services. Under contractual arrangements, the service companies provide, for a fee, a wide range of activities to the operating companies:

1. Advice to operating companies to insure that the policies they wish to establish are in their own best interests, and also in the interests of other operating companies in the group.
2. Advice and services in the handling of technical, financial, and commercial problems.
3. Design of refineries and other plants.
4. Research and development.

The service companies also serve as transmitters of information regarding new developments, ideas, and experiences from one company to another. Such information transfer helps prevent conflict of plans of operating companies and stimulates collaboration between operating companies on common projects. The service companies, in effect, serve as linking pins between the holding companies and the operating companies.

In addition to providing services, the service companies are themselves operators in some fields. They are responsible for international supply and shipping activities (supply operations) that do not fall within the jurisdiction of any one operating company. Closely linked with supply is a central marine organization that insures that the proper tonnage is available either from Shell fleets or by charter and a central sales division that deals with sales to international customers. It would be difficult for an individual operating company to handle such sales on its own.

Organization of the service companies. A "committee of managing directors" comprises the top management in the four service companies. Each of the eight men on the committee is a director within his company, as well as a director of the holding companies and one of the parent companies. In this way, a close liaison is effected between the various companies.

The chairman's primary responsibility is in the areas of finance and organization, and each of the other group managing directors is in charge of a portfolio covering one or more geographic areas and a number of functional and specialist fields. For example, there is a regional managing director for the Middle East and the United Kingdom and Irish Republic who is also the functional director for group trade relations, group materials, oil manufacturing, and the London legal and medical divisions. The organization of the service companies is given in Exhibit 43.

Under these circumstances, a managing director's attention is directed to each part of the world, which allows each managing director to maintain a global view of the group as a whole through one or more functions. Further breadth of involvement and knowledge is effected by changes that occur from time to time in distribution of the spheres of interest among the managing directors.

The heads of the various departments report to the managing directors and are known as coordinators. They fall into three separate classifications:

1. *Group functional coordinators* handle all matters applicable to oil and chemicals, including finance, planning, materials, research, and trade relations.
2. *Oil or chemical functional coordinators* handle marketing, manufacturing, exploration, and production and supply of oil or chemicals.
3. *Regional coordinators* handle oil and gasoline operations of operating companies in a given geographic area of the world.

The functional coordinators are the primary source of the varied technical services and advice in the daily operations of the company and have the additional responsibility of reviewing activities in their respective functional areas on a group basis for the managing directors.

The regional organizations provide and/or arrange the functions for the provision of varied technical and commercial advice and service, evaluate the plans and the performance of operating companies, make or recommend senior appointments within the operating companies, effect coordi-

Exhibit 43. Organization of the Royal Dutch/Shell Group Service Companies

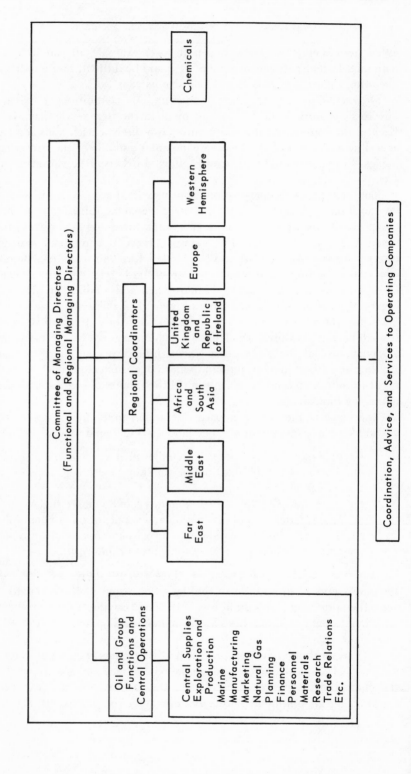

nation among the companies in their regions, and handle matters of common interest to the oil and chemical operations of operating companies. The regional organization represents virtually the whole of the service companies in those areas.

The geographical region assigned to each regional organization is defined as far as possible by the common interests or problems of the various operating companies concerned as well as by the most economic means of providing those companies with the necessary central services. The groupings are therefore subject to change with the circumstances.

Similarly, the structure of each regional organization varies with the circumstances inherent in each of the areas. An example is the Western Hemisphere region organization, which is the central office focal point for Canada and the United States. Another regional center is in Caracas, which handles Venezuela and the Caribbean. Still another regional center is in Buenos Aires; it serves most of the remainder of South America. Each regional organization, therefore, deals primarily with a small number of large sophisticated units that need relatively little central services and with some units, such as Shell Canada and Shell Oil in the United States, that operate under conditions of almost complete self-sufficiency. The region maintains a relatively small staff, therefore, and emphasizes the provision of services and the performance of staff work for the regional managing director. When functional services are needed, they are provided by the functional coordinators.

In contrast, the close interrelationship between what happens in one country and what happens in another country within the European area creates both the opportunity and the need for synergistic effort. As a result, the European regional organization is a sizable unit that is staffed with its own experts in fields such as marketing logistics, refinery coordination, personnel, and trade relations, but utilizes the functions of the more specialized services. In a similar manner, each of the other regions adapts its unit size and functions to existing circumstances.

The United Kingdom represents a special case. Taken with the Irish Republic, it constitutes a region, but the regional coordinator in this instance has no staff and is a member of the staff of the service companies for only a part of his time. The remainder of his time he spends as the managing director of Shell U.K., and he is, in that capacity, an operating company chief executive in that he handles Shell's oil and gas business in both the United Kingdom and Irish Republic. Because the United Kingdom and continental Europe constitute a single supply-logistic area in many respects, there is a very close collaboration between the two regional coordinators.

Other duties of Shell U.K., notably its responsibility for aspects common to the various parts of the business, illustrate one important aspect of the work performed by regional coordinators and operating company chief executives in the gas and oil areas. The responsibility is in such areas as local, public, and government relations, economic and environmental matters, and employee relations. In certain areas, the normal service company–operating company relationship is reversed. The London service companies find it to be more economical and effective to draw upon Shell U.K. for services in regard to the local matters than to provide them. A similar arrangement is evident in the Netherlands.

Chemicals. The chemical business is both smaller and more compact than its oil counterpart. Each service company organization is headed by a director of chemicals whose responsibilities are in the areas of marketing, manufacture, distribution, central trading, and intercompany coordination. The director performs the tasks that the regional coordinators and some of the functional coordinators perform in the oil business. Under his command are coordinators in the areas of manufacturing, marketing, finance, and experimental effort. The primary divisions of activity are in terms of product groups: agricultural chemicals, plastics and resins, elastomers, and industrial and base chemicals. Each product group has a product committee composed of the manufacturing, marketing, and experimental effort executives concerned with that product group in addition to other executives from such areas as finance and R&D. The product committee, therefore, constitutes a kind of interfunctional board for each product group.

The chemicals business runs its own specialist departments when it deals with matters peculiar to its business, but it draws on the resources of the service companies in all other matters.

The current organization structure of Royal Dutch/Shell has been in use since early 1966 or late 1965. Prior to that time, the group had adopted an organizational pattern for about six to seven years that did not work as expected. In the following paragraphs we shall examine the reasons that prompted management to adopt the new structure for a few years and later to discard it in favor of the present one. [4]

It all began as long ago as 1958. Oil profits were leveling off after several lucrative years. Standard Oil was revamping its entire U.S. structure, and Mobil Oil was involved in an extensive cost-cutting exercise. That was a period when it was essential to cut costs because it appeared to be the only way to boost profits. Royal Dutch/Shell decided to take a good hard look at its organization structure with the objective of eliminating any wasteful duplication of effort and resources.

The group had two head offices, one in London and the other in The Hague. Each was operating quite independently without much connection with the other. There were no fewer than seven managing directors supervising the group's activities from the two offices. Each managing director was in charge of a region or a function or both. "But in 1950 they were becoming too burdened by detailed management and paperwork to do a proper job of long-range planning." Top management of the group called in a leading management consulting firm in the United Kingdom to remove the fat from the organization and to recommend a new structure suitable for the challenges of the future ahead. The management consultants proposed the following changes:

1. The merger of the two head offices in London and The Hague into one central office mostly responsible for advice and service. The central office was to formulate the global strategies and policies of the whole group, but direct line control by the managing directors from the headquarters of their respective regions was to be eliminated.

2. Several regional and functional coordinators would have direct service responsibilities to the numerous operating companies in the field.

3. The day-to-day responsibility for getting things done was to be placed on the shoulders of a single top decision maker, namely, the director of coordination for oil (DCO). The directives of the DCO would be implemented by the several functional and regional coordinators.

4. The chemical side of the business would be split from the oil business. A director of coordination for chemicals (DCC) would run the chemical side under a setup similar to that on the oil side.

The recommendations made by the management consultants appeared to be very reasonable, but only on paper. Some of them were tried for a while, but others were completely ignored. The reason why the recommendations by the consultants did not work are many. The men at the top could not quite get used to their new roles as merely advisers to the operating companies. They apparently missed playing the part of prime movers and decision makers. The job of the DCC turned out to be very difficult, particularly with the several managing directors keeping a close watch on him. The operating companies resented the fact that they were reporting to numerous committees and not to one single person. For these and other reasons the managing directors abandoned the plan suggested by the consultants and assumed their original roles.

The experiment with the new structure, although it lasted for a short period only, was not a total waste. Although regionalism has returned to Royal Dutch/Shell, there exists today an extra layer of a new and more experienced corps of central coordinators than in the past. The new managerial layer insulates the managing directors from the everyday minor decisions and problems in the operating companies. What is more important is that the group now has a single central office. Centralized policy making and programming are now much easier. A director can decide from London or The Hague, with the aid of a giant computer, what kinds of resources to allocate to which part of the world and when they are to be made available. The optimization of the total Royal Dutch/Shell operations is now feasible. Centralized control of the various regional operations is much easier under the current organization.

What organizational changes are expected in the future? That depends upon the technological, political, and other environmental changes that may take place in the future. All of those factors affect the company's structure. For example, the Common Market may affect the company's European structure; the company's operations in Africa would not have been fragmented had Africa not been fragmented. As a matter of fact, a vastly extended global empire like Royal Dutch/Shell has to stay organizationally flexible all the time. There is no room for "organizational sclerosis."

Summary

In strict organizational terms, a company can be considered to have a world-oriented structure if it has grouped all its operations on a product or geographical basis without formal distinction between its domestic and foreign activities, if it has given its staff and functional staff groups worldwide responsibilities in their areas of specialization, and if its top management has informational inputs—product, geographical, and functional—that permit it to make decisions with their global impact in mind (pattern 8).

Organization structure of companies discussed under patterns 1 to 3, in a strict organizational sense, do not possess the essential characteristics of a world-oriented structure mentioned in the preceding paragraph. Companies discussed under patterns 4 to 6 have organization structures that approach the world-oriented structure to a far greater degree than those discussed under preceding patterns. A look at the companies presented under patterns 4 to 6 shows that all, except Ingersoll-Rand in pattern 5, are continental European companies. United States and British companies (Dunlop and Metal Box) dominate patterns 1 to 3.

A key difference that one notices in examining the organization structures of European and U.S. multinational companies is that European companies do not, as a rule, make an organizational distinction between their foreign and domestic operations. That could be because the European companies historically have had a small domestic market and have therefore been forced to think in terms of international markets fairly early in their life. As a consequence, top management personnel in European companies have acquired the international or world outlook and attitude. That has not generally been true of U.S. companies, which have had the advantage of having a large domestic market to worry about and have, as a result, treated their international operations as an arm of the comparatively large domestic ones. That, to a great extent, accounts for a large number of U.S. companies having an international department or division to handle their foreign operations (pattern 1).

Another key difference between European and U.S. companies is that the former put greater emphasis upon informal channels of communications and coordination than the latter put. United States companies have a tendency to adhere a bit too strictly to the concepts of line, staff, and functional staff authority relationships. Unity of command is much more sacrosanct to U.S. companies than to European companies. European companies are far less concerned with strict adherence to organization charts and job definitions, they have a tendency to make the organizational design suit the abilities and personalities of the executives rather than the other way around.

European companies give much greater freedom to their subsidiaries abroad than U.S. companies, who keep a close watch on their overseas operations. European companies also tend to give comparatively greater freedom to their larger subsidiaries than to the smaller ones. They appeared to be leaning over backward to give their subsidiaries in the United States relatively greater freedom than they give their subsidiaries in other countries.

Global planning and control and a worldwide perspective at the top management level do not come automatically with the elimination of the international division and the coordination of all operations worldwide organizationally along product or regional lines; nor does the presence of an international division mean that top management is unaware of the benefits that could be derived from the global approach.

One U.S. company executive said emphatically that his company uses the international division approach to manage its overseas operation, yet he believes that the company considers the world as its marketplace and plans on that basis. He said that an organization structure is merely a means to an end, a vehicle to be used for the purpose of achieving the company's goals. Nobody can deny the validity of that statement. It is my judgment, however, that an organization structure to a great extent reflects the attitudes and management philosophy of top management and that companies that wish to optimize their operations worldwide and desire not to treat their foreign operations as second-rate citizens are more likely to integrate their domestic and foreign operations on a regional or product basis. That may not apply in all situations and with all companies.

There is no company among those studied that has all the dimensions of the world-oriented organizational pattern described earlier. But of all the companies, the organization structures of Unilever and Royal Dutch/Shell come closest to resembling the world-oriented organization pattern.

REFERENCES

1. Information obtained from *What Unilever Is* (London: Unilever Ltd., 1966).

2. Information obtained from Charles Wilson, *Unilever, 1945–1965* (London: Cassell & Co., Ltd., 1968), chap. 2.

3. Information of the structure obtained from *Facts About Unilever* (London: Information Division, Unilever House).

4. Information obtained from "The Palace Revolt at Royal Dutch/Shell," *Dun's Review*, Séptember 1968.

Appendix

European Companies Interviewed

Country	Industry	Sales ($000)	Assets ($000)
Belgium			
Petrofina S.A.	Petroleum products	1,053,640	1,521,735
Solvay & Cie, S.A.	Chemicals	754,920	1,019,900
Germany			
Farbenfabriken Bayer AG	Chemicals	2,139,086	2,665,574
Great Britain			
The Dunlop Company Ltd.	Rubber products, engineering	1,188,000	977,491
Glaxo Group Ltd.	Special foods, pharmaceuticals	N.A.	N.A.
The Metal Box Company Limited	Packaging, containers and machinery	464,642	393,073
Imperial Chemical Industries Ltd.	Chemicals	3,252,240	4,676,160
Great Britain/Netherlands			
Royal Dutch/Shell	Petroleum products natural gas, chemicals	9,738,410	15,409,397
Unilever	Food, detergents, toiletries, feed	6,030,000	3,625,920
Italy			
Pirelli & Co. S.p.A.	Rubber products, wires, cables	1,067,100	1,169,000
Denmark			
Burmeister and Wain	Diesel engines, shipbuilding	N.A.	N.A.
The East Asiatic Company Ltd.	Shipping, plantations	N.A.	N.A.

European Companies Interviewed (continued)

Country	Industry	Sales ($000)	Assets ($000)
Sweden			
Alfa-Laval AB	Thermal equipment	N.A.	N.A.
Atlas Copco AB	Industrial tools	N.A.	N.A.
Telefon AB, LM Ericsson	Telecommunications equipment	561,887	803,377
AB SKF	Bearings, steel, castings	817,009	871,186
AB Volvo	Autos, tractors, harvesters, engines	850,574	823,841
Switzerland			
Brown, Boveri and Company, Ltd.	Machinery, clerical equipment	1,047,336	1,110,222
F. Hoffman-La Roche & Co. Ltd.	Pharmaceuticals	980,000	216,469
Landis and Gyr AG	Electrical equipment	N.A.	N.A.
Nestlé Alimentana S.A.	Food products	2,142,694	1,736,337
Sulzer Brothers Ltd.	Engines and machinery	397,379	683,970
Swiss Aluminium Ltd. (Alusuisse)	Aluminium, plastics, mining	482,712	818,614

Three companies that wish to remain anonymous

SOURCE: "The 200 Largest Industrials Outside the U.S.," *Fortune*, August 1970.

*United States Companies Interviewed**

Company	Industry	Sales ($000)	Assets ($000)
American Cyanamid Company	Medical, chemical	1,087,098	1,000,872
Campbell Soup Company	Food products	884,463	554,555
General Foods Corporation	Food products	1,893,760	1,176,174
Ingersoll-Rand Company	Industrial machinery	711,193	689,962
International Paper Company	Paper products	1,777,251	1,887,431
Scott Paper Company	Paper products	731,513	811,958
Johns-Manville Corporation	Construction materials and industrial products	583,606	501,829
Richardson-Merrell, Inc.	Pharmaceuticals	340,262	311,555
Union Carbide Corp.	Chemicals	2,933,015	3,355,913
Hercules Inc.	Chemicals	745,991	787,341

*Three companies that are included in *Fortune* 500 list wish to remain anonymous.
SOURCE: "The 500 Largest Industrial Corporations," *Fortune*, May 1970.

Index